ARTIFICIAL NEURAL NETWORKS FOR CIVIL ENGINEERS: Fundamentals and Applications

By the Committee on Expert Systems and Artificial Intelligence of the Technical Council on Computer Practices of the American Society of Civil Engineers

Edited by:

Nabil Kartam
Kuwait University, P.O. Box 5969, Safat, 13060, Kuwait

Ian Flood
University of Florida, Gainesville, USA

James H. Garrett, Jr.
Carnegie Mellon University, Pittsburgh, PA, USA

Contributing Authors:

G. Agrawal	The Earth Technology Corporation, Irvine, CA, USA
F. Amini	University of District of Columbia, Washington, DC, USA
P. L. Bourdeau	Purdue University, West Lafayette, IN, USA
J. A. Chameau	Golder Associates, Atlanta, GA, USA
P. Dayakar	Clarkson University, Potsdam, NY, USA
M. Demetsky	University of Virginia, Charlottesville, VA, USA
A. Faghri	University of Delaware, Newark, DE, USA
C. Ferregut	The University of Texas at El Paso, El Paso, TX, USA
I. Flood	University of Florida, Gainesville, USA
J. H. Garrett	Carnegie Mellon University, Pittsburgh, PA, USA
D. J. Gunaratnam	University of Sydney, Sydney, Australia
A. S. Hanna	University of Wisconsin-Madison, Madison, WI, USA
N. Ivezic	Carnegie Mellon University, Pittsburgh, PA, USA
N. Kartam	Kuwait University, Safat, Kuwait
D. Martinelli	West Virginia University, Morgantown, WV, USA
J. Ortiz	The University of Texas at El Paso, El Paso, TX, USA
R. A. Osegueda	The University of Texas at El Paso, El Paso, TX, USA
S. C. Park	University of Wisconsin-Madison, Madison, WI, USA
G. Z. Qi	University of Maryland, College Park, MD, USA
J. S. Russell	University of Wisconsin-Madison, Madison, WI, USA
A. E. Smith	University of Pittsburgh, Pittsburgh, PA, USA
M. A. Taha	University of Wisconsin-Madison, Madison, WI, USA
J. M. Twomey	University of Pittsburgh, Pittsburgh, PA, USA
J. C. S. Yang	University of Maryland, College Park, MD, USA

Published by

American Society of Civil Engineers

345 East 47th Street
New York, New York 10017-2398

D0074464

Abstract:

The purpose of *Artificial Neural Networks for Civil Engineers: Fundamentals and Applications* is to provide researchers with an understanding of the potential of artificial neural networks for solving civil engineering related problems, and guidance on how to develop successful implementation for a broad range of problem types. With this aim in mind, this monograph is divided into two parts. The first section addresses fundamental issues in the selection, development and use of neural networks, while the second section provides example applications such as using neural networks to: 1) locate structural damage; 2) control structures; 3) assist project owners in selecting bidders; and 4) model the stress-strain relationship of sand and clay type soils. Many of the ideas and techniques presented in the second section can commute across the disciplinary boundaries and, therefore, should be of interest to all civil engineers.

Library of Congress Cataloging-in-Publication Data

Artificial neural networks for civil engineers : fundamentals and applications / by the Committee on Expert Systems and Artificial Intelligence of the Technical Council on Computer Practices of the American Society of Civil Engineers ; edited by Nabil Kartam, Ian Flood, James H. Garrett, Jr. ; contributing authors, G. Agrawal ... [et al.].
p.   cm.
ISBN 0-7844-0225-6
1. Civil engineering--Data processing. 2. Neural networks (Computer science). 3. Computer-aided engineering. I. Kartam, Nabil. II. Flood, Ian. III. Garrett, James H. IV. Agrawal, G. (Girish) V. American Society of Civil Engineers. Expert Systems and Artificial Intelligence Committee.
TA345.A787 1997   97-159
624'0285'632--DC21   CIP

Preface

The 1990's have seen a tremendous growth in interest in the application of neurally inspired computing techniques to civil engineering. The driving force for this development has been the promise of certain information processing characteristics manifest in the brain that have, to a greater extent, eluded capture by conventional approaches to computing. The most commonly cited examples of these include an ability to learn and generalise from experience, to produce meaningful results to problems even when input data contain errors or are incomplete, to adapt solutions over time to compensate for changing circumstances, and to process information rapidly. Problems requiring such information processing capabilities are commonplace in civil engineering, and indeed, many successful applications have already been made.

The purpose of this monograph is to provide researchers with an understanding of the potential of artificial neural networks for solving civil engineering related problems, and guidance on how to develop successful implementations for a broad range of problem types. For this aim, the monograph is divided into two parts, the first section addressing fundamental issues in the selection, development and use of neural networks, while the second section provides example applications to each of the various disciplines of civil engineering. Many of the ideas and techniques presented in the second section can commute across the disciplinary boundaries and thus all chapters may be of interest to a reader, irrespective of their area of specialisation.

The first chapter provides an introduction to neural networks, explaining what they are, how they are relevant to civil engineering, and where they are being applied. Chapter 2 compliments this with a classification of the various forms of neural networking system available (architectures, modes of operation, and methods of development), and their relevance to different classes of problem. The first section concludes, in chapter 3, by addressing the issues of verification and validation of neural networks, tasks that are essential to the successful implementation of these devices.

The second section provides a selection of applications of artificial neural networks, balanced across the various civil engineering disciplines. Chapter 4 demonstrates the use of neural networks for assessing the location and magnitude of damage in structures, by recognising patterns in the vibration response of the structure. Chapter 5, in contrast, considers an application which may be used to prevent or minimise the damage caused to a structure when subject to excessive forces. In this case, neural models are used to predict response and actively control structures that are subject to potentially damaging dynamic loads. Chapter 6 considers an application of neural networks in the area of construction project management, that of assisting a project owner in selecting the most appropriate bidders for a construction project based on qualitative assessments of their performance. Chapter 7 provides a comprehensive review of the suitability and scope for application of neural network technology to transportation engineering, considering the potential areas for application, the successes to date, and the types of neural network paradigm relevant to different categories of transportation problem. Chapter 8 is concerned with the development of a neural network for modeling the stress-strain relationship of sand and clay type soils. Unusually, feedback loops are included within the network which enable it to build-up a stress strain curve incrementally. Finally, Chapter 9 considers a neural-fuzzy approach to the assessment of Liquefaction susceptibility of a site subject to a seismic event.

This monograph can be used to supplement educational textbooks in one-semester courses that introduce upper division undergraduate or graduate engineers to ANN concepts and their application. It is a valuable reference for ANN development, providing examples from each of the main disciplines in civil engineering.

Acknowledgements

This monograph is the result of the effort of the ASCE TCCP Expert Systems and Artificial Intelligence Committee. The objective in creating this monograph was to provide the civil engineering community with useful descriptions of practical applications of artificial neural networks to civil engineering related problems. This monograph represents an ongoing activity of the committee to prepare and carefully monitor a set of publications directly related to civil engineering and artificial intelligence. The editors appreciate the efforts of the members of the committee and the members of the civil engineering community, who reviewed the individual chapters in the monograph. A special thanks to Engineer A.P. Alex for his efforts in assembling and proof-reading the final copy of the chapters. The editors acknowledge the support and encouragement they received from Kuwait University -- College of Engineering, especially from the Dean "Dr. Hasan Al-Sanad" and the Civil Engineering Chairman "Dr. Omar Al-Saleh".

All chapters in this monograph have been rigorously reviewed by at least two reviewers according to the ASCE journal publication policy.

Biographies of Authors

Girish Agrawal

Dr. Agrawal is currently a Project Engineer and Technical Manager for the Cone Penetration Testing group at the Irvine, California, offices of EARTH TECH, Inc. A native of India, he did his undergraduate work in Civil Engineering at the Indian Institute of Technology in New Delhi, graduating in 1985. He holds a Master's degree (1987) and a Doctorate in Civil Engineering (1992) from Purdue University. In 1992 he joined the Civil Engineering faculty at Purdue University as a Visiting Assistant Professor. In August of 1993 he joined EARTH TECH as a Staff Geotechnical Engineer. Dr. Agrawal is a pioneer in the use of Artificial Neural Networks as computational tools for Geotechnical data analysis. In 1991, he introduced the idea and presented a detailed methodology for using ANNs as a tool to assess the liquefaction potential of soil deposits making direct use of field data. His technical interests include: Artificial Neural Networks, Fuzzy Sets, and Related Adaptive Learning techniques; Direct Push Technology for Geotechnical and Environmental Site Assessment; Earthquake Engineering; Numerical Modeling and Analysis; Dynamics of Pile Driving; Solid Waste Landfill Design; and Optimization of Earthwork Design and Construction. He has authored more than 15 publications.

Philippe L. Bourdeau

Dr. Bourdeau is currently an Associate Professor of Civil Engineering at Purdue University and a Lecturere at the Swiss Federal Institute of Technology in Lausanne, Switzerland. A native of France, he did his undergraduate and graduate work in Civil Engineering at the Swiss Federal Institute of Technology in Lausanne, obtaining his Bachelor, Master and Ph.D. degrees in 1976, 1978 and 1986, respectively, where he subsequently stayed on as a Senior Research Associate and Lecturer. In 1989 he also joined the Civil Engineering faculty at Purdue University. Dr. Bourdeau's research and teaching interests include: Stochastic Modeling of discontinuous geomaterials such as granular soils and fractured rocks; soil reinforcing and geosynthetics; uncertainty analysis; and application of probabilistic concepts in civil engineering designs. His research has been sponsored by government and private organisations within the U.S. as well as overseas. He has authored more than 50 publications in refereed journals and conference proceedings. He is very active in professional societies and is currently serving on the Education Committee of the International Geotextile Society and three ASCE technical committees.

Jean-Lou A. Chameau

Dr. Chameau is currently Vice Provost for Research and a Georgia Research Alliance (GRA) Eminent Scholar at the Georgia Institute of Technology. A native of France, he did his undergraduate work in Engineering at L'Ecole Nationale Superieure des Arts et Metiers and in Economics at La Sorbonne in Paris. He received his graduate education in Civil Engineering from Stanford University, completing Master and Ph.D. degrees in 1977 and 1980, respectively. In 1980 he joined the Civil Engineering faculty at Purdue University, where he subsequently became Full Professor and Head of the Geotechnical Engineering Program. In 1991, he became the Director of the School of Civil and Environmental Engineering at the Georgia Institute of Technology. In 1994 he became the President of Golder Associates, Inc. He returned to Georgia Tech in 1995 and now plays a key role in Georgia Tech's initiative to educate engineers who are environmentally sensitive. Dr. Chameau's technical interests include: Environmental geotechnology; sustainable development and technology; soil dynamics; micro-physical properties of soils; earthquake engineering; liquefaction of soils; and soil-structure interaction problems.

Penumadu Dayakar

Dr. Dayakar Penumadu obtained B.E (Honors) degree in civil engineering in 1986 from BITS, Pilani, India. He obtained Masters in civil engineering from University of Kentucky in 1989. He worked with Dr. Bobby Hardin on research related to consolidated drained triaxial testing and resonant column testing of clays. Dr. Penumadu came to Purdue University in 1989 to pursue doctoral study with Dr. Jean-Lou Chameau. He obtained his second Masters degree in civil engineering from Purdue in 1991. He then moved to Georgia Institute of Technology to continue his doctoral study on calibration chamber testing and pressuremeter in clays with Dr. Chameau. He obtained his Ph.D. in June, 1993. He has been an assistant professor in the department of civil and environmental engineering at Clarkson University, Potsdam, NY from July 1993.

Michael Demetsky

Dr. Demetsky is a professor of civil engineering at the University of Virginia where he teaches and conducts research in transportation systems engineering. Professor Demetsky is also the chairman of the Transportation Research Board Committee on Artificial Intelligence.

Ardeshir Faghri

Dr. Faghri is an assistant professor of civil engineering at the University of Delaware. His research focuses on applications of computer methods such as simulation, geographic information systems, artificial intelligence and virtual reality in transportation engineering.

Carlos Ferregut

Dr. Carlos Ferregut is an associate professor of civil engineering and is the associate director of the Centre for Structural Integrity of Aerospace Systems. He holds a Ph.D. degree in civil engineering from the University of Waterloo, Canada. He has an extensive background in risk-based analysis and design, structural engineering, simulation and non-destructive evaluation methodologies He has been engaged in research and development work involving the reliability analysis of civil, offshore and space structural systems, risk analysis, and mathematical modeling using the theories of probability and statistics. Since his arrival at UTEP, Dr. Ferregut has developed research programs in probabilistic structural mechanics and on the application of artificial intelligence techniques to damage detection.

Ian Flood

Dr. Flood is Director of the Fire Research Centre and a faculty member of the M. E. Rinker Sr. School of Building Construction, at the University of Florida, Gainesville, USA. Prior to this, he held academic positions in the Department of Civil Engineering at the University of Maryland, College Park, and in the School of Building and Estate Management at the National University of Singapore. He has published extensively in the areas of construction management and computer-based modeling in engineering. His current areas of research include the development of intelligent methods of modeling construction processes (for which he received the National Science Foundation Research Initiation Award), neural network-based approaches to the weigh-in-motion of trucks crossing steel bridges, and the modeling of uncertainty in construction costs and schedules.

James H. Garrett, Jr.

Dr. James H. Garrett, Jr. is an associate professor of civil and environmental engineering at Carnegie Mellon University. His research and teaching interests are oriented toward the application of computing technology to the engineering tasks of analysis, synthesis and evaluation. He is a co-recipient of both the 1993 ASCE Wellington Prize and the 1990 ASCE Moisseiff Award. He is also received National Science Foundation Presidential Young Investigator Award in 1989 and was a recipient of the 1992 IABSE Prize from the International Association of Bridge and Structural Engineers. He received his B.S. (1982), M.S. (1983), and Ph.D.(1986) in civil engineering from Carnegie Mellon University.

David J. Gunaratnam

Dr. David J. Gunaratnam is senior lecturer in the department of architectural and design science of the University of Sydney. He has previously held faculty positions at the University of Sri Lanka and the University of the West Indies. His research interests include application of machine learning techniques to design and the enhancement of neural network learning and performance for engineering applications. He received his Ph.D. in structural engineering from the University of Cambridge.

Awad S. Hanna

Dr. Awad S. Hanna is an assistant professor at the University of Wisconsin-Madison, construction administration program and civil engineering department. He earned a Masters and Ph.D. in civil engineering "Construction engineering and Management emphasis" from Pennsylvania State University in 1986 and 1989 respectively. He worked as an assistant then associate professor at the Memorial University of Newfoundland, Canada from 1989 to 1993. He has a total of nineteen years of industrial and academic experience in different countries including the U.S. His experience extends to many fields including project and design engineer, teaching and research. Dr. Hanna is the winner of a major Canadian competition for best innovative ideas in construction for 1990.

Nenad Ivezic

Dr. Nenad Ivezic received his M.S. degree in civil engineering from Carnegie Mellon University in 1992 and currently he is pursuing his Doctoral degree at the same department. From 1986 to 1990, he worked as a research engineer in the Research and Development group at the Institute for Material Testing of Serbia in Belgrade, Yugoslavia. His research interests include computational support for engineering design, machine learning, and decision support systems for collaborative design.

Nabil Kartam

Dr. Nabil Kartam is an associate professor of civil engineering at Kuwait University. He received the M.S. degree in construction engineering and management in 1985 from the University of Michigan, the M.S. degree in computer science in 1988, and the Ph.D. degree in civil engineering in 1989 from Stanford University. He worked as an engineer, planner, professor, and consultant for the last twelve years in the USA and Kuwait. Dr. Kartam is the sole investigator for more than a half million dollars of industrial research in the area of microcomputer applications, construction engineering, project management, construction safety, construction estimating and scheduling, artificial intelligence and CAD. He is the first recipient in Maryland's College of Engineering of the distinguished Lilly Teaching Award in 1991.

David Martinelli

Dr. Martinelli is an assistant professor of civil and environmental engineering at West Virginia University. Professor Martinelli's research interests include applications of new and emerging artificial intelligence paradigms such as neural networks and genetic algorithms in transportation engineering.

Jaime Ortiz

Engg. Jaime Ortiz holds a B.S. degree in civil engineering from the University of Texas at El Paso where he is currently a graduate research assistant pursuing a M.S. degree with an emphasis on structural engineering. He has been involved in the development of non destructive evaluation methodologies for the last four years. He has built several ANN during the course of his research. During the Summer of 1995 he participated in the Outstanding Student Summer Program at Sandia National Laboratories.

Roberto A. Osegueda

Dr. Roberto A.Osegueda is an associate professor in civil engineering and the Director of the Centre for Structural Integrity of Aerospace Systems His specialisation is in structural and solid mechanics. He holds Ph.D., M.S. and B.S. degrees from Texas A&M University. He has about eight years of expertise in global non-destructive damage evaluation of structural systems from vibration measurements. Dr. Osegueda has received grant awards to investigate the detection of damage in composite materials using laser Doppler velocimeter. His experience has expanded to NDE of offshore structures, where vibrational approaches can rely on accelerometer based technology. Dr. Osegueda has more than 15 publications on damage detection in structures, from a list of over 60 journal, conference proceedings articles and technical reports.

S.C. Park

Dr. S.C. Park is an assistant professor in the School of Business at the University of Wisconsin Madison. He obtained an M.B.A. in management information systems from Curtis L. Carson School of management at the University of Minnesota in June 1985. Professor Park then obtained his Ph.D. degree from the University of Illinois at Urbana-Champaign in 1990. Dr. Park's teaching and research experience are in the areas of data processing, knowledge-based decision support systems, machine learning and neural networks. Dr. Park acted as a reviewer for IIE Transactions, ORSA, Journal on Computing, Decision Support Systems, Decision Sciences, and IEEE Transactions on Computer.

G. Z. Qi

Dr. G. Z. Qi is an expert in seismology, geology and signal processing. The last eight years he worked at the Structure Dynamics Laboratory of the mechanical engineering department at the University of Maryland as a faculty research associate. He directed a number of earthquake projects in the area of dynamic soil characteristics. He assisted in the development of the random decrement technique as applied to the in-situ damping measurement in soil. Dr. Qi is also experienced in the analysis of strong motion earthquake records.

Jeffrey S. Russell

Dr. Jeffrey S. Russell, is assistant professor of civil and environmental engineering for the construction engineering and management program at the University of Wisconsin-Madison. He received his MSCE and doctorate from Purdue University, department of civil engineering. Dr. Russell has extensive experience in construction contractor evaluation, surety contract bonds, contractor failure, construction automation and robotics, and constructability.

Alice E. Smith

Dr. Alice E. Smith is assistant professor - Industrial engineering at University of Pittsburgh. Her research interests are in modeling and optimisation of complex systems using computational intelligence techniques, and her research has been sponsored by Lockheed Martin Corporation, the Ben Franklin Technology Centre of Western Pennsylvania, and the National Science Foundation, from which she was awarded a CAREER grant in 1995. She is an associate editor of ORSA Journal on Computing and engineering Design and Automation, and a registered Professional Engineer in the state of Pennsylvania. Dr Smith is a member of IEEE, ASEE and INFORMS, and a senior member of IIE and SWF.

Mahmoud Taha

Dr. Mahmoud Taha was born in Minia-Elkamh, Egypt, on July 10, 1959. He entered faculty of engineering at Cairo University, in Egypt, in 1977. After graduation, he was appointed as a demonstrator in the structural engineering department at Cairo University where he taught from 1982 to 1988. During this period, he completed his M.S. in structural engineering in 1986. He joined to the civil and environment engineering department at the University of Wisconsin-Madison in 1991 where he pursued his Ph.D. studies in construction engineering and management. He worked as research assistant since 1992.

Janet M. Twomey

Dr. Janet M. Twomey is assistant professor of industrial and manufacturing engineering at Wichita State University. She received Ph.D., M.S. and B.S. degrees in industrial engineering from the University of Pittsburgh and a B.A in psychology/sociology from Duquesne University. Her research interests are in neural network modeling and stochastic simulation modeling. Her research has been published in IIE Transactions and Journal of Mathematical and Computer Modeling. She is a member of IIE and SWE.

Jackson C.S. Yang

Dr. Jackson C.S. Yang is a professor of mechanical engineering and Director of Structural Dynamics and Robotics Laboratory at the University of Maryland for over thirty years. He was involved in the development of the random decrement technique and its application to the measurement of damping in soil and the detection of damage in structures for the past fifteen years with over 100 journal publications. Dr. Yang was the principal investigator on contracts with NSRDC, NSF, ONR, USGS, NBS, ARADCOM and NSWC, which measured damping in soil and structures and detected cracks in buildings, mobile homes, bridges, offshore platforms, wind tunnels, beams, plates, machinery systems, piping systems and compressors.

Contents

Chapter 1

Introduction

J. H. Garrett, Jr,[1]. M. ASCE, D. J. Gunaratnam[2], and Nenad Ivezic[3]

Abstract: This chapter is organized around three questions: *What are artificial neural networks? Why should a civil engineer be interested in them? Where are they being applied in civil engineering?* The intent of this chapter is to provide a basic understanding of artificial neural network (ANN) concepts and where ANNs can be applied within civil engineering.

1.1 What are Artificial Neural Networks?

Artificial neural networks (ANNs), quite simply, are computational devices. They can be either implemented in the form of a computer chip or they can be simulated on conventional serial computers. Most researchers and application developers at this time simulate their neural networks using software simulation. A neural network is a highly interconnected network of many simple processors as depicted in Figure 3. Each processor in the network maintains only one piece of dynamic information (its current level of activation) and is capable of only a few simple computations (adding inputs, computing a new activation level, or comparing input to a threshold value). The pattern of activation at the input processing units represents the problem being presented to the network and the pattern of activations seen at the output processing units represents the result of the computation performed by the neural network. A neural network performs "computations" by propagating changes in activation (i.e., level of stimulation) between the processors; it stores what it has "learned" as strengths of the connections between its processors. The propagation of activation, and thus the nature of the "computation" performed by the network, is strongly affected by the topology and strengths of the connections between the processors.

---

[1] Dept. of Civil and Environmental Eng., Carnegie Mellon University
[2] Dept. of Architectural and Design Science, University of Sydney
[3] Dept. of Civil and Environment Eng.,Carnegie Mellon University

As an example, consider the problem of interpreting ground-penetrating radar (GPR) signals taken from railroad ties (Tsai 1993; Heiler, Motazed and McNeil 1993). The basic idea for using an ANN in this situation is as follows. A GPR signal is collected by an antennae and receiver as shown in Figure 1. The received signal has information in it as to the condition of the tie from which the signal was reflected as shown in Figure 2. This signal is then discretized into 60 points along the time dimension (i.e., the amplitude of the signal is discretized for 60 time increments) for 5 locations over the width of the tie. Thus, a total of 300 discretized points, normalized by a maximum expected amplitude value, form the input presented to the neural network shown in Figure 3. This discretized signal is then propagated through the *trained* neural network to produce values at its output layer representing the classification of the tie (a *trained* neural network is one which has been presented a large number of examples and from these examples acquired the mapping from input to output). This classification is represented as values for one of five output processing units, representing classifications from new to very bad.

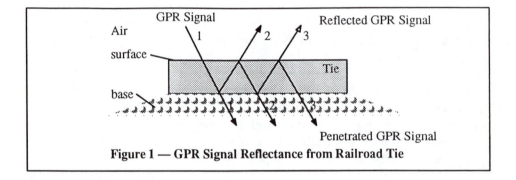

Figure 1 — GPR Signal Reflectance from Railroad Tie

One does not program a neural network as we are used to programming a computer. To program a conventional computer, we write a computer program consisting of a sequence of steps for the computer to follow. Rather, to program a neural network one presents it with *examples* of the computation to be performed. These examples consist of collections of input and output patterns, where the patterns are represented as patterns of activation. In the above

2

described application, the examples consist of patterns of discretized GPR signals (300 values scaled between 0 and 1) and patterns of classifications (values of 0 for all inapplicable classes and values of 1 for the applicable class). Then, the weights are iteratively modified to be able to reconstruct the presented examples. Hence, the "program" or definition of the computation, is embodied within the connection strengths of a neural network, the topology of the network, and the mechanism of activation propagation.

It is the above described ability to modify its own weights, i.e., to self-organize, that makes neural computing feasible, for it would be impossible to set the connection strengths manually for all but the simplest of neural networks. In addition, self-organization leads to the observed neural network characteristics of robustness and the ability to generalize. By modifying the connection strengths between processors, neural networks can automatically create internal features that: 1) might not be apparent from the data and thus would have defied the manual setting of connection strengths; and 2) can be recognized in previously unseen input patterns and used to produce appropriate patterns of output.

Rumelhart, et al., (chs. 1–3, in PDP 1986) provide an excellent description of the basic anatomy of all neural networks, which they divide into seven basic aspects: 1) a set of processing units, 2) the state of activation of a processing unit, 3) the function used to compute output of a processing unit, 4) the pattern of connectivity among the processing units, 5) the rule of propagation employed, 6) the activation function employed, and 7) the rule of learning employed.

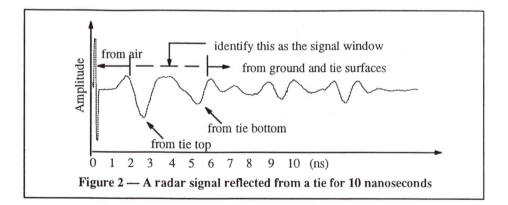

Figure 2 — A radar signal reflected from a tie for 10 nanoseconds

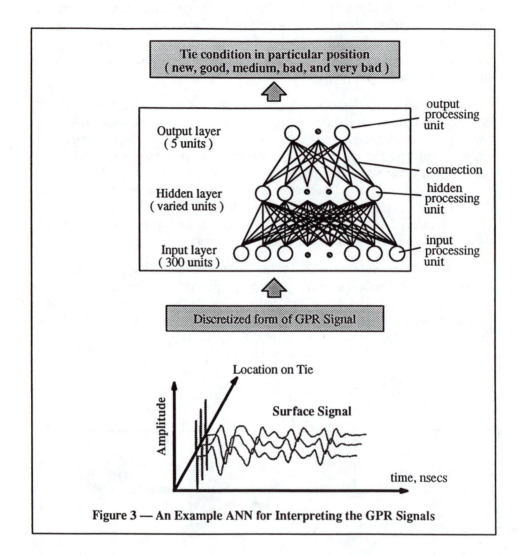

Figure 3 — An Example ANN for Interpreting the GPR Signals

An overview of these seven basic aspects described by Rumelhart, et al. (ch. 2, in PDP 1986) is presented in the next seven subsections and serves as a foundation for discussions in later chapters of the various types of neural networks.

Set of processing units. All neural networks are composed of a set of processing units, also called nodes, neurodes, or units depending on who is describing the network. Processing units may represent:

- a specific concept, such as features, letters, words, etc (the idea that one processing unit is equal to one concept); or

- an indescribable part of a larger concept, such as a sub-pattern within a larger pattern (i.e., this is the idea that many processing units may together equal one concept) (Rumelhart et al. 1986).

All processing in a neural network is carried out by these processing units (i.e., there is no centralized control mechanism that computes values for processing units). Although in certain software simulations of neural networks on sequential machines there is a centralized procedure that controls the order in which processing units are addressed and actually does the computing for all processing units, this is not truly what was envisioned for these networks. Neural networks are envisioned to be collections of individual processors, each capable of a few simple computations and control being completely via the passing of output between the processing units.

The main tasks associated with a processing unit is to receive input from its neighbors providing incoming activations, compute an output, and send that output to its neighbors receiving its output. Such a system is inherently parallel, because many processing units can be carrying out their computations at the same time. The processing units in a neural network can be classified as one of three types:

- input processing units, which receive input from external sources, compute their activation level, compute their output as a function of activation level, and transmit this output to the rest of the network;

- output processing units, which upon receipt of input from the rest of the network, compute and broadcast their output to external receivers (i.e., manipulators, speakers, or other networks) or feed their output back to the input layer of the network for further processing (e.g., recursive networks) ; and

- hidden processing units, which only receive input from, and broadcast their computed output to, processing units within the network (i.e., no "outside" contact).

State of activation. After calculating the activation level at each processing unit based on its net input, each processing unit then has an activation level, a, which is most often represented as a continuous quantity between the values of 0 and 1.

It is the activation level of all the processing units in a network that represents the state of the network:

- input processing unit activation levels represent the current external input to the network;

- output processing unit activation levels represent the current output being broadcast to the external receivers; and

- hidden processing units in a neural network represent the features within the input pattern that are present and influence the pattern of output produced by the network (Rumelhart et al. 1986).

It is the hidden layer that allows neural networks to represent more complicated mappings. To capture the features and sub-features within a set of data, there usually should be one or two hidden layers in which to represent this hierarchy of features (Hornik et al. 1989; Cybenko 1989). For a new input pattern, certain sub-features present within the pattern (which were "learned" from previously trained patterns) will be activated. These sub-features may activate certain features at the next level, which will cause the network to produce an output pattern. If the sub-features and features the network "learned" and applied are correct, the output pattern produced should be appropriate for the presented input pattern. Hence, it is important that the network "learn" about as many of the features and sub-features present within the input patterns so as to be able to adequately respond to all instances of input patterns. This need is met by presenting the network with many varied example input patterns. The set of training cases should embody examples of all features and sub-features the network is to "learn." For this reason, the selection of training cases can be considered an important part of the "programming" activity of a neural network. What you present to the neural network in the form of training cases (input patterns and expected output patterns) very much affects what the network "learns" and subsequently how well it performs and generalizes.

Output function. Each processing unit transmits its output to its neighbors. This output, also a scalar value usually between 0 and 1, is determined from the level of activation of the processing unit. Associated with each processing unit is an output function, f, which defines how the output value for the processing unit is determined from its activation. Hence, the relationship between the activation level and output value for any processing unit i can be described mathematically as follows:

$$o_i = f_i \left[a_i \right] \tag{1}$$

In some neural network models, the output function, f_i, is unity. In other neural network models, the output function is a threshold function, i.e., a

6

processing unit produces no output unless the activation exceeds some predefined level of activation (Rumelhart et al. 1986). Having an output function performing threshold logic prevents the network from making "wild guesses" when the input pattern presented does not really have any of the features or sub-features resembling those that the network has "learned."

Pattern of connectivity among the processing units. As stated previously, processing units are connected to other processing units and communicate with each other only via these connections. It is this pattern of connectivity and the strengths of the connections that mostly influences how a network will respond (the various rules for activation, output, etc., will also affect how a network actually responds, but for a constant set of rules, the topology and connection strengths will most affect what it computes). For example, for networks that use a sigmoidal activation function, if the weight of a connection going from the ith processing unit to the jth processing unit, w_{ij}:

- is positive, the connection is called *excitatory*, as in processing unit i encourages the activation in processing unit j (represented as an arrow);

- is zero, the connection is called *inactive*, as in processing unit i has no effect on the the activation in processing unit j;

- is negative, the connection is called *inhibitory*, as in processing unit i discourages the activation of processing unit j (represented as a line with a filled circle at end).

The absolute value of the weight, $| w_{ij} |$, represents the strength with which the ith processing unit excites or inhibits the jth processing unit.

Most often, a network starts out with the processing units being connected to many other processing units and then the self-organizing ability of the network is utilized to determine which weights are excitatory, which are inhibitory, and which are zero. Hence, the topology can also be self-organized to a certain extent, but starting out with a large number of connections expecting many to go to zero is not a recommended practice because of the large weight update cost incurred, not to mention the convergence problems encountered. Researchers are now looking at ways in which the number of processing units and the connection topology can be adapted as the network is in the process of learning, i.e., ways in which processing units and connections can be added and deleted as the training process progresses (Ash 1989; Tenorio and Lee 1989; Fahlman and Lebiere 1990; Wu 1992).

Rule of activation propagation. Processing units compute their output using their output function and then communicate that output to their neighbors. The rule of propagation describes how the inputs impinging on a processing unit (i.e., the outputs from other processing units) and the strengths of the connections are combined to compute the net input, N, to the processing unit. Most often, this rule is simply a weighted summation, described mathematically as follows:

$$N_j = \sum_i w_{ij}\, o_i \tag{2}$$

If one looks at the outputs from other processing units and the weights of connections from other processing units coming into a processing unit as vectors, e.g., $(o_1,\ o_2,\ ...,\ o_n)$ and $(w_1,\ w_2,\ ...,\ w_n)$, the net input by the above rule of propagation is simply the dot product of these two vectors (Caudhill 1987). The dot product is simply the projection of one vector onto the other, i.e., $|w|\ |o|$ $cos b$, where $|w|$ is the magnitude of the weight vector, $|o|$ is the magnitude of the vector of output impinging on the processing unit and b is the angle between these two vectors (see Fig. 4). Note that the maximum activation will be achieved when b $=$ 0, i.e., the input and the weights vectors are in the same direction, and smallest when they are in opposite directions. Learning an output pattern in a backpropagation neural network is basically the process of moving the direction of the weight vector, w, towards the direction of the output vector, o.

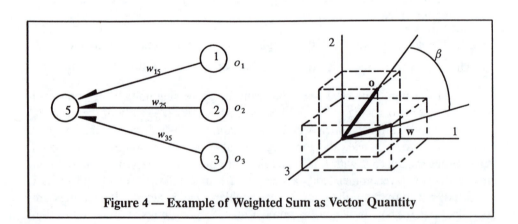

Figure 4 — Example of Weighted Sum as Vector Quantity

From this simple description, the usefulness of neural networks in recognition problems should become apparent. One would simply have to define the different weight vectors (representing the different inputs to be recognized), and the network would activate the output processing unit(s) having the weight vector that most closely matches the input pattern. Note also, that the input vector does not have to exactly match any one weight vector. If the vector is slightly off, a fairly high net input will still occur.

Activation function employed. The activation function, F, defines how the net input received by a processing unit is combined with its current level of activation to compute a new level of activation. The activation function is usually expressed mathematically as follows:

$$a_{inew} = F\left[a_{iold}, N_i\right] \tag{3}$$

However, in simple network simulators the activation function is equated to the value of the net input arriving at the processing unit:

$$a_{inew} = N_i \tag{4}$$

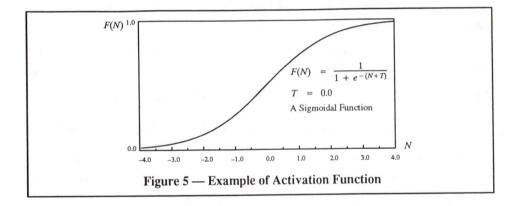

Figure 5 — Example of Activation Function

Whenever the activation function is continuous and bounded (as it most often is), it is common to use a sigmoidal function for F as shown in Fig. 5. The sigmoidal function, which is continuous and differentiable (an important property for use in backpropagation learning), is used to maintain the value of activation for a processing unit within the bounds of 0 and 1.

Rule of learning. The learning rule defines how the network is modified in response to experience (i.e., training cases presented to the system). In the past, only three ways were considered in which the network could be modified:

- develop new connections between the processing units;

- remove existing connections between the processing units; and

- modify the strength of the existing connections between processing units.

The first two types of network modification can be considered as special cases of the third. In addition to adding connections, these researchers have considered adding new processing units and their concomitant connections as another way of modifying the neural network (Ash 1989; Fahlman and Lebiere 1990; Wu 1992). However, most neural network simulators still only provide the capability to modify existing connection strengths.

A large number of rules for modifying the connection strengths of existing connections in unsupervised learning models are a variant of Hebbian Learning. Hebb's rule of learning, also referred to as "Hebb" synapse, is stated as: "*When an axon of cell A is near enough to excite a cell B and repeatedly or persistently takes part in firing it, some growth process or metabolic change takes place in one or both cells such that A's efficiency, as one of the cells firing B, is increased.*" (Hebb 1949)

Using the terminology defined in this section, we can put Hebb's rule of learning as: if a processing unit, u_i , receives an input from another processing unit u_j, and both are active, then the weight, w_{ij} , should be strengthened .

For simple Hebbian Learning, the learning rule can be simply stated as:

$$\Delta w_{ij} = \eta \, a_j \, o_i \tag{5}$$

where η is the learning constant (a value between 0 and 1) representing the degree by which the weights are changed when both processing units are excited. If η is close to zero, the connection strength is modified slightly, while if η is close to one, the connection strength is modified significantly.

Another common form of learning rule is called the *delta rule:* (Widrow and Hoff 1960)

$$\Delta w_{ij} = \eta \left[t_j - a_j \right] o_i \tag{6}$$

It is called the delta rule because learning is proportional to the difference between the actual activation and the expected activation (teaching input). In learning via the delta rule, the weight between i and j is changed only when: 1) the output from processing unit i is non-zero; and 2) the difference between the actual activation of processing unit j and its expected activation is non-zero.

1.2 Why are Artificial Neural Networks Applicable in Civil Engineering?

To better understand why ANNs are interesting tools for supporting the practice of civil engineering, we must first take a closer look at the different types of tasks that engineers in general, and civil engineers in particular, address.

Engineers recognize and formulate problems. They interpret incomplete, noisy data in order to recognize the existence and nature of a problem. For example, consider the problem of detecting damage in a building, with thousands of structural members, by interpreting data collected from accelerometers and displacement transducers placed at various locations on the structure. This is an inverse problem recognizing a state from the observed behavior of a system. In other words, incomplete and uncertain data about a system is mapped into a description of the state of a system. This type of problem is often referred to as classification, but classification can be more generally described as an inverse mapping problem, where the mapping is from observed attributes to the classes for which the set of observed attributes satisfy the necessary conditions for class membership. Because the sufficient conditions may not be observable, the mapping is likely to be non-unique. Non-uniqueness of the mapping is a common characteristic of such inverse mapping problems.

Engineers synthesize solutions to formulated problems. Engineers search over the space of potential problem solutions recognizing potentially feasible parts of this space (i.e., those that deliver desired system behavior) and eliminating infeasible parts of the space (i.e., those that will not deliver such behavior) as quickly as possible. They then focus on refining the potentially feasible solution space. In other words, engineers map from a space of desired system behaviors to a space of system form attributes that deliver that behavior. Again, this process is an inverse mapping problem and as with all inverse mapping problems, the mapping is again non-unique.

Engineers analyze potential solutions to problems. In our attempts to design and control the behavior of systems, both man-made and natural, engineers find that they must be able to *predict* the complex behaviors of these systems, knowing the configuration of the system and the environmental loads to which it is exposed. This is obviously a problem of determining a mapping from cause to effect. Engineers are thus modelers of material and system behaviors, from which they are able to make predictions about the expected behaviors of specific system configurations. However, this behavior 1) is often governed by nonlinear multi-variate (and sometimes unknown) interrelationships, 2) varies over time due to degradation of material properties, and 3) occurs within "noisy" less controllable physical environments. In addition to predicting system behaviors, another aspect of engineering analysis is the *estimation* of unmeasured attributes based on measured attributes. Estimation and prediction, while often used interchangeably, have distinct meanings in this discussion. Prediction is an extrapolation process—i.e., predicting what will happen in the future based on what is known currently about the state of the system and its environmental loads, or predicting how a model will behave beyond the bounds of its observed behavior. Estimation is defined to be an interpolation process—i.e., estimating attributes of a system in its current state based on other known or observed attributes and their relationship to the unknown attributes, or estimating how a model will behave by interpolating between other observed behaviors.

Engineers evaluate potential solutions to problems against a variety of criteria (possibly in conflict) and select a solution from among the available alternatives. They have to take a set of criteria and recognize which potential solutions satisfy most or all of the important criteria and compare and contrast the advantages and disadvantages of each potential solution. The best decision is seldomly one that satisfies all criteria maximally. The evaluation of solutions is an estimation problem, where the values of the evaluation criteria (i.e., effects) are estimated using the set of known form and behavior attributes of the system (i.e., causes) .

Engineers plan, schedule, and allocate resources for the activities required to manufacture/construct a selected alternative. They have to first map a selected alternative into the set of activities required to build it. This is again an inverse mapping from the finished product (i.e., effect) to the activities that cause it to exist (i.e., causes). Once the needed activities are determined, engineers must then determine the types and amounts of resources needed to complete each activity. This is again the result of two inverse mappings. The first is an inverse mapping from the estimated total time and cost of the project (i.e., effect) to the individual activity finish times and costs (i.e., causes). Currently, this is done by starting out with a schedule that uses resources for the critical path activities that ensures the estimated completion time is met. The second inverse mapping is from the finish time and the final cost of each activity (i.e., effect) to the amounts of resources to be applied in completing the activity (i.e., causes).

Engineers manage projects in which they must monitor the state of resource usage and predict the resources required to complete the project. They must continually monitor the state of resource usage and predict whether the project will exceed the expected budget. The prediction of final costs is obviously a direct mapping from the existing state of the project and the nature of resource usage to the total cost of the project. This type of mapping is identical to the

Engineers control and operate dynamic systems acting as solutions to formulated problems. For some problems, dynamic systems are posed as solutions to a problem and must be controlled to provide the desired response, such as an HVAC system within a large multi-function building. Such systems provide the flexibility to deliver desired behavior in situations of dynamic environmental loadings or site conditions, but a control strategy must then be specified. In determining the control strategy, the engineer must determine the mapping between the space of system states and the space of applied control forces, based on some control objective. Again, this is an inverse mapping problem—determining the desired control forces (i.e., a desired cause) for a given system state (the desired effect). Engineers must develop such control strategies for complex systems for which a model of behavior and expected performance is unknown, or not very accurately known, and must be predicted. The thermal performance of a building is such a system for which an accurate model is not available.

In the preceding discussion, the engineering tasks described at one level were: analysis, design, system identification, diagnosis, prediction/estimation, control, and planning/scheduling. However, all of these problems appear to be one of two more abstract types of problem: (1) causal modeling (i.e., mapping from cause to effect for estimation and prediction); and (2) inverse mapping from effects to possible causes.

Engineers have in the past used a variety of *tools* for performing both causal modeling and inverse mapping. This set of tools includes statistics and regression, probabilities and Bayes rule for combining probabilistic evidence, optimization, rules of thumb and knowledge-based systems, and others. The very nature of a neural network is to map from one space of patterns (i.e., the input patterns) to a space of output patterns (i.e., the output patterns). As such, an artificial neural network is thus another tool that can be used for determining such causal models and inverse mappings. For this reason, ANNs should be interesting to engineers as a tool for supporting the tasks that they must perform. For some problems, the ANN may be the best tool. In other cases, it may not. In the next section, examples are presented of where ANNs have been applied in civil engineering to acquire both causal and inverse mappings.

1.3 Where can Artificial Neural Networks be Applied in Civil Engineering?

As discussed in the previous subsection, ANNs can be applied to problems where patterns of information represented in one form need to be mapped into patterns of information in another form. If the direction of the mapping is from the independent to the dependent information, this is a causal mapping; if the direction is from dependent to independent, this is an inverse mapping. For example, the problem of trying to interpret the signals coming from a collection of sensors into some meaningful set of properties on which a decision can be made is a common application of artificial neural networks for solving an inverse problem.   On the other hand, predicting the strain state in a material based on the loading path and the applied stress increment is an example of a causal mapping.   This section is intended to illustrate some of the different types of problems to which ANNs are being applied within the domain of civil engineering.

The major types of tasks in civil engineering to which neural networks are currently being applied are: classification/interpretation tasks (i.e., inverse mapping from observations to known classes), diagnosis (i.e., inverse mapping from observed effect to cause), modeling (mapping from cause to effect), and control (inverse mapping from observed state to control forces function to apply).

Classification and interpretation problems are common applications for ANNs.   Heiler, et al., are investigating the use of ANNs to assist in classifying ground penetrating radar (GPR) signals taken from in-service railroad ties to classify their condition (Heiler, Motazed and McNeil 1993).   They are using signals taken from railroad ties in various states of damage to train a neural network to be able to classify GPR signals from in-service ties.   They are developing a similar approach for classifying bridge deck pavements.   In Chapter 6, the use of an ANN for another classification problem—contractor prequalification evaluation—is described.   As another example, Chapter 9 describes the use of an ANN to classify the liquifaction susceptibility of a site from penetration testing results.

Artificial neural networks are also being applied to solve inverse mapping problems, where the network is trained on a set of cause-effect data and trained to diagnose observed effects in terms of unknown causes.   For example, in Chapter 4 the application of an ANN to detect damage in a cantilever structure from vibrational measurements is described.   Wu, et al., proposed the use of a neural network for the purpose of damage detection in a structural frame (Wu, Ghaboussi and Garrett 1992).   The structural frame was modeled using existing structural modeling and analysis techniques.   Then, the model was artificially "damaged" and subjected to base excitation from several recorded earthquakes. The results from these analyses were then used as training cases to train a network to take displacement observations and predict the location and severity of individual member damage.   Szewczyk and Hajela also developed a neural network-based approach to detecting damage in structural systems (Szewczyk and Hajela 1994).   The ANN they developed is able to quickly acquire and compute the mapping from patterns of displacement information to damage states (i.e., member stiffness reductions).   Gagarin, et al., have applied neural networks to another inverse mapping problem—predicting the attributes of a passing truck from strain response readings taken from the bridge over which it passes (Gagarin, Flood and Albrect 1994).   The benefit of this approach is that bridge loading statistics can be acquired using more conventional, and more reliable, strain gauge technology, and without the need to stop and weigh vehicles.

Chapter 5 presents an application of an ANN for the identification and control of civil engineering structures. In this application, an ANN-based model is first developed from observed structural response to applied loadings. This model is then used to learn the appropriate control forces for observed dynamic behavior of a specific structure. This particular application is another example of an inverse mapping problem. Chapter 7 presents applications of ANNs in Transportation Engineering.

Another area where neural networks are being applied in engineering is for creating models for making predictions and estimations. For example, Chapter 8 presents an ANN geomaterial model used to estimate the strain behavior of the geomaterial in response to changes in its stress state. As another example, Karunanithi et al. developed an ANN to predict the flow of a river (Karunanithi et al. 1994). The ANN is trained to take a period of historical river flow data and to predict the flow beyond immediately beyond that period. As another example, Chao and Skibniewski describe the use of an ANN as an estimator (Chao and Skibniewski 1994). The authors describe how they can use an ANN to estimate the productivity of various construction activities. The authors present an interesting approach for acquiring the data they need to train the network—they observe bench-scale operations and construction simulations. Using ANNs as a means of capturing and efficiently utilizing simulation data is an interesting and effective application of this technology.

A slightly different application is that of using the neural network as a surrogate for more complicated and time-consuming prediction models. Such ANN-based models can be used to quickly pare-down a problem space, after which the more costly, time-consuming predictive models can be applied to the much smaller problem space. For example, this is the approach taken by Ranjithan, et al., in developing a tool for estimating the difficulty of remediating a contaminated ground water aquifer with an unknown hydraulic conductivity field (Ranjithan, Eheart and Garrett 1993). In his approach, Ranjithan used an existing remediation design system to design a remediation plan for a large number of different hypothesized hydraulic conductivity fields, and then used this data to train a neural network to predict the cost of dealing with other hydraulic conductivity fields. Such a tool, once created, can seriously reduce the number of possible hydraulic conductivity fields that need to be considered by a remediation designer. As another example, Rogers applied an ANN to the problem of structural behavior modeling or prediction of behavior (Rogers 1994). Rogers describes the use of an ANN as a surrogate behavior model for a more complicated and time-consuming finite element-based structural analysis procedure. The critical question in these types of applications of neural networks is one of generality—i.e., is the network that is trained by solving a large number of problems able to solve other different types of problems. If not, then the question of overall impact of the trained network arises. Ranjithan was able to show that hydraulic conductivity fields generated from a reasonably diverse range of field statistics could be predicted with sufficient accuracy using his neural network approach. Rogers claimed that such a ANN-based behavior prediction capability could be justified for use in optimization systems where many iterations of behavior prediction occur.

1.4 Summary

As illustrated by the above described applications, neural networks can play a role in addressing the tasks of classification/interpretation (i.e., mapping observations to known classes), diagnosis (i.e., mapping effect to cause), modeling (mapping cause to effect), and control. The advantages of using ANNs for these problems are that they are universal approximators of multi-variate nonlinear mappings, some are able to acquire this mapping automatically, they are able to compute these mappings when there are small amounts of error in the input patterns, and they are able to compute these mappings very fast due to their inherent parallel nature if implemented in hardware. The intent of this monograph is to provide the civil engineering audience with a focused discussion and illustration of appropriate civil engineering problems to which ANNs should be applied and why. Later chapters will present in depth discussions of several more applications of neural networks to specific civil engineering problems.

1.5 References

Ash, T. (1989). "Dynamic Node Creation in Backpropagation Networks," *Proceedings of the International Joint Conference on Neural Networks*, Washington D. C., June 18-22.

Caudhill, M. (1987). "Neural Networks Primer - Part I," *AI Expert*, December, 1987.

Chao, L. C. and Skibniewski, M. "Estimating Construction Productivity: A Neural Network-Based Approach," *J. of Computing in Civil Engineering,* Vol 8., No. 2, pp. pp. 234-251, April.

Cybenko, G. "Approximations by Superpositions of A Sigmoidal Function," *CSRD Report No. 856*, Center for Supercomputing Research and Development, University of Illinois, Urbana, Illinois, Feb., 1989.

Fahlman, S. E., and Lebiere, C. (1990). "The Cascade–Correlation Learning Architecture," *Technical Report CMU–CS–90–100*, School of Computer Science, Carnegie Mellon University, Pittsburgh, PA.

Gagarin, N., Flood, I. and Albrecht. P. (1994). "Computing Truck Attributes with Artificial Neural Networks," *J. of Computing in Civil Engineering,* Vol 8., No. 2, pp. pp. 179-200, April.

Hebb, D. O. (1949). *The Organization of Behavior: A Neuropsychological Theory,* Wiley, New York.

Hornik, K., Stinchcombe, M., and White, H. (1989). "Multilayer Feedforward Networks are Universal Approximators," *Neural Networks*, 2, 356-366.

Karunanithi, N., Grenney, W. J., Whitley, D. and Bovee K. (1994). "Neural Networks for River Flow Prediction, *J. of Computing in Civil Engineering,* Vol 8., No. 2, pp. pp. 201-220, April.

Heiler, M., Motazed, B. and McNeil, S. (1993). "Exploration of Ground Penetrating Radar for Railroad Tie Maintenance Scheduling," in Proceedings of *Infrastructure Management: New Challenges, New Methods*, ASCE, Denver, June 1993.

Ranjithan, S., J. W. Eheart, and J. H. Garrett, Jr. (1993). "A Neural Network-Based Screening Tool for Groundwater Reclamation Under Uncertainty," *Journal of Water Resources Research*, Vol. 29, No. 3, pp. 563-574.

Rogers, J. L. (1994). "Simulating Structural Analysis with a Neural Network," *J. of Computing in Civil Engineering,* Vol 8., No. 2, pp. pp. 252-265, April.

Rumelhart, D. E., McClelland, J. L., and the PDP Research Group. (1986). *Parallel Distributed Processing - Volume 1: Foundations.* The MIT Press, Cambridge, MA.

Rumelhart, D. E., Hinton, G. E., and Williams, R. J. (1986). "Learning Internal Representations by Error Propagation," in *Parallel Distributed Processing: Explorations in the Microstructure of Cognition, Vol. 1: Foundations,* D. E., Rumelhart, and J. L., McClelland, Eds., The MIT Press, ch. 8.

Rumelhart, D. E., Hinton, G. E., and McClelland, J. L. (1986). "A General Framework for Parallel Distributed Processing," in *Parallel Distributed Processing: Explorations in the Microstructure of Cognition, Vol. 1: Foundations,* D. E., Rumelhart, and J. L., McClelland, Eds., The MIT Press, ch. 2.

Szewczyk, Z. P and Hajela, P. (1994). "Damage Detection in Structures Based on Feature-Sensitive Neural Networks," *J. of Computing in Civil Engineering*, Vol 8., No. 2, pp. 163-178 , April.

Tenorio, M. F., and Lee, W.-T. (1989). "Self–Organizing Neural Network for Optimum Supervised Learning," *Technical Report TR–EE–89–30*, School of Electrical Engineering, Purdue University, West Lafayette, Indiana.

Tsai, C. C. (1993). "Classification of Radar Signals using Neural Networks for Railroad Tie Inspection." Unpublished M.S. Thesis, Department of Civil Engineering, Carnegie Mellon University, Pittsburgh, PA, 70 pages.

Widrow, B., and Hoff, M. E. (1960). "Adaptive Switching Circuits," *1960 IRE WESCON Convention Record,* New York, IRE, 96–104.

Wu, X., (1992) "Neural Network-Based Material Modeling." Unpublished Ph.D. Thesis, Department of Civil Engineering, University of Illinois at Urbana-Champaign, Urbana, Illinois, 202 pages.

Wu, X., J. Ghaboussi, and J. H. Garrett, Jr. (1992). "Use of Neural Networks in the Detection of Structural Damage," *Computers and Structures*, Vol. 42, No. 4, pp. 649-659.

Chapter 2

Systems

Ian Flood[1] and Nabil Kartam[2]

Abstract : The chapter provides an introduction to the diverse range of alternative artificial neural network systems currently available. This is achieved with reference to a decomposition and classification of the key features of artificial neural systems. An identification is first made of the different types of processing that can be performed at the neuron level, the lowest level in a neural network. This is followed by an identification of the different ways in which neurons can be combined into an integral processing device capable of solving non-trivial problems. The range of alternative function types that can be implemented by neural networks are then examined. Finally, a review is made of the primary methods of developing/training neural networks to solve a given problem. At each stage of the discourse, relevant neural paradigms are referenced and areas of application pertinent to civil engineering are identified.

2.1 Introduction

The objective of this chapter is not to provide a comprehensive listing and description of all relevant neural network systems (such information is readily available in several excellent texts, such as that by Hecht-Nielsen (1990)). Rather, the intent is to provide a clear insight into the diverse range of neural networking systems that have been developed over the years, and an understanding of their applicability to different types of problem. This is achieved by reference to Fig. 1, which shows a decomposition and classification of the main features comprising neural networking systems. Double lines are used to denote a decomposition into inclusive features (that is, features that are all present in some form within a neural system), while shaded lines are used to classify exclusive features (features that usually exist independently of each

---

[1] ME Rinker Sr. School of Building Construction, Florida, USA
[2] Dept. of Civil Eng., Kuwait University, P.O.Box.5969, Safat, 13060, Kuwait

other). It should be noted, however, that some hybrid systems may incorporate several exclusive features within a single neural system.

2.2 Operation Of Neurons

An important feature of any neural networking system, critical to the type of problem it can solve, is the mode of operation of its neurons. The key features of neuron operation are listed in the top box of Fig. 1, and are discussed in turn in this section.

The neuron, a schematic of which is shown in Fig. 2, is the basic building block of a neural network. For the purposes of this discussion, it is convenient to talk about a neuron as comprising both the cell body and its input links, as illustrated in the figure. Neurons come in an indefinite variety of functional forms. The specific form is determined by the type of signal received and transmitted by the neuron (whether it is a stream of pulses, or a real value), and the functions performed on signals as they pass across the links and through the main body of the neuron (see Fig. 2).

In principle, there are no restrictions on the form of a neuron in any of these respects (the activation function could be a high order polynomial for example), though in practice the tendency is to maintain simplicity in function at the neuron level and allow complexity in the function of the network to result from the interaction between the neurons.

Signal type

A dichotomy of neurons (in terms of the type of signal they process) is into those that use pulse coding of data, and those that represent data as single values. In the later case, the types of coding can be further divided into discrete-change value neurons (making changes in activation value at discrete points in time), and continuous-change value neurons (with continuously varying activation values, such as occurs in electronic analog circuitry).

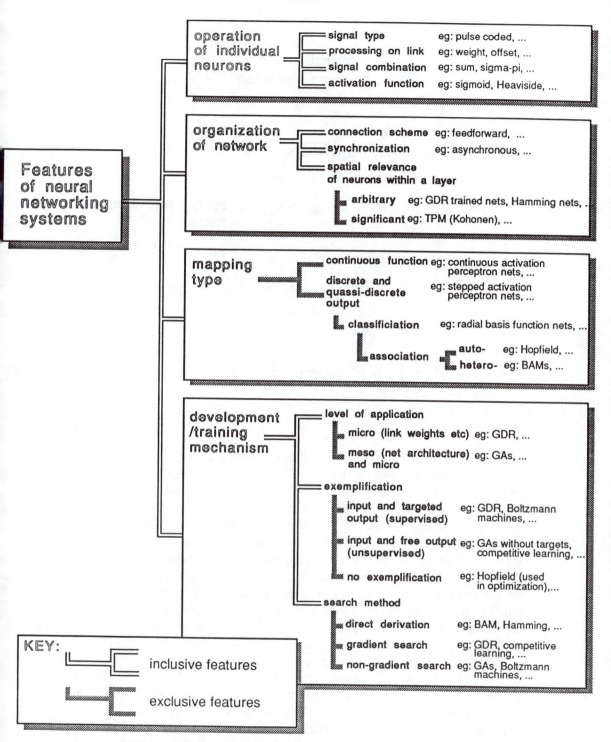

Fig. 1: Decomposition-Classification of Neural Networking Systems

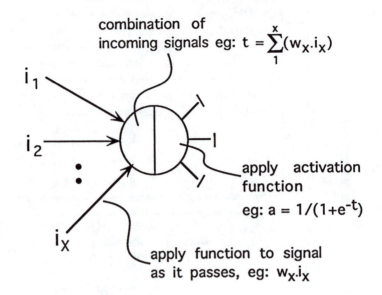

combination of
incoming signals eg: $t = \sum_{1}^{x}(w_x \cdot i_x)$

i_1

i_2

apply activation
function

eg: $a = 1/(1+e^{-t})$

i_x

apply function to signal
as it passes, eg: $w_x \cdot i_x$

Fig. 2: Main Elements of a Neuron

In the pulse-coded approach, information is received by and transmitted from a neuron as a stream of pulses (see Fig. 3(a)). It is the frequency of the pulses, rather than their amplitude, that represents the information. While this mode of operation is close to that of biological neurons, limited work has been undertaken applying pulse-coding neurons to engineering problems. However, certain advantages are claimed for this type of neuron, in particular an ability to encode a large amount of information within the pulse structure (Dayhoff, 1990). The frequency with which a neuron emits pulses is dependent on its potential or charge (measured in the main cell body) at the current point in time. This potential tends to discharge as the neuron emits pulses. Pulses arriving along the input links to the neuron may tend to further decrease this potential (for an inhibitory connection between the link and the main cell body) or increase the potential (if the connection is excitatory). Usually, neurons of this type include a saturation level beyond which the potential in the main cell body (and thus the rate of output of pulses) cannot be increased. The inherent temporal dependency of the output from these neurons could possibly be exploited in the solution of dynamic problems arising in civil engineering (modeling the dynamic behavior of structures for example). Indeed, Goerke et al. (1990) have developed a network composed of these neurons that can generate different sequences of pulse codes suitable for the dynamic control of actuators. Clearly, there is a need for exploration of the potential of this type of element for civil engineering applications.

Continuous-change value neurons, on the other hand, represent their level of activation as a single value that may change in a continuous manner over time, as illustrated in Fig. 3(b). Again, networks based on this method of coding data have received little or no attention within civil engineering, but would seem to have potential for application to any of the wide variety of dynamic problems arising in this discipline.

The method of representing information received by and transmitted from a neuron as a discretely changing value (such as illustrated in Fig. 3(c)) is currently the favored approach in civil engineering. In this set-up, a neuron outputs a value (often a real number) which is held until the neuron is put through another processing cycle.

The most widely used variant in this class is the sigmoidal neuron (a schematic of which is shown in Fig. 4(a)) which operates in accordance with the following system of equations and has been discussed in more detail in Chapter 1:

$$t_n = \sum_{x=1}^{x} (w_{x,n} \cdot i_x) + b_n \tag{1}$$

$$a_n = \frac{1}{1 + e^{-t_n}} \tag{2}$$

where: t_n is the summed weighted input to the n-th hidden neuron; $w_{x,n}$ are the weights on the connections to the hidden neuron; b_n is a weighted bias associated with the neuron; and a_n is the activity level generated at the hidden neuron.

Processing of signal

The above sigmoidal neuron is just one of an indefinite range of discrete-change value neurons. This class can be further subdivided according to three stages of processing implemented at the various locations across a neuron, as indicated in Fig. 2. The first stage is the operation applied to signals received across the input links, the second stage refers to the way in which signals arriving at the main body of the cell are combined, and the third stage refers to the activation function applied to this combined value. The significance of each of these stages of processing can readily be understood from a graphical interpretation of the operation of the neuron. For this purpose, a plot is made of the level of activation generated by the neuron in response to a range of values presented across its inputs.

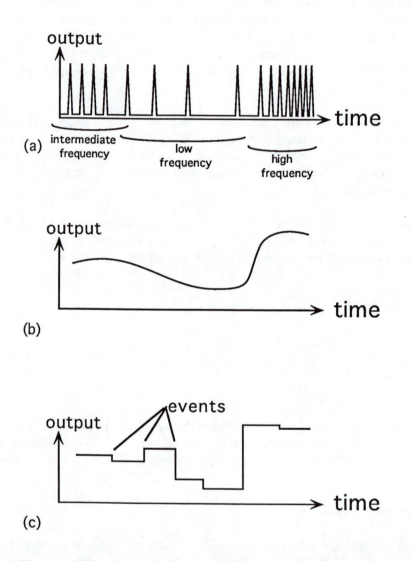

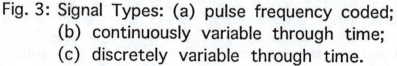

Fig. 3: Signal Types: (a) pulse frequency coded;
(b) continuously variable through time;
(c) discretely variable through time.

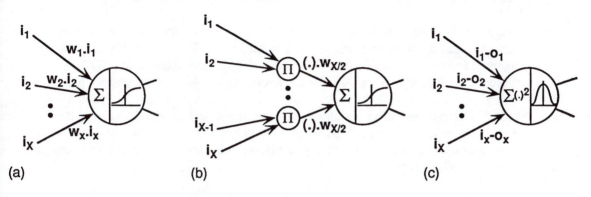

Fig. 4: Neuron Types: (a) laminar function; (b) sigma-pi function; (c) radial function.

Fig. 5(a) shows typical output from the sigmoidal neuron operating in accordance with Eqns. (1) and (2) and comprising two inputs. Note, the surface assumes the form of a sigmoidal step. This basic form would be produced by any neuron of this type, although its specific attributes (direction in which the step rises, its steepness, and its displacement from the origin) will vary depending on the values of the weights on the input links and the value of the neuron's bias, as discussed by Flood and Kartam (1994). This interpretation can be extended to neurons with any number of input links, though it is not possible to plot the results as they are hyper-surfaces involving more than three dimensions. Contrast this first activation surface with the others shown in Fig. 5 produced by a variety of different types of neuron. The surfaces shown in Figs. 5(b) and 5(c) are also produced by neurons of the type shown in Fig. 4(a), operating in accordance with Eqn. (1), but utilizing the Gaussian and sine activation functions, equations (3) and (4), respectively:

$$a_n = e^{-s_n t_n^2} \tag{3}$$

$$a_n = sine(t_n) \tag{4}$$

Note that the basic shape of these surfaces is defined by the form of activation function adopted. Also note that all three of these surfaces have contour maps composed of a series of parallel straight lines. This is true for any neuron that operates in accordance with Eqn. (1), irrespective of its activation function.

There are a number of other widely used neuron types that have functional surfaces radically different from those discussed so far. The first of these are the sigma-pi (or second order) neurons (see, for example, Rumelhart et al. (1986a)), illustrated in Fig. 4(b). The name is a reference to the fact that they apply both summation (Σ) and product (Π) operations to the signals arriving from the input links. The number of permutations of summations and products that can be performed on a set of input signals grows rapidly with the number of inputs. Consequently, only a subset of these permutations are usually performed, such as in the following equation:

$$t_n = \sum_{x=1}^{x/2}(w_{x,n} \times i_{2x-1,n} \times i_{2x,n}) + b_n \qquad (5)$$

Figs. 5(d) to 5(f) show the surfaces produced by a two input sigma-pi neuron operating in accordance with Eqn. (5), utilizing the sigmoid, Gaussian, and sine activation functions respectively. Note that, the contour maps of these surfaces are non-linear in form. The advantage of using this type of neuron seems to be, though not fully established, facilitation of training in situations where the solution surface is particularly complicated in form.

A third class of neurons in relatively widespread use are the radial neurons, so called because their contour maps comprise a series of concentric circles (or spheres or hyper-spheres for neurons with three or more input links), radiating from a single point in the input plane. Fig. 4(c) shows the basic form of these neurons, the operation of which, prior to application of the activation function, is given by:

$$t_n = \sqrt{\sum_{x=1}^{x}(c_{x,n} - i_x)^2} \qquad (6)$$

where: $c_{x,n}$ is a vector of offsets associated with the input connections to the neuron.

This simply measures the magnitude of the distance between the vectors i and c. Applying the sigmoid, Gaussian, or sine activation functions result in surfaces of the forms illustrated in Figs. 5(g) to 5(i). Radial neurons, in particular those utilizing the Gaussian or similar activation function, are often used in classification type problems since they can be focused over a localized region of input space thereby grouping problems with similar input patterns (Moody and

Darken, 1989). In addition, the localized nature of these functions (if using a Gaussian-like activation function) provide better control when constructing a composite from these functions (see Flood (1991)).

There are many variations on the above theme at each of the three stages of processing. In principle, the activation function (the third stage of processing) can take on any form and may include discontinuities, a common example of which is the Heaviside or step function:

$$H(t_n) = \begin{cases} 0 & \text{when } t_n \leq b_n \\ 1 & \text{when } t_n > b_n \end{cases} \tag{7}$$

Neurons of this type are widely used in networks used in classification type applications where there are a finite number of alternative results that can be conveniently represented by discrete values such as the binary 0 and 1. Common examples of networking systems that use this mode of operation include Hamming networks (Lippmann, 1987) and Boltzmann machines (Hinton and Sejnowski, 1986).

In the extreme case, a neuron may not include an activation function. This is particularly common for neurons that operate in accordance with Eqn. (1). In this case, the neuron acts as a simple integrator of incoming signals, adding together the results from the preceding layer of neurons in the quantities denoted by the weights on the corresponding links. Neurons that operate in this manner are often used at the output layer of a network, providing a convenient mechanism for combining the sub-tasks performed by other sections of the network into a single result.

Another important variant are the neurons used in the functional link networks (Pao, 1989). Here, non-linear functions are applied to the values transmitted across the input links (the first stage processing) of a single layer of neurons. The application of non-linear functions at this location facilitates modeling non-linear problems without the use of hidden neurons and activation functions. This can greatly increase the rate at which a network can be trained, though there is no clear guide for selecting an appropriate function to apply across the links.

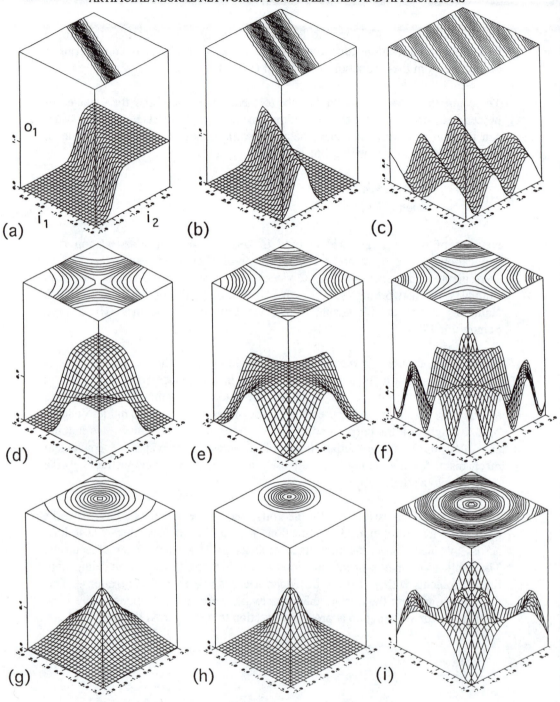

Fig. 5: Neuron Activation Surfaces:
(a) laminar-sigmoid; (b) laminar-Gaussian; (c) laminar-sine;
(d) sigma-pi-sigmoid; (e) sigma-pi-Gaussian; (f) sigma-pi-sine;
(g) radial-sigmoid; (h) radial-Gaussian; (i) radial-sine;

2.3 Spatio-Temporal Organization Of A Network

The function performed by a neuron is, typically, very simple and thus capable of solving only a very limited set of problems. It is, however, the collective operation of a large number of neurons that provides the richness and versatility necessary to solve more complicated problems such as those considered in the later chapters of this book. For this purpose, neurons are connected into a network, so that the levels of activation generated at certain neurons becomes the input to other neurons. The way in which neurons are connected as such has a major effect on the behavior and, ultimately, the function performed by the network. Conversely, for some networking systems, the spatial orientation of neurons within a network forms, as a result of training, an analog of some aspect of the problem to be solved. In addition, the temporal organization of a network (that is, the firing scheme or the relative timing by which the neurons execute their processes) is also significant in determining the precise nature of the function it implements. These organizational details, listed in the second box of Fig. 1, are the subject of this section.

Connection schemes

Fig. 6 shows the two most fundamental neural network connection schemes: the fully connected network; and the layered feedforward network. The fully connected network is the most comprehensive connection scheme, with all neurons linking to all other neurons, including themselves.

All other connection schemes can be thought of as a subset of this structure, that is with some connections absent. The layered feedforward network, on the other hand, divides the neurons into distinct layers, with some or all of the neurons in one layer feeding into some or all of the neurons in the subsequent layer. Neurons within each layer are considered to operate in parallel with each other, while those in different layers are effectively operating in series. Importantly, all networks can be converted into a layered feedforward equivalent.

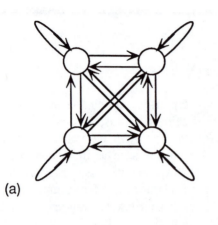

(a)

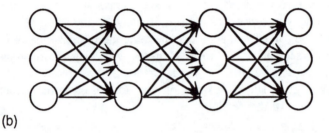

(b)

Fig. 6: Fundamental Connection schemes:
(a) fully connected; (b) layered feedforward.

Fig. 7 illustrates the above points, using a simple network comprising four neurons, with a feedback link from neuron C to neuron B, and a recurrent link on neuron B (feeding back to itself). Fig. 7(a) shows the original form of the network, while Fig 7(b) shows its interpretation as a subset of a fully connected system - the actual links are shown in bold and the missing links are presented as shadows. Fig. 7(c) shows the layered feedforward equivalent of the network. Here, each layer represents a subsequent cycle of processing in the original feedback network.

Feedforward networks have become the most widely adopted connection scheme for civil engineering applications. This results from there simplicity and the fact that they lend themselves to training by the popular error-backpropagation techniques such as the Generalized Delta Rule (Rumelhart et al., 1986b). Error backpropagation can, however, be applied to networks that incorporate feedback links (see Chapter 12). Moreover, there are many neural networking systems where feedback is a prerequisite. One such example is the Brain-State-in-a-Box network (Anderson et al., 1977), which uses a fully connected architecture as given in Fig. 6(a). Three other examples, illustrated in Fig. 8, are: (i) the Hopfield network (Hopfield, 1982; Hopfield and Tank, 1985) which is fully connected but with no recurrent links; the Bidirectional Associative Memory network (BAM) (Kosko, 1988) which comprises two layers fully connected to each other; and the Hamming network (Lippmann et al., 1987) which is a hybrid consisting of a layered feedforward network followed by a fully connected network. In each of these examples, the architecture of the network is critical to the function they perform, often with the links designed to inhibit activity in neighboring neurons. Interestingly, most neural networks with a high degree of feedback (such as discussed here) are used for some form of pattern classification.

The concept of feedback is particularly useful for modeling dynamic processes (see Chapter 12 for example). Feedback can allow a network to undergo a sequence of state transitions, over an indefinite period of time, that is analogous in some way to the time-wise behavior of physical processes. Flood and Worley (1995) have demonstrated the feasibility and validity of this approach for modeling the dynamic behavior of construction processes.

Finally, many neural networking systems are composed of several interconnected networks (or network modules). Hamming networks (see Fig. 8(c)) are a clear example of this, where the first level network is designed to measure how close (in Hamming distance terms) an input pattern is to each example in a set of prototype patterns, while the second level network is designed to select the closest prototype pattern. Breaking down a problem into a number of sub-tasks, as such, and then solving each with its own network module has been adopted in several applications in civil engineering. The advantages are: (i) training is less likely to fail since each network module can focus on a simpler task that is less likely to contain conflicting information (see, for example, the problem of determining truck attributes from bridge strain data (Gagarin et al., 1994)); (ii) greater ease in maintaining the system since new functions can be added without the need to retrain the entire network (see, for example, the problem of estimating earthmoving equipment production (Karshenas and Feng, 1992)); and, (iii) increased scope of application in that a user can be allowed to assemble an appropriate combination of modules, from a menu, to solve any of a broad class of problems (see, for example, the task of constructing neural-based construction simulation models (Flood and Worley, 1995)).

Synchronization

Most neural networks function in a synchronous manner so that, at any point in time, all neurons are operating at the same stage in their processing cycle. Alternatively, neurons may operate asynchronously, that is out of phase with each other, often in some random fashion. Hopfield networks (Hopfield, 1982) are an example of devices that operate in this manner - in this case neurons update their states at random points in time, though with equal probability. Asynchronous operation, as such, adds an element of noise to the function implemented by the network, and is particularly useful in pattern classification type problems for reducing the likelihood that a network will converge on a spurious result representing an unspecified class in the problem.

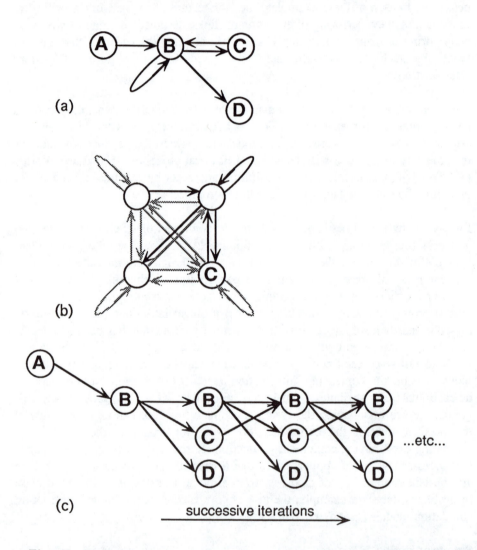

Fig. 7: Reinterpretations of a Simple Recursive Network: (a) original network topology; (b) as a subset of a fully connected network; (c) layered feedforward interpretation.

Spatial relevance of neurons

For most neural networking systems, the physical location of a neuron within the network is of no particular relevance. For example, the initial assignment of input neurons to independent variables, and output neurons to dependent variables, can usually be made in

an arbitrary manner, so long as the chosen scheme is maintained subsequent to training. Likewise, each hidden neuron develops, through training, a contribution to the function provided by the network that has no relevance to its physical location within the layer.

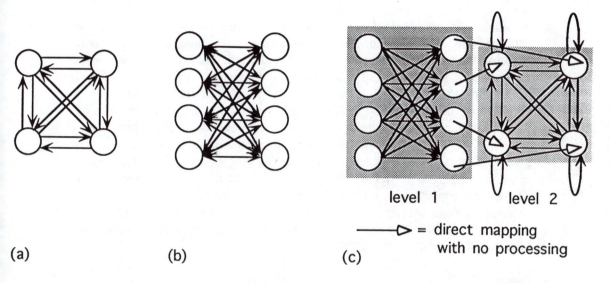

level 1   level 2

━━━▷ = direct mapping
with no processing

(a)   (b)   (c)

Fig. 8: Common Network Connection Schemes: (a) Hopfield network; (b) BAM network; (c) Hamming network.

However, there are a few networking systems where the location of a neuron within a network is of significance. In Kohonen's self-organizing Topology-Preserving Maps (TPMs) (Kohonen, 1989), for example, the network organizes itself during training so that output neurons in close proximity will respond to input patterns that are physically similar. Another example occurs in radial-Gaussian neural networks developed using the incremental training algorithm (Flood, 1991). In this case, the position of a hidden neuron determines the extent of its contribution to solving the overall problem. The hidden neurons are ordered with the most significant on one side and the least significant on the other side. This is particularly useful if it is required at some later date to cut down the size of the network, since it facilitates removal of the least significant neurons.

2.4 Mapping Types

Continuous Functional Mapping

A useful means of classifying neural networks is in terms of their method of interpreting a problem and representing its solution, the third feature type presented in Fig. 1. Fig. 9, shows the most general form of problem-to-solution mapping performed by neural networks, that of continuous functional mapping.

A problem is presented to the network as a vector of real values, such as described above. This vector marks an instance in an X dimensional input space (X being the number of inputs to the neural network). The solution produced by the network is also a vector of values (real and/or integers), this time marking an instance in a Y dimensional output space. A key characteristic of this mode of operation is, as illustrated by the figure, that problems in close proximity in the input space tend to map onto solutions in close proximity in the output space. Networks that incorporate neurons with continuous activation functions, such as given by Eqns. (2)-(4) , generally provide this type of mapping. Continuous function mapping is by far the most common mode of operation used in civil engineering applications. Examples include the estimation of construction productivity from both quantitative and qualitative system attributes (Chao and Skibniewski, 1994), and extrapolating river flow measurements to unmetered locations (Karunanithi et al., 1984).

Discrete Output

An alternative class of mapping types is that in which the output generated by the network is discrete in value. As before, these networks map from points in input space to points in output space. However, in this case, problems falling within distinct regions of the input space tend to map to a single common point in the output space (see Chapter 11, for example). Input to the network may be either continuous or discrete.

The output of discrete values is usually achieved by means of a stepped function such as the Heaviside function given in Eqn. (7). However, in some circumstances, continuous activation functions may be used and the neurons forced to output values that approximate any of a finite set of discrete values. This may be achieved through training - networks with sigmoidal activation functions, for example, are often trained using the Generalized Delta Rule (Rumelhart et al., 1986b) to output values close to either 0.0 or 1.0.

Alternatively, neurons with continuous activation functions (such as given by Eqns. (2) to (4) may be forced to converge, in an iterative process, on values close to one of a finite number of discrete values. In this case, the output from the network is fed back in such a way that each output neuron tends to weaken the signal of its competitors while, in some set-ups, reinforcing its own signal. This process is repeated many times until the values generated at the outputs have all converged on stable values. An example of this latter approach is the Hopfield network with continuous activation functions (Hopfield and Tank, 1985), which forces the values generated at its outputs to converge on either 0.0 or 1.0. Hopfield networks, however, cannot be used as general purpose discrete output mapping devices, but fall into the more specific class of pattern associators discussed below.

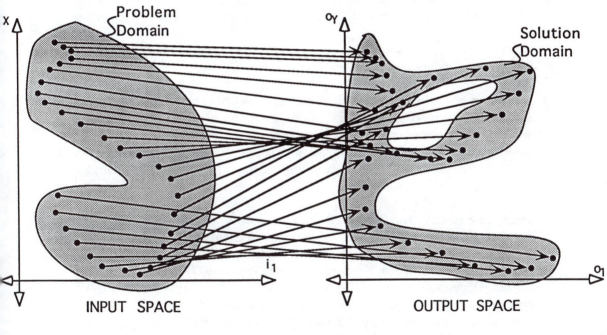

●───▶●= problem to solution mapping

Fig. 9: Mapping From Continuously Variable Input Space to Continuously Variable Output space.

35

Pattern Classifiers

Pattern classifiers are an important sub-class of the discrete output networks. These devices are characterized by the mapping of several mutually exclusive input regions to the same point in output space, as illustrated in Fig. 10 (see regions A and D in this figure, for example).

All the points comprising a region in the input space (such as any of the marked input regions in Fig. 10) may represent either true or noisy variants of a prototype input pattern. Gagarin et al. (1994) describe a neural network system part of which is designed to classify trucks according to the FHWA method, from the strain behavior of the structure over which they are traveling. The classification system is based primarily on the configuration of truck axles. Trucks with similar axle configurations tend to produce similarly shaped strain-time response curves, and thus tend to fall within a contiguous region of the input space. Slight differences in the spacings of axles provide true variants within a class of trucks. However, the strain response of a structure includes noise caused by other traffic and the dynamic response of the structure. Such noise has the effect of increasing the area of each region in input space that maps to an output class.

Associative Networks

Associative networks are a group of devices that operate in a manner very similar to classifiers, providing mappings of the form indicated in Fig. 10. The distinction is primarily one of application, with the output vector of an associator more specifically thought of as a pattern (usually an image) rather than an identity for a class. This view has been inspiration for the design of some highly specialized network architectures.

There are essentially two types of associative network: (i) autoassociators which associate an input pattern with an idealized version or prototype of itself (examples include the Hopfield Network (Hopfield, 1982; Hopfield and Tank, 1985), Brain State in a Box Network (Anderson et al., 1977), and the Hamming network (Lippmann et al., 1987)) and in this sense map points in input space directly back to other points in input space as illustrated in Fig. 11; and (ii) heteroassociatiors which map between different patterns in separate spaces (examples include the Adaptive Resonance Theory (ART) (Carpenter and

Grossberg, 1988) (see Chapter 5), and the Bidirectional Associative Memory (Kosko, 1988)). Autoassociative networks are most usually used for removing noise from an image or completing an incomplete pattern, though the Hopfield Network, in particular, is often used for solving optimization problems.

Tongthong (1993), for example, has considered the use of Hopfield networks for resource level optimization in construction projects.

2.5 Network Development And Training Mechanisms

The fourth key feature of a neural networking system indicated in Fig. 1 is that of developing or training the network. This usually refers to the process of determining the specific values for the network parameters, such as the weights and biases, that will make it perform the required function, though it may also include establishing certain network architectural details.

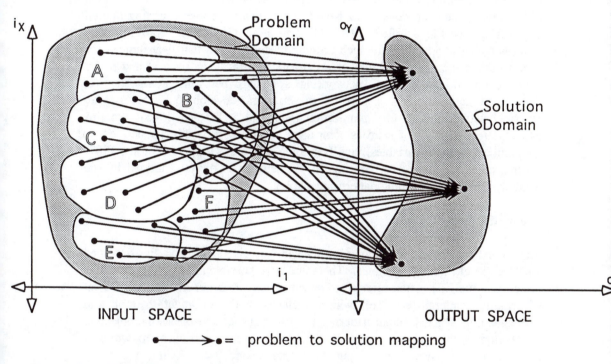

Fig. 10: Classification Mapping

Level of application

There are, according to Fig. 1, three sub-features to any training mechanism. The first is the level within the network at which training occurs. Most usually, this is at a low level, determining values for the weights, biases, and so on, in the network, though in some mechanisms training may also operate at a higher level determining architectural factors such as the number of neurons to include in the network. The Generalized Delta Rule (GDR) (Rumelhart et al., 1986b) is the most widely used example in civil engineering of a training mechanism that operates solely at a low level within a network (see Chapters 1, 5, and 9 to 13). Genetic algorithms (Srinivas and Patnaik, 1991), the radial-Gaussian incremental training algorithm (Flood, 1991), network pruning algorithms (Karnin, 1990), and the Cascade Correlation Algorithm (Fahlman and Lebiere, 1990), on the other hand, are all training methods that determine network structure (in addition to low level parameter values) that have been applied to problems arising in civil engineering (see Flood (1989; 1990), Gagarin et al. (1994), and Karunanithi et al. (1994)). The advantage of such training mechanisms is that they remove the need to select the exact structure of a network arbitrarily or by trial and error. Other common examples of networking systems where the architecture is determined automatically as part of the network development process, are Hopfield networks used for optimization (Hopfield and Tank, 1985) (in this case, the total number of neurons comprising the network is directly defined by the number of output variables), and Hamming networks (Lippmann et al., 1987) (in this case, the number of neurons in the network is directly defined by the number of prototype training patterns available).

Exemplification

The second sub-feature of training mechanisms, as given in Fig. 1, is concerned with the use of training examples. There are three possible approaches under this category. The first (often referred to as supervised training) makes use of a set of training patterns each of which includes both an input pattern and corresponding targeted output pattern. The training mechanism has the objective of developing the network into a state whereby it can reproduce, to within a given error tolerance, these input to output mappings. Again, the GDR (Rumelhart et al., 1986b) is the most widely used example of this mechanism in civil engineering. Other examples include learning in Bidirectional Associative Memory (BAM) (Kosko, 1988), and learning in Boltzmann Machines (Hinton and Sejnowski, 1986).

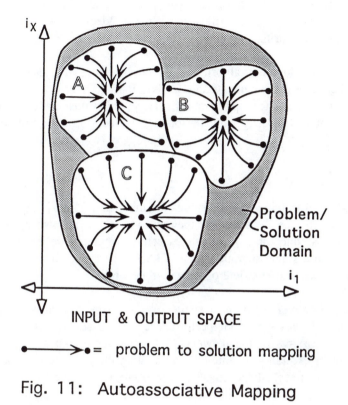

Fig. 11: Autoassociative Mapping

Alternatively, some training mechanisms make use of training examples that do not include targeted outputs. This approach is adopted when there is no *a priori* knowledge of what solutions should be produced by the network for a given problem (perhaps because appropriate solutions are not available, or are too expensive to obtain) or when there is a desire to let the system identify by itself underlying groupings in a set of data. Genetic Algorithms (GAs) (see for example Srinivas and Patnaik (1991) can be used in this way, and have, for example, been applied to the determination of optimal sequences of construction processes (Flood, 1989; Flood, 1990). GAs operate by evolving a network (or family of networks) in a manner analogous to natural evolution, with successive generations being selected or rejected according to some fitness function. (Note that GAs can also be used in a supervised manner with targeted output).

39

Likewise, competitive learning algorithms, such as those developed by Kohonen (1989), operate without the use of output patterns. In this case, the algorithm uses the proximity of input patterns in input space to determine how to adjust the responses of neurons, and are thus particularly adept at grouping patterns according to their clustering.

Some network development algorithms operate without the use of training patterns. The clearest example of this is the Hopfield network (Hopfield and Tank, 1985) when used for optimization. Here, the values of the connection weights are computed directly from the objective function of the problem to be optimized.

Search method

The final feature of training mechanisms is the method, or algorithm, they use to compute values for the network parameters and, where necessary, define the specific network architecture. The fastest operating methods define the specifics of the network in a single-step algorithm. BAMs operate in this manner, as do Hamming networks, and Hopfield optimization networks.

Most methods, however, operate in an iterative manner, starting with an initial set-up (that usually has very poor performance) then gradually moving through ever improving variants of the network. The changes to the network may be directed by either explicitly or implicitly computing the gradient (and sometimes higher order derivatives) of the objective function with respect to the parameter to be modified, and using this information to determine the modification to be made. This is efficient in the sense that modifications are more likely to lead to an improvement in the networks performance. On the other hand, the network can quickly become trapped in a locally optimal solution (though this can be overcome by the introduction of noise such as used in non-gradient search methods discussed in the next paragraph), and the method can only be adopted in situations where the objective function is differentiable with respect to the parameters to be modified. The GDR (Rumelhart et al., 1986b), and Kohonen's competitive learning algorithms (Kohonen, 1989) are examples of directed iterative methods of training.

Alternatively, iterative search methods may be undirected in the sense that they do not, in any way, make use of the gradient of the optimization function to determine the modifications to be made to the network. Modifications are made in a random manner and their utility (and consequently their acceptance or rejection) is assessed retrospectively. Training in Boltzmann machines, and GAs operating in either a supervised or unsupervised mode, are example search methods that fall into this category. The primary disadvantage of these techniques is that convergence on a solution can be slow.

2.6 Conclusions

The chapter has provided a comprehensive review of the diverse range of neural networking systems, in terms of both their computational characteristics and applicability to different types of problem. For many of the systems, or classes of system, discussed, no attempt has yet been made to apply them within the civil engineering disciplines. Indeed, all the systems discussed above demonstrate information processing characteristics that could have significant application within civil engineering, and establishment of their performance (relative to classical methods of solution, where available) would seem to offer a rich source for future research.

2.7 References

Anderson, J.A., Silverstein, J.W., Ritz, S.A., and Jones, R.S., (1977). "Distinctive Features, Categorical Perception, and Probability Learning: some Applications of a Neural Model", *Psych. Review,* 84, pp 413-451.

Carpenter, G.A. and Grossberg, S., (1988). "The ART of Adaptive Pattern Recognition", *Computer*, pp 77-88.

Chao, L.C., and Skibniewski, M.J. (1994). "Estimating Construction Productivity: Neural Network-Based Approach." Journal of Computing in Civil Engineering, 8(2), ASCE, New York, NY, pp 234-251.

Dayhoff, J.E., (1990). "Regularity Properties in Pulse Transmission Networks", *Proc. Third Int. Conf. on Neural Networks,* San Diego, CA, part III, pp 621-626.

Fahlman, S.E. and Lebiere, C., (1990). "The Cascaded-Correlation Learning Architecture", *Rep. CMU-CS-90-100,* Carnegie Mellon University, Pittsburgh, PA.

Flood, I., (1989). "A neural network approach to the sequencing of construction tasks." Proc. 6th Int. Symp. on Automation and Robotics in Construction, Construction Industry Institute, Austin, Texas, pp 204-211.

Flood, I., (1990). "Solving construction operational problems using artificial neural networks and simulated evolution." Proc. the CIB W-55 and W-65 Joint Symposia on Building Economics and Construction Management, Vol. 6, University of Technology, Sydney, Australia, pp 197-208.

Flood, I. (1991). "A Gaussian-Based Feedforward Network Architecture and Complementary Training Algorithm", *Proceedings of the International Joint Conference on Neural Networks* , 1, Singapore, IEEE and INNS, pp 171-176.

Flood, I. and Kartam, N., (1994). "Neural Networks in Civil Engineering. I: Principles and Understanding", *Journal of Computing in Civil Engineering,* ASCE, 8(2), pp 131-148.

Flood, I., and Worley, K., (1995). "An Artificial Neural Network Approach to Discrete-Event Simulation", Artificial Intelligence for Engineering Design, Analysis and Manufacturing, 9, pp 37-49.

Gagarin, N., Flood, I., and Albrecht, P., (1994). "Computing Truck Attributes with artificial neural Networks", *Journal of Computing in Civil Engineering*, ASCE, 8(2), pp 179-200.

Goerke, N., Schone, M., Kreimeier, B., and Eckmiller, R., (1990). "A Network with Pulse Processing Neurons for Generation of Arbitrary Temporal Sequences", *Proc. Third Int. Conf. on Neural Networks,* San Diego, CA, part III, pp 315-320.

Hecht-Nielsen, R. (1990). *Neurocomputing*. Addison-Wesley, 1990.

Hinton, G.E., and Sejnowski, R.J., (1986). "Learning and Relearning in Boltzmann Machines", *Parallel Distributed Processing*. Vol. 1, (Rumelhart, D.E., et al., Eds.) MIT Press, Cambridge, Mass. pp 282-317.

Hopfield, J. (1982). "Neural networks and physical systems with emergent collective computational properties." Proc. National Academy of Sciences, USA, Vol 79, 2554-2558.

Hopfield, J., and Tank, D. (1985). "Neural computation of decisions optimization problems." Biological Cybernetics, Vol. 53, 141-152.

Karnin, E. D. (1990). "A simple procedure for pruning back-propagation trained neural networks." Transactions on Neural Networks, 1(2), Institute of Electrical and Electronic Engineers, New York, N.Y., 239-242.

Karshenas, S., and Xin, F., (1992). "Application of Neural Networks in Earthmoving Equipment Production Estimating." Proceedings of the 8th Conference in Computing in Civil Engineering and Geographic Information Systems, ASCE, New York, NY, pp 841-847.

Karunanithi, N., Grenney, W.J., Whitley, D. and Bovee, K., (1994). "Neural Networks for River Flow Prediction" Journal of Computing in Civil Engineering, 8(2), ASCE, New York, NY, pp 201-220.

Kohonen, T. (1989). *Self-organization and associative memory.* Third Edition, Springer-Verlag, Berlin.

Kosko, B., (1988), "Bidirectional Associative Memories", *IEEE Trans. Systems, Man, and Cybernetics, SMC-L8,* pp 49-60.

Lippmann, R.P., Gold, B. and Malpass, M.L., (1987). "A Comparison of Hamming and Hopfield Neural Nets for Pattern Classification" *MIT Lincoln Laboratory Technical Report 769,* Lexington, MA.

Moody, J. and Darken, C.J., (1989). "Fast Learning in Networks of Locally-Tuned Processing Units", *Neural Computation*, vol. 1, pp. 281-294.

Pao, Y-H., (1989). *Adaptive Pattern Recognition and Neural Networks*, Chapter 8, Addison-Wesley, Reading, MA.

Rumelhart, D.E., Hinton, G.E., and McClellend, J.L., (1986a). "A General Framework for Parallel Distributed Processing", *Parallel Distributed Processing.* Vol. 1, (Rumelhart, D.E., et al., Eds.) MIT Press, Cambridge, Mass. p 73.

Rumelhart, D.E., Hinton, G.E., and Williams, R.J., (1986b). "Learning Internal Representations by Error Propagation", *Parallel Distributed Processing.* Vol. 1, (Rumelhart, D.E., et al., Eds.) MIT Press, Cambridge, Mass. pp 318-362.

Srinivas, M., and Patnaik, L., (1991). "Learning neural network weights using genetic algorithms - improved performance by search-space reduction." Proc. Int. Joint Conf. on Neural Networks, IEEE and INNS, Neuro-Dynamics II, Vol. 3, Singapore, pp 2331-2336.

Tongthong, T., (1993). *Solving Resource Leveling Problems using Artificial Neural Networks*, Ph.D. Thesis, University of Maryland.

Chapter 3

Validation and Verification

Janet M. Twomey[1] and Alice E. Smith[2]

Abstract: This chapter discusses important aspects of the validation and verification of neural network models including selection of appropriate error metrics, analysis of residual errors and resampling methodologies for validation under conditions of sparse data. Error metrics reviewed include mean absolute error, root mean squared error, percent good and absolute distance error. The importance of interpretive schedules for pattern classification tasks is explained. The resampling methods - bootstrap, jackknife and cross validation - are compared to the popular neural network validation methods of train-and-test and resubstitution. While the techniques covered in this chapter are especially aimed at supervised networks where errors during training and validation are known, many of the techniques can be applied directly, or in a modified form, for unsupervised (self-organizing) neural networks.

3.1. Introduction to Validation and Error Metrics

Artificial neural networks are increasingly used as non-linear, non-parametric prediction models for many engineering tasks such as pattern classification, control and sensor integration. Neural network models are data driven and therefore resist analytical or theoretical validation. Neural network models are constructed by training using a data set, i.e. the model alters from a random state to a "trained" state, and must be empirically validated. This chapter will concentrate on the class of supervised networks, where the target (or teaching) outcome is known for the sample of data used to construct and validate the network. Many of the issues raised in this chapter can also be applied to self-organizing (unsupervised) networks as well, however the issue of identifying

---

[1] Dept. of Industrial and Manfacturing Eng., Wichita State University, Wichita, Kansas.

[2] Dept. of Industrial Eng., University of Pittsburgh, Pittsburgh, PA.

what is an error, and how severe it is, must be separately addressed. When error is discussed in this chapter, it refers to the prediction or classification error remaining in a completely trained neural network.

The evaluation and validation of an artificial neural network prediction model are based upon one or more selected error metrics. Generally, neural network models which perform a function approximation task will use a continuous error metric such as mean absolute error (MAE), mean squared error (MSE) or root mean squared error (RMSE). The errors will be summed over the validation set of inputs and outputs, and then normalized by the size of the validation set. Some practitioners will also normalize to the cardinality of the output vector if there is more than one output decision, so the resulting error is the mean per input vector and per output decision.

A neural network performing pattern classification where output is generally binary or ternary will usually use an error metric that measures misclassifications along with, or instead of, an error metric which measures distance from the correct classification. For a specific pattern class A, misclassification error can be broken down into two components - Type I errors and Type II errors. Type I errors, sometimes called α errors, are misclassifications where the input pattern, which belongs to class A, is identified as something other than class A. These misclassifications are akin to missed occurrences. Type II errors, sometimes called β errors, are misclassifications where the input pattern belongs to a pattern class other than A, but is identified by the neural network as belonging to class A. These misclassifications are akin to false alarms. Of course, a Type I error for one class is a Type II error for another class.

Since the objective of a neural network model is to generalize successfully (i.e., work well on data not used in training the neural network), the True Error is statistically defined on "an asymptotically large number of new data points that converge in the limit to the actual population distribution" (Weiss and Kulikowski 1991). True Error should be distinguished from the Apparent Error, the error of the neural network when validating on the data set used to construct the model, i.e. the training set. True Error is also different from Testing Error, the error of the neural network when validating on a data set not used to construct the model, i.e. the testing set. Since any real application can never determine True Error, it must be estimated from Apparent Error and / or Testing Error. True Error can be expressed as a summation of Apparent Error plus a Bias (usually positive):

True Error = Apparent Error + Bias

While most current neural network practitioners use Testing Error as the estimate for True Error (the so-called train-and-test validation method), some use Apparent Error, and a few use combinations of both. The terminology used here, Apparent Error and Bias, originates from the work of Bradley Efron, a statistician who is well known for the bootstrap method and his work in the area of statistical model error estimation (Efron 1982, 1983).

To summarize, when facing neural network validation, the error metric(s) must be selected and the validation data set must be selected. These decisions should ideally be made prior to even training the neural network as validation issues have direct impact on the data available for the training, the number of neural networks required to be trained, and even on the training method. The next part of this chapter will discuss selecting an error metric for function approximation networks and for pattern classification networks. It is assumed, for simplicity, that data is ample and the popular train-and-test method of neural network validation is used. The need for analysis of error residuals is then examined. Later in the chapter, the problem of sparse data is revisited, and resampling methodologies for neural network validation are discussed.

3.2. Selecting an Error Metric

Validation is a critical aspect of any model construction. Although, there does not exist a well formulated or theoretical methodology for neural network model validation, the usual practice is to base model validation upon some specified network performance measure of data that was not used in model construction (a "test set"). In addition to trained network validation, this performance measure is often used in research to show the superiority of a certain network architecture or new learning algorithm. There are four frequently reported performance measures: mean absolute error (MAE), root mean squared error (RMSE), mean squared error (MSE) and percent good (PG) classification. Typically, for the sake of parsimony, most researchers present only one performance measure to indicate the "goodness" of a particular network's performance. There is, however, no consensus as to which measure should be reported, and thus direct comparisons among techniques and results of different researchers is practically impossible.

3.2.1 Comparison Among General Error Metrics

For networks with smooth, i.e. analog or continuous, output targets, a continuous error metric such as MAE or RMSE is desirable. These error metrics are very often used for pattern classification networks as well, where the output targets are discrete (usually binary) but the actual outputs are continuous. The definitions for RMSE, MSE and MAE are given in the following equations, where n is the number of patterns in the validation set, m is the number of components in the output vector, o is the output of a single neuron j, t is the target for the single neuron j, and each input pattern is denoted by vector $\mathbf{i}$:

$$RMSE = \sqrt{\frac{\sum\limits_{i=1}^{n}\sum\limits_{j=1}^{m}(o_{ij}-t_{ij})^2}{n}}$$

(1)

$$MSE = \frac{\sum\limits_{i=1}^{n}\sum\limits_{j=1}^{m}(o_{ij}-t_{ij})^2}{n}$$

(2)

$$MAE = \frac{\sum\limits_{i=1}^{n}\sum\limits_{j=1}^{m}|o_{ij}-t_{ij}|}{n}$$

(3)

We will regard MSE as essentially analogous to RMSE, and concentrate on comparisons between RMSE and MAE. While the choice between these two metrics may seem inconsequential, there are cases where they would lead to conflicting interpretations during validation, especially for pattern classification networks. The following example is from (Twomey and Smith 1993a, 1995). The pattern classification problem is a well known two class classification problem depicted in Figure 1. Two Gaussian distributions are classes A and B, where class A has a mean of 0 and a standard deviation of 1 and class B has a mean of 0 and a standard deviation of 2. There is considerable overlap between the classes, making this is a straightforward "hard" pattern classification task. Both training and testing sets contained equal numbers of observations from each class.

Typically, networks are trained to decreasingly lower training tolerances in an attempt to achieve the "best" performing network. This assumes that lower training tolerances equate with improved performance, which is certainly not always the case. To examine the relative differences between RMSE and MAE, several networks were trained and tested in order to measure the effects of lowering the training tolerance for the two pattern classification problem where the correct output for class A is 0 and the correct output for class B is 1.

A total of 13 different networks were trained, each to a different training tolerance. Training tolerances ranged from 0.08 to 0.6 for normalized input between 0 and 1. During training, a response was considered correct if the output was within a pre-specified absolute training tolerance of the target value (0 or 1). Training iterations continued for each network until each of the training samples was deemed correct according to the specified training tolerance. Note that the tolerance that was used to train the network is an upper bound to the final training tolerance of the trained network, since the maximum acceptable error is applied to the worst training vector.

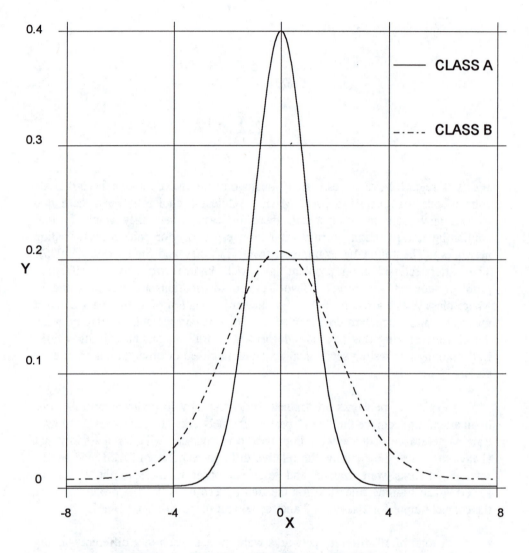

Figure 1. Two Class Classification Problem.

Figure 2 is a plot of RMSE vs. training tolerance for the test set of 1000. This plot indicates that the RMSE resulting from networks trained at tolerances between 0.08 and 0.13 vary to some degree about a RMSE of 0.14. The RMSE for networks trained to tolerances from 0.14 to 0.40 steadily declines to a minimum of 0.11. At training tolerances of 0.5 and 0.6 there is a sharp increase to a RMSE of 0.24. The result of the mid-range training tolerances having the smallest RMSE is not expected. Minimum RMSE is often used as a criteria for determining the best trained network. Based on this criteria, the network trained to a tolerance of 0.4 would be chosen as the best performing among all those trained. This inconsistent phenomenon will be explained below.

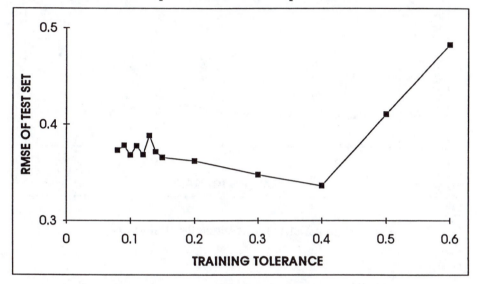

Figure 2. RMSE as a Metric for Selecting the Best Trained Network.

Figure 3 is a plot of the test set results for Mean Absolute Error (MAE) vs. training tolerance. These results, aside from some slight variations at the lower training tolerances, are closer to what is usually predicted: a steady decrease in MAE with a decrease in training tolerance. Criteria for selecting the best trained neural network is, again, to choose the network with the smallest MAE, in this case a training tolerance of 0.1.

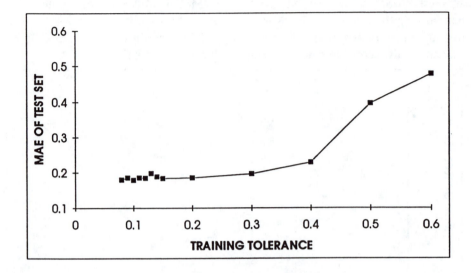

Figure 3.   MAE as a Metric for Selecting the Best Trained Network.

In order to explore these issues, the relative frequency histograms of test set residuals, or output errors, were constructed for each network.   Six distributions that are representative of the 13 networks are presented in Figure 4. The network trained at a 0.1 training tolerance exhibits a trimodal distribution of errors.   The large center peak indicates very small errors, or output that is very close to the targeted values.   The smaller endpoint spikes denote clearly incorrect responses (i.e. a B signal for an A, or an A signal for a B); the right hand side shows a larger proportion of misclassifications for data sampled from class B, suggesting a harder classification task.   There is a smaller proportion of errors in the region between the spikes, representing uncertain classifications (i.e. a 0.35 for A or a 0.65 for B).   As the training tolerance increased, all three modes decrease until the error distribution takes on a Gaussian like distribution shape at tolerance of 0.4.   At tolerances of 0.5 and 0.6, the distributions become bimodal with an increase in distance between the modes at a tolerance of 0.6.   At these large training tolerances, more vectors are classified in the less sure region because the networks have not been allowed to learn the classification model. Therefore, the RSME (and similarly, the MSE) penalizes distant errors, i.e. clear misses, more severely and therefore favors a network with few or no distant errors.   This can cause networks with many uncertain predictions to have a lower

RSME than a network with a few clear misses. MAE takes large errors into account, but does not weight them more heavily.

3.2.2 Specific Pattern Classification Error Metrics

In pattern classification, interpretive schedules or rules are employed for classifying a correct response to a given input vector, **i**. This is because there is a discrete (generally binary or ternary) target but an analog output (generally between 0 and 1). For example, where the targets are either 0 or 1, it must be decided how to classify an output such as 0.65. There are two commonly used interpretive schedules for binary output, where subscript p is the number of patterns and there is a single output j per input vector **i**. For interpretive schedule I:

$$if \ |o_p - t_p| \leq 0.5 \ then \ C_p = 1, \ else \ C_p = 0 \qquad (4)$$

and for interpretive schedule II:

$$if \ |o_p - t_p| \leq 0.4 \ then \ C_p = 1, \ else \ C_p = 0 \qquad (5)$$

Percent good (PG) classification is a measure of the number of correct classifications summed over all n patterns using one of the interpretive schedules from above:

$$PG = \frac{100}{n} \sum_{p=1}^{n} (1 - |C_{tp} - C_{op}|) \qquad (6)$$

The effect of interpretative schedule on the reported performance was investigated by (Twomey and Smith 1993a, 1995) on the two class classification problem shown in Figure 1. Their results are summarized below. Figure 5 is a plot of the test set results measured in terms of percent good (using interpretative schedules) vs. training tolerance. This plot displays two curves representing interpretive schedule I and interpretive schedule II. Since the output for these networks are binary (0,1), interpretive schedule I classifies all output less than 0.5 as coming from class A and all output greater than 0.5 as coming from class B. For interpretive schedule II, an output less than 0.4 is classified as coming from class A and output greater than 0.6 is classified as coming from class B. Note that for interpretive schedule II, an output that falls between 0.4 and 0.6 is always counted as incorrect. In both methods the network with the highest proportion of correct responses would be deemed as the "better" network. As anticipated, the curve for schedule I is consistently greater than curve for schedule II since schedule II is a subset of schedule I and the networks themselves are identical. The preferred networks according to interpretive schedule I were trained using tolerances between 0.08 and 0.5, while training tolerances between 0.08 and 0.2 yielded the preferred networks according to interpretive schedule II. The choice of interpretive schedule allows the user to decide how close an output should be to correctly signal a classification. The most generous rule possible, interpretive schedule I, allows for the possibility that many uncertain classifications (i.e. outputs between 0.4 and 0.6) will be considered correct, while the network may in fact have little or no knowledge of how to correctly classifying these input patterns.

Martinez et al. (1994) derived an alternative pattern classification error metric, the absolute distance error (ADE) to quantify the normalized absolute distance from the highest activated class to the correct class using an ordered set of classes, e.g. a sequenced set of categories. This normalization is needed because in some cases the highest activated class is not equal to 1. ADE is defined as:

$$ADE = \left| \frac{\sum_{c=1}^{m} (c * o_c)}{\sum_{c=1}^{m} o_c} - c_a \right| \tag{7}$$

where c is the class number using a scale of 1 to m, o_c is the network output for a class c, and c_a is the number of the actual (i.e. correct) class. This error captures how far away the predicted class is from the actual class, when the classes are ordered.

3.2.3 Classification Errors

The relative importance of Type I and Type II errors are now considered for pattern classification networks. A two class problem defines the probabilities (p) of each type of error:

p(Type I error) = α = p(Class B | Class A) and

p(Type II error) = β = p(Class A | Class B).

In many statistical models and neural network models the objective is to minimize the sum of these relative errors. However, some models will prefer to minimize Type I errors while others will prefer to minimize Type II errors, within some reasonable constraint on the other error type rate. In neural networks, the interpretive schedules discussed above may not meet the desired objective. In addition, networks are generally trained with the implicit, and perhaps the unrecognized, assumption that $\alpha = \beta$.

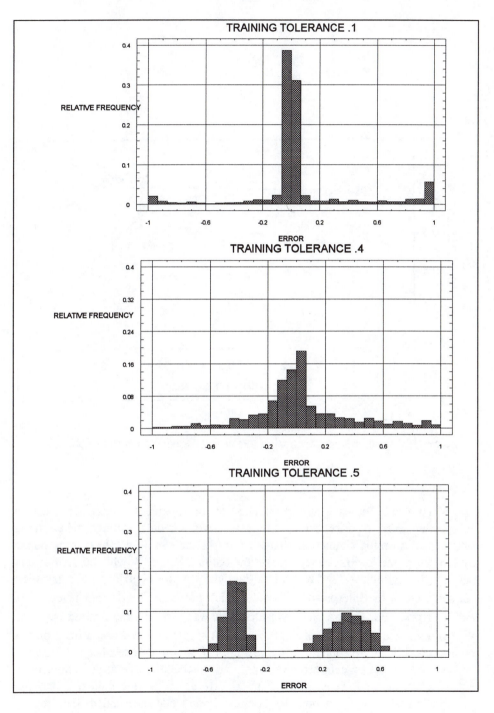

Figure 4. Relative Frequency Histograms of Residuals.

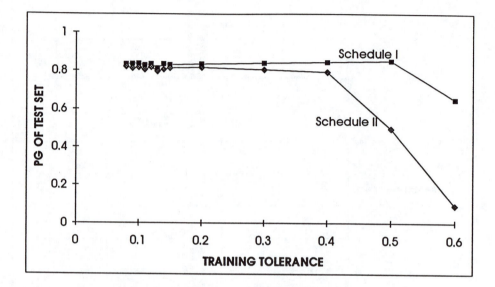

Figure 5.   Performance According to Percent Good Interpretive Schedules.

To enable the explicit consideration of the relative seriousness or cost of committing each type of error, an interpretive schedule strategy taken from statistical discriminant function analysis (Draper and Smith 1981) was proposed by (Twomey and Smith 1993a): locate the optimal boundary which discriminates between the two classes. The optimal boundary is the boundary point between classes used in the interpretive schedule which produces the desired levels of α and β errors. For the problem considered, it was assumed the desired outcome was to minimize the sum of α and β errors. A single network was trained on the pattern classification problem shown in Figure 1 to a tolerance of 0.1. Figure 6 is a plot of test set percent error vs. interpretive schedule. Total percent error is equal to the sum of Type I and Type II errors. The plot indicates that the minimal error occurs at a boundary point between classes equal to 0.3, that is output < 0.3 is considered class A while output > 0.3 is considered class B. This interpretive schedule produces minimal errors and is appropriate where the seriousness of committing a Type I error is equivalent to that of a Type II error.

Note that this decision of interpretive schedule boundary point is made after the network is trained.

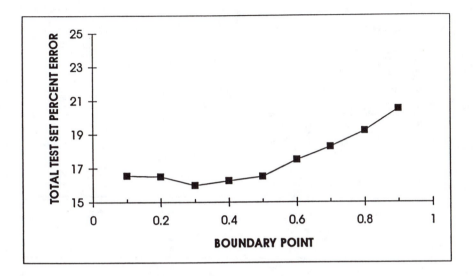

Figure 6. Minimization of the Sum of α and β.

To demonstrate the relationship of α to β, and to examine the effects of weighing the relative seriousness of one error type more heavily than the other, a plot of percent test set error vs. interpretive schedule is shown in Figure 7. The solid line represents percent incorrect classifications of Class A or Type I error (α). The dotted line represents percent incorrect classifications of Class B or Type II error (β). The plot indicates that as α decreases, β increases. The lines intersect at decision boundary 0.2, where percent error is 0.17 for both error types. The ratio, or relative seriousness of Type II error to Type I error, is 1.0. Moving the decision boundary from 0.2 to 0.1 decreases the ratio of a Type II error to Type I error from 1.0 to 0.6. Moving the decision boundary in the opposite direction toward a value of 0.9 increases the ratio from 1.0 to 6.3, where the chances of committing a Type II error is more than 6 times as great as committing a Type I error; i.e. at 0.9, a Type I error is much less likely to occur than a Type II error. At 0.3, where the minimum sum of the two errors occurs, the ratio of Type II to Type I errors is 1.5. For interpretive schedule I, where the decision boundary occurs at 0.5, it is incorrectly assumed that both type of errors are given equal importance. In fact there are more than two times as many Type II errors as Type I errors at a value of 0.5.

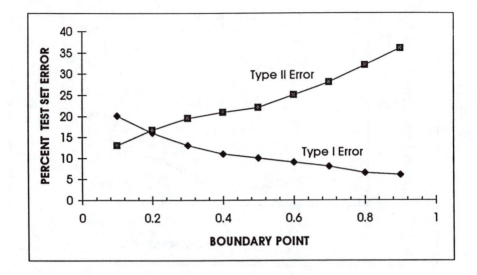

Figure 7.   The Effects of Changing the Decision Boundary on Relative Errors.

This plot illustrates how the decision boundary of the classification schedule can be adjusted a posteriori to reflect the relative seriousness of Type I vs. Type II errors for a given neural application.   In fact it demonstrates that error type curves must be examined to ascertain the relative proportion of classification errors to be expected for the model under consideration.   Reliance upon an implicit assumption of $\alpha = \beta$ will usually prove false when the actual trained network and its classification error characteristics are investigated.

3.3. Analysis of Residuals

Statistical model builders check residual plots, and neural network model builders should do likewise.   The residual, or error, for pattern p is simply the target minus the network output:

$$r_p = o_p - t_p \qquad (8)$$

There are three primary discoveries to be made from residual plots.   These are discussed in turn.

The first phenomenon to look for on a residual plot is bias.   **Bias** is a systematic distribution of the residuals.   In neural networks, bias often takes the form of undershoot or overshoot.   Undershoot is where the network model does not reach the upper and lower extremes of the target data.   Overshoot is the opposite phenomenon. Undershoot is a more frequently found bias, especially for networks using the popular sigmoid transfer function, and can often be remedied by retraining the network on an expanded normalization range.

Another form of bias is disproportionate errors on exemplar vectors or classes with under-representation, such as outliers or rare events. When the training data set includes classes or instances which happen relatively rarely in the training set, the neural network will often train to the dominant class(es), producing poor performance on the rarer class(es). This can be remedied by focused training on the rarer class(es), that is by artificially increasing their share of training vectors. An articulated architecture which is not globally connected, can also equalize performance among classes. In a globally connected architecture, such as the popular multi-layered perceptron, all weights will be affected by all input patterns. This will cause dominant patterns or classes to dominate weight training. An articulated architecture where certain weighted connections are allocated to individual patterns or classes will alleviate this dominance problem. Such architectures which use supervised training include the probabilistic network and the cascade correlation network.

The second phenomenon which can be easily recognized using residual plots is **relative magnitude** of individual errors. This was discussed in the earlier section where the squared error term (RMSE or MSE) was more favorable to many small errors than to a few large errors. The application will dictate which kinds of errors are permissible, but the modeler will want to check on distribution of the errors. Sometimes, a well performing network will produce a few large errors (clear misses) for outlying data points. These outliers can be further investigated for correctness and appropriateness to the model.

The third aspect of residual analysis is related to the second. Residual plots of the testing and training sets must be compared. While it is expected that the overall magnitude of the error for the training set will be as low or somewhat lower than that of the testing set, both distributions should behave similarly. Significantly different residual distributions of **training and testing errors** can indicate bias in either or both of the data sets (i.e., the sets are inherently different from each other), or too small of a sample in one or both sets. Also, a large increase of magnitude of error from the training set to the testing set can be indicative of overtraining, i.e. memorization of the training set with poor generalization ability. Many remedies have been published addressing overtraining (also called overfitting). These include reducing the network size, pruning trained connections with small weights, and ceasing training before the test set error significantly degrades.

3.4. Validation With Sparse Data

Neural network validation is especially problematic when dealing with sparse data where the decision on how to best use the limited data - for model construction or for model validation - is critical. Validation still needs improved methodologies for the neural network community, however there is a corresponding body of literature on validation of statistical models such as regression or discriminant function analysis (Mosier 1951, Stone 1974, Lachenbruch and Mickey 1968, Efron 1982, Efron 1983, Gong 1986). Several resampling methods have been developed which have two important aspects. First they use all data for both model construction and model validation. Second they are nonparametric techniques and do not depend on functional form or probabilistic assumptions. Below, after describing the two most common methods of neural network validation, these resampling methods are briefly described.

1. Resubstitution - resubstitutes the data used to construct the model for estimating model error, i.e. this is the training set error. Therefore the estimate of True Error equals the Apparent Error, and Bias is assumed to equal zero. Resubstitution is sometimes used in neural network validation, however it is usually noted to be biased downward (sometimes severely). It does use all of the data for both model construction and model validation, and requires only one model to be constructed.

2. Train-and-test - divide the data set into two sets. Use one set to construct the model (train the neural network) and use the other set to validate the model (test the neural network). This is the most common method of neural network validation. True Error is estimated directly as the testing set error, and Bias could be calculated by subtracting off the Apparent Error (training set error) from the testing set error. The proportion set aside for training of the available data has ranged, in practice, from 25% to 90%. The training set error (and therefore the estimate of True Error) is highly dependent on the exact sample chosen for training and the exact sample chosen for testing (which are completely dependent on each other since they are mutually exclusive). This creates a highly variable estimate of True Error, especially for small sample sizes. A modification of this method is to divide the data into three sets - a training set, a first testing set used during training and a second testing set used for validating the trained network. The first testing set is used during training to decide when training should cease, that is, before overfitting takes place. The second testing set is used to estimate the True Error of the trained network. This method may result in a better generalizing final network, but the available data sample is divided three ways instead of two ways, decreasing the number of data points used for model construction. For both versions of train-and-test, only one model is constructed, but both training and testing are done on a subset of the available data.

3. Grouped cross validation - divides the available data into k groups. A total of k models are then constructed, each using k-1 data groups for model construction, and the hold out group for k[th] model validation. A final model which is used for application is built using all the data. True Error is estimated using the mean of testing set errors of the k grouped cross validation models. This method uses all available data for both model construction and model validation, but requires the construction of k+1 models, i.e. training k+1 neural networks. Bias is estimated by subtracting the Apparent Error of the application network from the estimate of True Error.

4. Grouped jackknife - this is identical to the grouped cross validation except the Apparent Error is determined by averaging the Apparent Errors of each jackknifed model. (Where each jackknifed model is the same as each grouped cross validated model, described in the preceding paragraph.) The Bias is then estimated by subtracting this new Apparent Error from the estimated True Error. Therefore, the validation using grouped cross validation and grouped jackknife will be identical except for the calculation of Apparent Error.

5. Bootstrap - a data set of size n is drawn with replacement from the original data set of n observations. This sample constitutes the bootstrap training set. The bias of each bootstrapped network is estimated by subtracting the Apparent Error of that network (training set error) from the error of the network evaluated on the original total data set. This is repeated b times, each with a different randomly drawn data set. The overall estimate of Bias is obtained by averaging over the b estimates of bias. The final application model is constructed using all of the data, therefore b+1 models are constructed, i.e. b+1 neural networks are trained. True Error is estimated by adding the estimate of Bias to the Apparent Error of the application model. The bootstrap is generally noted to be less variable than the grouped cross validation or grouped jackknife, but it can be downwardly biased.

A simple example of the performance and variability of these methods on a one variable function approximation problem, previously used in both the statistical and the neural network literature for validation research, was presented by (Twomey and Smith 1993b). A total of $N = 1010$ (x, y) observations were generated according to: $y = 4.26(e^{-x} - 4e^{-2x} + 3e^{-3x})$; x ranged from 0.0 to 3.10 (see Figure 8). Ten observations were randomly selected to make up the training and validation sample, n=10. The remaining 1000 observations were set aside as the *true* estimate of Bias. The prediction models, fully connected feedforward multi-layer networks, were all constructed of 1 input node (x variable), 1 hidden layer of 3 nodes and 1 output node (y). All networks were trained using the standard backpropagation algorithm. Training was terminated when either all training pairs were deemed correct within 10% of the targeted output, or after 10,000 presentations of the training sample. The error metric for testing was mean squared error (MSE).

The standard method of train-and-test was considered first. Twenty percent (2 observations) of the sample were removed for testing and the remaining 80% (8 observations) were used for training. To examine the variability of the Bias estimate, 45 networks, each with a different combination of train/test (8/2) samples, were trained and tested according to the method described above. True Bias was evaluated for each of the 45 networks over the 1000 observations. The results, shown in Table 1, indicate that model Bias estimated according to the train-and-test methodology, $\hat{\beta}_{\text{T-T}}$, on average over estimates the true model Bias and is highly variable. Considering the 10 observations chosen as the total sample for training/testing, this result is not surprising. It does illustrate the potential problems associated with the standard train-and-test methodology; that is - model performance can be highly dependent on which observations are chosen for training/testing.

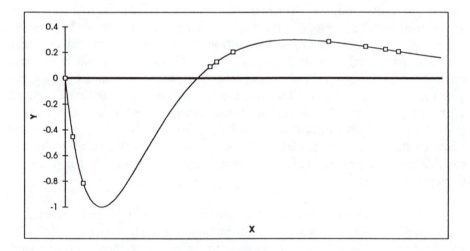

Figure 8. Function Approximation Problem: $y = 4.26(e^{-x} - 4e^{-2x} + 3e^{-3x})$.

This can best be seen in Figure 9, where the True Error and Test Set Error (MSE) are plotted for each of the 45 networks. This plot illustrates that Test Set Error can under estimate the True Error approximately 50% of the time and over estimate the True Error approximately 50% of the time, sometimes drastically missing True Error.

Table 1. Results of Train-and-Test Methodology.

	Apparent Error	Estimated Bias	True Bias
Mean	0.016	0.075	0.028
ariance	4.3E-05	0.016	0.001

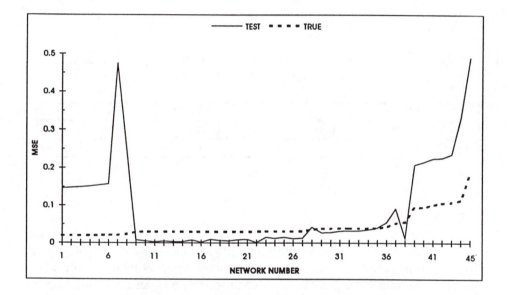

Figure 9.   True and Test Set Error According to Train-and-Test Method.
(Data Sorted by True MSE.)

The resubstitution, cross validation, jackknife and bootstrap methods were also examined using the same sample of 10 observations. In order to make the computational effort comparable, 10 bootstrap samples (b=10) were constructed and the group size (k) of the cross validation and the jackknife was set to 1. Thirty additional bootstrap samples (b=40) were constructed to examine the effects of increased b. True Bias was again evaluated over the 1000 observations. The results are shown in Table 2. The Apparent Error estimate of Bias, obtained by the resubstitution method, under estimated True Bias, however it was the closest estimate and only required the construction of single network. The bootstrap method (b = 40) gave the next closest estimate of Bias, but with the highest computational effort of 41 total networks constructed.

The resampling methods have been shown to be superior to the train-and-test and resubstitution methods when used in statistical prediction models under conditions of sparse data (Mosier 1951, Stone 1974, Lachenbruch and Mickey 1968, Efron 1982, Efron 1983, Gong 1986). Clearly, more research is needed to fully investigate the usefulness of resampling methodologies for neural network validation when constrained by small samples. The main point is that if data is the primary constraint, then it may be prudent to expend more computational effort for construction and validation of multiple networks, and construct the final neural network model using all the data for training.

Table 2. Estimates of Bias from Resampling Methodologies Compared to Resubstitution and Train-and Test.

	True	Apparent	CV (k=1)	Jack (k=1)	Boot (b=10)	Boot (b=40)
Bias	0.013	0.00	0.065	0.058	0.037	0.034
Networks	-	1	11	11	11	41

3.5. Conclusions

Because neural networks are purely empirical models, validation is critical to operational success. Most real world engineering applications require getting maximal use of a limited data set. Careful selection of an error metric(s) will ensure that the error being minimized is in fact the one most applicable to classification or approximation problem at hand. The trained network must be examined for signs of bias, even if error tolerances are met. Identification of bias will alert the user so that the network can be modified, or its outputs altered to reflect the known bias. Residuals of the training and testing sets can warn the user of the phenomena of overtraining and overfitting. When using an interpretive schedule because of discrete target outputs, care must be taken to ensure the proper balance of Type I and Type II errors.

In sparse data situations, a resampling methodology will allow all the data to be used to construct (train) the final operational neural network, while still providing for validation. The size of the groups in grouped cross validation or grouped jackknife, and the number of bootstrapped samples will depend on the computational resources available, the data set size and the precision needed in the validation step. The resampling methodologies do expend significantly greater resources in training and testing the neural networks, so in cases of ample data, the traditional train-and-test method may be the best choice.

3.6 References

Draper, N. R. and Smith, H. (1981). *Applied Regression Analysis*. New York: Wiley and Sons.

Efron, B. (1982). The Jackknife, the Bootstrap, and Other Resampling Plans. *SIAM NSF-CBMS, Monograph* **38**.

Efron, B. (1983). Estimating the error rate of a prediction rule: Improvement over cross-validation. *Journal of the American Statistical Association* **78**, 316-331.

Gong, G. (1986). Cross-validation, the jackknife, and the bootstrap: Excess error estimation in forward logistic regression. *Journal of the American Statistical Association* **81**, 108-113.

Lachenbruch, P. and Mickey, M. (1968). Estimation of error rates in discriminant analysis. *Technometrics* **10,** 1-11.

Martinez, S., Smith, A. E. and Bidanda, B. (1994). Reducing waste in casting with a predictive neural model. *Journal of Intelligent Manufacturing* **5**, 277-286.

Mosier, C. I. (1951). Symposium: The need and the means of cross-validation. I. Problem and designs of cross-validation. *Education and Psychological Measuremen*t **11**, 5-11.

Stone, M. (1974). Cross-validory choice and assessment of statistical predictions. *Journal of the Royal Statistical Society Series B* **36**, 111- 147.

Twomey, J. M. and Smith, A. E. (1993a). Power curves for pattern classification networks. *Proceedings of the 1993 IEEE International Conference on Neural Networks*, 950-955.

Twomey, J. M. and Smith, A. E. (1993b). Nonparametric error estimation methods for the evaluation and validation artificial neural networks. *Intelligent Engineering Systems Through Artificial Neural Networks: Volume 3* ASME Press, 233-238.

Twomey, J. M. and Smith, A. E. (1995). Performance measures, consistency, and power for artificial neural network models. *Journal of Mathematical and Computer Modelling,* Vol.21, 243-258.

Weiss, S. M., and Kulikowski, C. A. (1991). *Computer Systems that Learn.* San Mateo, CA: Morgan Kaufmann Publishers, Inc.

Chapter 4

Damage Detection From Vibration Measurements Using Neural Network Technology

Jaime Ortiz[1], Carlos Ferregut[2] and Roberto A. Osegueda[2]

Abstract: A detailed study of the capabilities of artificial neural networks to detect damage in a cantilever structure is presented. This chapter includes the definition of the architecture for a three layer backpropagation neural network, that processes the changes in the resonant frequencies of a beam due to damage, to locate and quantify the damage. The network was trained and tested with deterministic and random information of the resonant frequencies of the damaged beam generated analytically, and it was also tested with experimentally measured resonant frequencies. Several sensitivity tests were conducted with three levels of damage at different locations.

4.1. Introduction

With the aging of the United States civil infrastructure comprised of buildings, bridges, offshore structures, dams, pipeline systems, highways, etc., it will be necessary to review retrofitting practices for an effective utilization of limited resources. At present, decision-makers in the public and private sectors are aware of the need to implement infrastructure management programs to extend the life span of facilities. Such programs rely on user demands, qualitative and quantitative assessment of the conditions of the facilities, and on the costs of repairing and/or replacing them to prioritize maintenance activities. Therefore, measurements of the conditions of facilities are essential. In many cases, assessing the condition of a structure is primarily done with purely visual inspections and using subjective ratings and engineering opinions. Visual inspections, however, are usually time consuming and expensive because of the increased size and complexity of today's structures.

---

[1] Grad. Res. Asst., Dept. of Civil Eng., The University of Texas at El Paso, El Paso, TX. 79968.
[2] Associate Professor, Dept. of Civil Eng., The University of Texas at El Paso, TX. 79968

The above concepts of infrastructure management are currently being utilized by many state highway agencies for pavement and bridge management, and by regulatory government bodies for the assessment of damage of buildings after major catastrophic events. A structural damage may be defined as any deficiency and/or deterioration of material properties caused by external loading, environmental conditions and human errors in design and construction. When the damage is not large enough to be evident or if it occurs in hidden or unaccessible locations, the damage may be undetected and unaccounted for.

In recognizing this problem, some agencies have adopted specific technologies to detect and assess damage for the particular type of structural systems they manage. Among those technologies, the use of ultrasound, eddy currents, x-rays, seismic sensors, and others are not at all uncommon. However, an effective inspection employing most of the above technologies requires the positioning of instruments in the vicinity of the damage or defect. In contrast, vibration-based methods rely on measurements of the global dynamic properties of structures to attempt to detect and quantify damage. Such dynamic measurements can be made with transducers placed at few or several locations of the structure.

Vibration damage detection methods are based on the fact that as damage accumulates in a structure, the stiffness of the structural location decreases, thus decreasing the global stiffness of the structure. The loss of stiffness, in turn, produces changes in the dynamic characteristics of the structure (i.e., resonant frequencies, mode shapes and damping ratios). These characteristics can be experimentally determined through standard modal analysis techniques with accelerometers and impact hammers and/or shakers. Therefore, vibration measurements before and after damage can help to infer the location and magnitude of damage.

Several sensitivity methods have been proposed in the literature for the utilization of changes of vibrational characteristics of structures for the detection of damage [Stubbs 1985, Stubbs & Osegueda 1990, Stephenson 1993]. These methods relate measurable changes in the vibrational characteristics of a structure to changes in the stiffness and mass of structural locations through a set of linear sensitivity equations. Usually, each vibration frequency generates one equation, and thus, a large number of frequency measurements is needed to avoid an underdetermined system of equations, making the methods somewhat unreliable [Osegueda et al. 1990]. Furthermore, since these sensitivity methods take the changes in stiffness as a record of the damage, they seldom discriminate the type of the damage (ie. crack, corrosion, fatigue, etc.).

One promising approach to infer the location and magnitude of damage in structures with vibration measurements may be neural networks technology. The seemingly overwhelming task of reviewing vast amounts of data generated from a dynamic response can, in theory, be easily carried out using this technology. Neural networks generally deal with pattern recognition; thus, it seems natural to think that neural networks may work in identifying pattern changes (not necessarily linear) in the vibration characteristics of a structure associated with different damage locations and magnitudes and types of damage.

This chapter discusses the application of neural networks for damage detection in structures using vibration measurements. It includes a case study of the applications of neural networks to the detection of damage in a cantilever beam with resonant frequency information. However, due to the expected uncertainties in frequency measurements, the methodology selected in developing the training data consisted of artificially inducing uncertainties at different levels of variability. This chapter also includes a description of the architecture of the neural network, a discussion of the training process, and verifications of the neural network model using analytical and experimental input data.

Previous Related Work

The application of neural networks in structural damage assessment is still in its infancy and only a limited number of papers have been written on the subject. A brief review of some of these papers follow.

Szewczyk and Hajela (1992) formulated the damage detection in a structural system as an inverse problem. They modeled damage as a reduction in the stiffness of structural elements which is associated with observable static displacements under prescribed loads. The neural network that they developed, generated the inverse mapping between the stiffness of individual structural elements and the global static displacements. They employed numerical simulation to demonstrate the ability of the network to detect damage in the presence of noise and incomplete information.

Wu et al. (1992) developed a backpropagation neural network to detect the damage states of a three story frame. The Fourier spectra of the computed relative acceleration time history of the top floor, when the frame is subjected to an earthquake excitation, was taken as a training set. Spectra corresponding to various damaged members were used. Their network architecture had 200 input processing elements, three output processing elements and ten processing elements in a hidden layer.

Elkordy et al. (1993) developed a back propagation neural network to assess the damage of a five story frame. The network was trained with analytically generated data and tested with experimental data. A possible limitation of this network was that it only attempted to detect large damage magnitudes. No results were given to evaluate the ability of the network to detect and quantify small damages.

Several other applications of neural networks in the structural engineering field have been reported in the literature; however, their focus is outside the topic of this chapter and they will not be reviewed here.

4.2. Summary Of Approach

Because of the availability of resonant frequency data for damaged and undamaged cantilever beams in the literature, it was decided, for the purpose of exploring the use of artificial neural networks as applied to damage detection, that the structure considered would be a cantilever beam. However, since the data in the literature is not enough to perform a comprehensive training of a neural network, an analytical model was thus imperative to carry out the learning process.

The modeling of a cantilever beam may be viewed as simple. However, the utilization of an Euler-Bernoulli model may be erroneous due to inherent errors for the lack of shear deformations and rotary inertia effects. For this reason, a finite element modal analysis program that is based on Timoshenko beam elements was selected. These elements provide more accurate frequency results for higher order modes with fewer elements. The details of the model are described in Section 3.

With this model, a database of resonant frequencies as functions of the damage magnitude and the location, was generated. For the purpose of locating damage, the cantilever beam was divided into 10 locations. The damage was defined as the fractional loss of the second moment of area over one location. During the training, the resonant frequency information was provided in the form of fractional changes between the undamaged and damaged beam due to a given magnitude of damage at a single location; the fractional change information makes the database applicable to any cantilever structure with a uniform section. Originally, the training was performed for a wide range of damage magnitudes ranging from 1% to 25%. However, due to naturally expected uncertainties in resonant frequency measurements, it was decided to also investigate the performance of the network when trained with uncertain data. The uncertain data was simulated through a Monte Carlo approach (Stephenson 1993).

The final network architecture, the method of entering the data, and the length of training were set through an iterative process until good results were obtained. Several architectures were tried and are discussed in Section 4.

The neural net was tested in two ways. First, it was tested using analytical results of the resonant frequencies due to damage magnitudes that were not included in the training set. Second, it was tested with experimental resonant frequencies reported by Stubbs and Osegueda (1990). Furthermore, the effects of uncertainties on the input data were also investigated by generating random sets of damaged frequencies.

4.3. Test Structure

The cantilever beam selected for this study is depicted in Figure 1 along with its damage locations. The cantilever beam was 40 in. (101.6 cm) long and had a cross sectional area of 1.0 in. x 0.5 in. (2.54 cm x 1.27 cm). The material is aluminum with properties of E = 10,000 ksi (70 GPa) and a mass density of 0.098 lbm/in^3 (2,710 Kg/m^3).

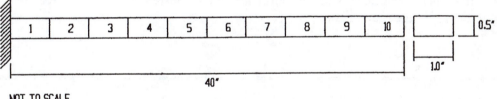

NOT TO SCALE

Figure 1.   Cantilever Beam with Numbered Damage Locations

40 FINITE ELEMENTS, 41 NODES

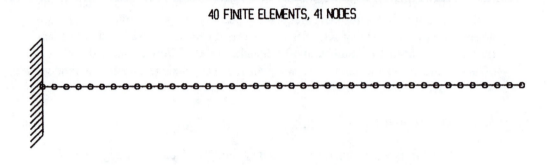

Figure 2.   Finite Element Model of Cantilever Beam

For the purpose of accurately modeling the resonant frequencies, the beam was equally subdivided into 40 elements. And for the purpose of detecting damage, the beam was divided into 10 locations, each location was made of four contiguous finite elements. As mentioned earlier, the finite elements were Timoshenko beam elements. Figure 2 depicts the finite element model of the beam. Location 1 is at the support and location 10 is at the tip. The resonant frequencies generated with the analytical model served as the basis for the training of the neural network.

Mode	1	2	3	4	5	6
Freq. (Hz)	10.02	62.73	175.45	343.22	566.10	843.37

Table 1.   First Six Resonant Frequencies in Cantilever Beam.

Table 1 lists the resonant frequencies obtained for the first six modes of the undamaged beam.

4.4. The Neural Network

A backpropagation neural network was developed during this study. To define the architecture of the network, it needs to be recognized that the available input data consists of a vector of resonant frequency information, and that the desired output would correspond to the damage magnitude and the most likely location where that damage may occur. Therefore, the first step was to decide on the format of the input and output of the network, which in essence defines the number of Processing Elements (PE's) to be placed in the input and output layers. Once these layers were defined, the number of hidden layers and the number of PE's for each of them were determined by the Root Mean Square (RMS) error associated with the output layers as a decision quantity. If the RMS errors are not sufficient in making this decision, different network architectures may be trained and tested. At the end, a neural network with an input layer consisting of 6 PE's, a hidden layer with 15 PE's and an output layer with 11 PE's was found to be an effective architecture. All PE's of one layer were interconnected with all PE's of the adjacent layer. Details of this process follow.

Deterministic Data

In determining the format for inputing the resonant frequency information for the cantilever beam, several schemes were attempted. One was simply to use the resonant frequencies obtained for the beam from the finite element program. Other attempts included obtaining the logarithm of the frequencies as the input data vector, and taking the logarithm of the difference between the undamaged and damaged frequencies. Of the above, the input format that was best at assessing the damage on the beam was the vector containing the resonant frequencies. However, after further consideration, it was concluded that this format was not acceptable because it was only appropriate on the specific beam for which the network was trained. After careful considerations and other attempted formats, a workable set of input data was determined. With this scheme, the difference of resonant frequency values corresponding to a given damage situation and the undamaged values were divided by the undamaged values, thus, resulting in a vector of six values containing the fractional difference of the undamaged and damaged resonant frequencies as shown below.

$$z_i = \frac{f_{u_i} - f_{d_i}}{f_{u_i}}$$

where, z_i is the fractional difference (change) in the ith mode, and f_u and f_d are the undamaged and damaged frequencies.

		Output Node									
	1	2	3	4	5	6	7	8	9	10	11
Method A	5	3									
Method B	0	0	5	0	0	0	0	0	0	0	
Method C	5	0	0	1	0	0	0	0	0	0	0

Table-2. Formats for Introducing the Output Training Data

The next step was to determine a method of introducing the output training data so as to yield the most satisfactory results. Here, several methods were tested. Method A had two output nodes, the first node for the damage magnitude and the second for the location, as seen in Table 2 for 5% damage at location three. This method proved to be unsatisfactory. Method B consisted of ten output nodes corresponding to one damage magnitude per location. This format was also unsatisfactory. After testing several other methods, eleven output nodes provided the most acceptable results of all methods tested. In Method C, the first node corresponds to the damage magnitude and the remaining ten were zeros or a one coding the location of the damage. A value of zero corresponds to an undamaged state and a value of one identifies the damaged location.

The next step was to determine the number of hidden layers and the number of PE's per layer. Attempts were made with multiple hidden layers, however, the results obtained were not better than those obtained from networks having a single hidden layer. In addition, the time required in training a network with two or three hidden layers was longer than that required in training a network with a single layer. Therefore, it was determined that neural networks with one hidden layer would be best. A decision on the number of PE's for the single hidden layer was made based upon computations of the average RMS error while varying the number of PE's.

In determining the above described architecture, the neural network was trained and tested with deterministic cases from the finite element model. In creating the training data which consisted of 60 input vectors of fractional changes in the resonant frequencies and their corresponding output vectors that described the magnitude and location of the damage, a deterministic set of resonant frequencies of the cantilever beam was obtained for the undamaged situation and for damage magnitudes of 1%, 5%, 10%, 15%, 20% and 25% in each of the ten locations. This, in essence, created the training input and output data.

For testing the network, an input set of fractional changes in the resonant frequencies was similarly obtained for each location for a damaged magnitude of 13%. To decide on the number of PE's in the single hidden layer, damage predictions were obtained varying the number of PE's in the layer. For each set of output values the RMS error was computed. Table 3 lists the average RMS errors obtained for the damage magnitude of 13% at each location for the different numbers of PE's in the hidden layer of the network. It should be noted that there was not a definite pattern on the effects of decreasing the number of PE's on the average RMS error. Whereas by increasing the number of PE's past 15, resulted in less accurate networks. Having built many networks with different numbers of PE's, different learning rates and cycles, and other aspects that affect the results obtained from a network, it was decided that a network with 15 PE's in the hidden layer was the best of all networks attempted. Therefore, the number of PE's in the hidden layer of the neural networks throughout this study were set at 15.

Number of PE's	Average RMS error
4	1.63
6	1.30
8	0.80
10	0.94
12	0.91
14	1.52
15	0.72
16	0.99

Table 3. Average RMS Error versus Number of PE's in single hidden layer of the Neural Network.

In summary the neural network selected for this study consisted of an input layer of 6 PE's, an output layer of 11 PE's and a single hidden layer with 15 PE's. The network was trained at a fast learning rate for 30,000 cycles and an epoch size of 16..

Data Containing Uncertainties

Because measured resonant frequencies are contaminated with errors, it is essential to consider the effects that the uncertainties in these frequencies have on the neural network damage detection ability. This was done by considering uncertainties in the training and in the testing data. Uncertainties were artificially added to the training database described in Section 5 using a Monte Carlo simulation approach. Stephenson [1993] noted that resonant frequencies measured through standard experimental modal analysis techniques followed a Normal distribution. Thus, it was decided that the artificially induced uncertainties in the training database should also be normally distributed. For each of the above training cases at all levels of damage, ten different randomly generated uncertainties were incorporated into the resonant frequency values of each damage case, resulting in a database consisting of 600 cases. This process was repeated for various levels of uncertainty which were defined by the magnitude of the coefficient of variation (COV) (mean value divided by the standard deviation) during each of the Monte Carlo simulations. Five values for this coefficient were selected for this study: 0.1%, 0.5%, 1%, 2% and 5%. With the random data generated for each coefficient, five additional neural networks were trained with a database consisting of 600 cases. During the Monte Carlo simulation the elements of the set of resonant frequencies pertaining to a particular case were assumed perfectly correlated. The results obtained from the six different networks, one trained with deterministic data and five trained with data contaminated with uncertainties, were used to observe how uncertainties in the training data for a neural network influence its ability to assess damage.

4.5. Damage Detection Results

Once the neural networks were trained, the performance of the networks in predicting the location and the magnitude of the damage was evaluated. The goals set for this evaluation process were: 1) to observe the effects that the damage magnitude, uncertainties in the training data and uncertainties in the input data have on the networks' abilities to assess damage, and 2) to evaluate if an analytically trained network with and without uncertainties can be utilized to assess damage on an actual situation.

Analytical Damage Simulations

The neural networks were evaluated using several sets of data that were analytically generated. For the evaluation process, three magnitudes of damage were selected that were different from the magnitudes used in the training process. Therefore, three deterministic data sets were generated. Each deterministic set contained ten cases, one damage case at each of the ten locations. The damage magnitudes for the evaluation phase were 3%, 13% and 23%. These levels of damage were artificially introduced in the finite element model, in each of the ten locations, to generate a total of 30 deterministic cases. For each case an input vector of fractional changes of the first six resonant frequencies was also generated. In addition, uncertainties were also introduced in the input data sets, using the Monte Carlo simulation approach. Uncertainties in the resonant frequencies were assumed to be represented by the COV of each frequency. Five values for these coefficients were considered, these are: 0.1%, 0.5%, 1%, 2% and 5%. For each damage magnitude, for each location, and for each COV, ten randomly generated vectors were additionally created, generating 1,500 additional cases contaminated with uncertainties. In all a total of 1,530 input cases were generated. All input cases were processed in each of the six neural networks discussed in Section 6.

The test data were utilized to evaluate the six different networks in terms of their ability: a) to detect the correct location and b) to predict the magnitude of the damage. To assess these, the detectability of damage and the expected damage magnitude needs to be defined. These definitions are aided through the use of Table 4. This table lists the actual location and magnitude of damage (column 1), a typical set of output results consisting of a damage magnitude (second column) and ten prediction coefficients (Columns 3 through 12), and the expected damage (last column) which is defined in this paper as the damage magnitude of the output layer (column 2) times the largest of all prediction coefficients. This product was subjectively chosen as a means to account for the fact that the output of the neural networks was in real numbers which may be interpreted as the likelihood of a particular location being damaged. Negative values of the prediction coefficients may be effectively taken as zeros.

A successful detection of the damage location occurs when the largest prediction coefficient in the output layer corresponds to the actual damaged location. Thus, a measure of the ability of the network to detect damage is defined as the number of successful detections over the total number of attempts. This is defined as detectability.

Furthermore, to aid in the presentation of the vast number of results it was necessary to use the expected damage of the last column of Table 4. To compare the effectiveness of the damage predictions over all locations, the expected damage values are then graphed as a function of the location, giving graphs like the one shown in Figure 3. Each bar of Figure 3a represents one case, while the graph of Figure 3b is a summary of ten damage cases.

Detectability versus Uncertainties in Training Data

The effects of uncertainties in the data set employed to train the neural networks were assessed with all 1,530 cases. Each network was evaluated independently using, as inputs, the fractional changes in the resonant frequencies corresponding to damage magnitudes of 3%, 13% and 23% at all locations. The detectability of the three damage magnitudes as a function of the COV in the training data can be seen in Figure 4. This figure shows the aggregated results for all locations and all damage cases. Each of the six values on the horizontal axis are associated with each of the neural networks developed, while the values on the vertical axis show the detectability of each network.

As expected, each neural network predicts the location of damage at larger degrees of damage magnitude better than it does at smaller magnitudes. What was not expected, however, was the role different degrees of uncertainties in the training data sets play in a network's damage assessment capabilities. From Figure 4, it is evident that a network trained with deterministic data performs poorly at predicting damage locations. The network trained with deterministic data only identified the correct location about 30% of the time. However, with only deterministic data, the ability of this network to locate damage increases significantly to almost 100% regardless of the damage magnitude.

The results improve considerably for the neural networks trained with data with coefficients of variation of 0.1%, 0.5%, 1%, 2%. In these cases the detectability was above 80% for the larger damages. However, the detectability of the neural network trained with uncertain data, in which the COV is 5% decreases. At the time of writing this chapter, the reasons for this behavior remain unclear to the authors and are currently under investigation.

Plots similar to Figure 4 were also generated for the results on each location. Figure 5 shows the results obtained for locations 1, 4, 6, and 9, providing a spectrum of the detectability near the support, around the center and near the free end of the beam. These plots follow the same general pattern as that seen on Figure 4. The results from Figure 5 clearly show that the detectability is a function of the location, being erratic in the middle third of the beam. Also the detectability near the free end is relatively good at high damage values. This behavior may be because the sensitivity of damage, at the locations in the middle third, on the fractional changes of the resonant frequencies are similar. Thus damage may be erroneously predicted at an adjacent location.

Detectability versus Uncertainties in Test Data

To assess the effect that the magnitude of the uncertainty in the test data has on the detectability, plots that show the detectability of each network with respect to the COV of the test data were prepared using the results for all locations. These plots are shown in Figure 6.

TABLE 4. Output results for 13% damage using deterministic input and neural network trained at COV level of 0.1%.

Actual location and magnitude of damage	Damage Magnitude (%)	Prediction Coefficient Location										Defined Predicted Magnitude (%)
		1	2	3	4	5	6	7	8	9	10	
Loc. 1 (13%)	18.45	1.06	-.01	-.01	.00	-.04	-.09	-.03	.02	-.04	-.12	19.52
Loc. 2 (13%)	18.46	-.02	1.03	-.01	-.04	-0.6	-.04	-.02	.00	-.13	.00	19.01
Loc. 3 (13%)	18.83	-.11	.01	1.05	.05	-.09	-.06	-.02	-.12	-.12	.03	19.71
Loc. 4 (13%)	17.62	-.07	-.02	.05	.90	.21	-.12	-.10	-.06	-.04	-.03	15.77
Loc. 5 (13%)	12.31	.02	.00	.00	.26	.46	-.09	-.06	.03	.01	-.03	5.60
Loc. 6 (13%)	11.70	.04	.06	.02	-.12	-.06	.73	.17	.03	-.06	.03	8.50
Loc. 7 (13%)	19.80	.00	-.04	-.05	-.13	-.12	.13	.50	.13	-.10	-.03	9.82
Loc. 8 (13%)	18.62	-.02	-.08	-.12	-.11	-.12	-.12	.09	1.06	.00	-.03	19.76
Loc 9. (13%)	18.32	-.09	-.12	.00	-.05	-.12	-.12	.05	-.02	.99	-.03	18.17
Loc 10. (13%)	15.03	-.13	.01	-.02	-.03	-.07	-.04	-.02	-.02	-.05	1.07	16.08

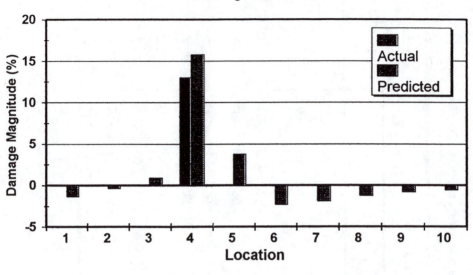

(a)

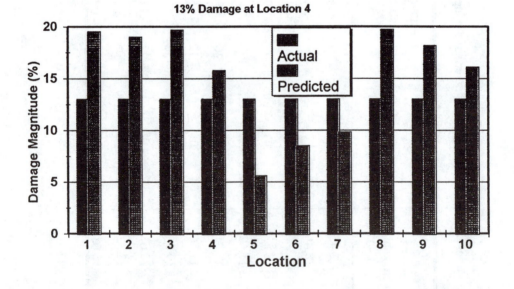

(b)

Figure 3.   Expected Damage Magnitudes.   (a) Predicted Damage Magnitudes as function
of location (actual damage of 13% at location 4).   (b) Summary of Expected
Damage Magnitude of all cases of Table 4.

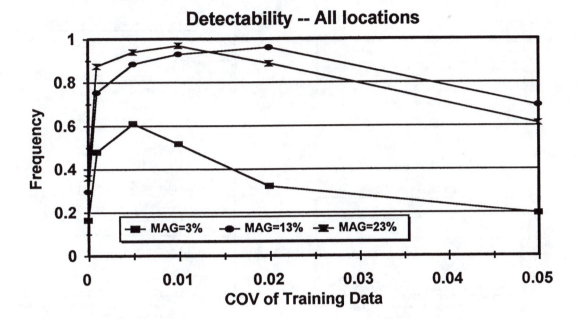

Figure 4.   Overall Detectability versus COV in the Training Data.

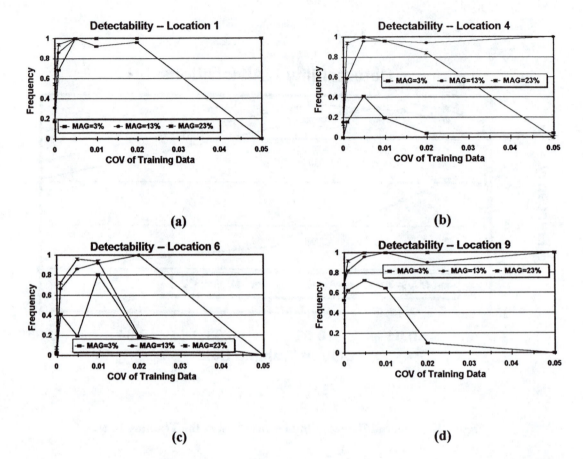

(a)

(b)

(c)

(d)

Figure 5.   Detectability versus COV in Training Data for (a) Location 1, (b) Location 4, (c) Location 6 and (d) Location 9.

In general, it is observed that as the uncertainty in the input test data increases, the detectability of all networks decreases. The rate at which the detectability decreases with the uncertainty in the test data is the largest for the network trained with deterministic data. Detectability is improved, for all damage levels as the COV of the training data increases up to a value of 1%. A reversal in this trend is observed for the remaining networks. Again, further analysis is needed to explain this behavior.

Damage Magnitude Quantification

Influence of the COVs of the test data and the COVs of the training data on the quantification of damage is shown in Figures 7 through 9. Each figure shows the results for the neural network trained with a data set with a coefficient of variation of 0.5%. These plots were chosen because they represent the best cases of the study. The neural network trained with a data set with a COV of 0.5% was consistent and much more accurate at quantifying the damage for the three test levels considered in this study. These results also show that damage at the middle section of the beam is more difficult to assess accurately.

Experimental Simulations

To evaluate if the analytically trained networks can assess damage on an actual situation, experimental resonant frequencies published in the literature were used. The experiments performed by Stubbs and Osegueda (1990) consisted of measurements of the resonant frequencies of undamaged and damaged cantilever beams. They performed a total of nine experiments of single damage for magnitudes 2%, 10% and 30% at three locations, equivalent to locations 1, 5 and 9 of Figure 1. For eight of the experiments, six resonant frequencies were available, but for the case of 2% damage at location 1 only 5 frequencies were listed. From the published measured frequencies, nine input test data of fractional changes of frequencies were built. The experimental input data was then tested in each of the six networks already described.

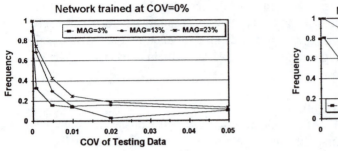

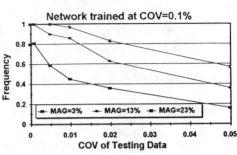

(a)   **(b)**

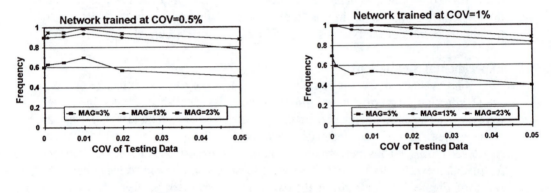

(c)   **(d)**

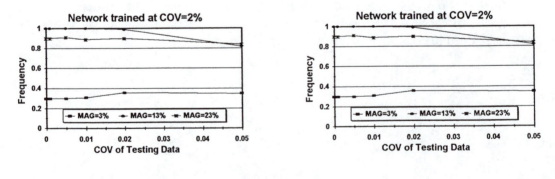

(e)   **(f)**

Figure 6.   Detectability of each Network versus COV in the Test Data. (a) COV=0%, (b) COV=0.1%, (c) COV=0.5%, (d) COV=1%, (e) COV=2%, (f) COV=5%.

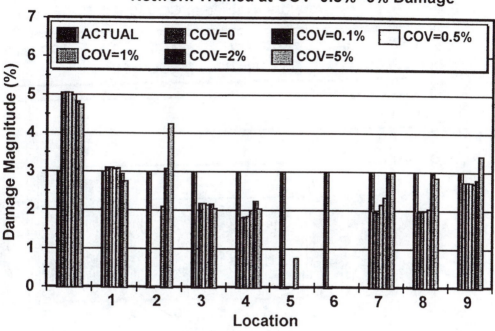

Figure 7. Summary of Expected Damage Magnitudes for a 3% Actual Damage for Networks Trained with COV=0.5%.

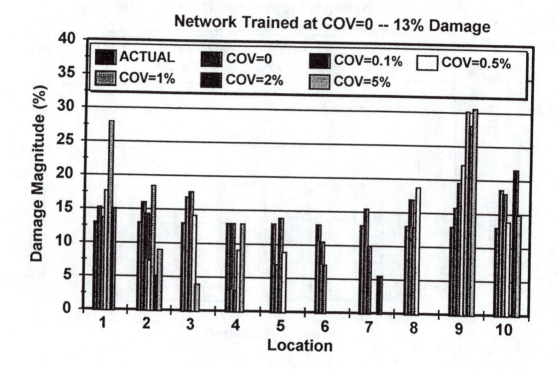

Figure 8.   Summary of Expected Damage Magnitudes for a 13% Actual Damage for Networks Trained with COV=0.5%.

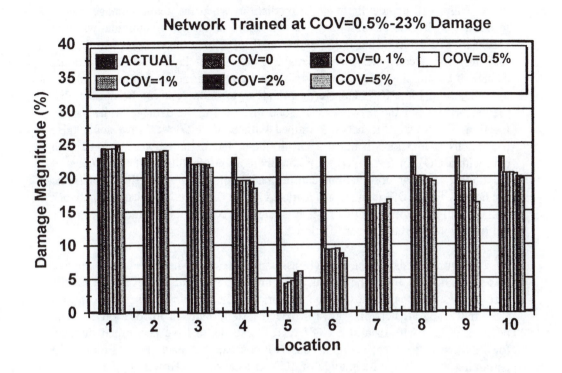

Figure 9.   Summary of Expected Damage Magnitude for a 23% Actual Damage for Networks Trained with (a) COV=0 and (b) COV=0.5%.

Figure 10 depicts the damage predictions when the actual damage was at location 1. It can be observed that the damage of 2% magnitude was not predicted, this could be attributed to the small magnitude of damage or to the fact that only five frequencies were available in the input layer and the fractional change of the missing frequency was assigned a value of zero. Figure 10b shows the predictions for a 10% damage magnitude at location 1, it can be noticed that the performance of the networks was good in detecting the damage at the correct location. However, the network trained without uncertainties gave some false predictions at locations 3 and 6. On the other hand, the network trained with data with a COV of 5% failed to predict the correct magnitude of the damage at location 1. Similar observations can be made from Figure 10c that depicts the predictions for a 30% damage at location 1, with the exception that the network trained with data with a COV of 5% predicted the correct magnitude at location 1 but made a false prediction at location 2.

Figure 11 shows the damage assessment results when the actual damage was at location 5. From the results of Figure 11a, it can be observed that for the case of the 2% damage, most of the networks predicted some damage at locations 1, 5 and 8 and all networks always detected some damage in location 5. The network trained with data at a COV of 0.1% seems to have performed the best for this particular case. Similar observations can be made from Figure 11b pertaining to a damage magnitude of 10% at location 5. However, the network trained with the deterministic data made a significant false prediction at location 9. For the case of 30% damage magnitude at location 5, the performance of the networks was not satisfactory; only the network trained with data with a COV of 0.1% detected a significant damage at the correct location. Most of the networks falsely predicted significant damage at location 1. The relatively poor performance of the networks in predicting damage at this location, being in the middle third of the beam, had already been observed with the analytical results and thoroughly discussed previously.

Figure 12 shows the prediction results for the cases where the damage was located at location 9. The three different magnitudes of damage were successfully predicted at the correct location as can be observed in the graphs. However, for the prediction with the 2% damage, false predictions were made at locations 4 and 5. It should be noted from Figure 12a, that it seems that the network trained with deterministic data works the best in detecting the 2% damage. The networks with data with high COV values do not conclusively detect the damage. All networks performed satisfactorily to assess the damage of magnitudes 10% and 30% at location 9 (Figures 12b and 12c), with the exceptions of the ones trained with data having high COV values.

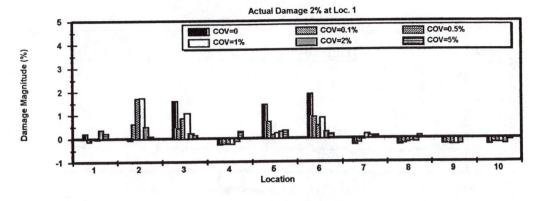

(a)

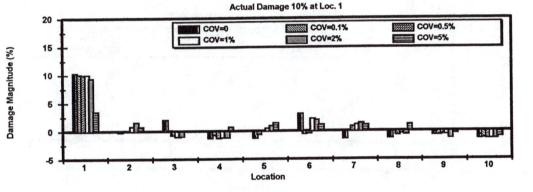

(b)

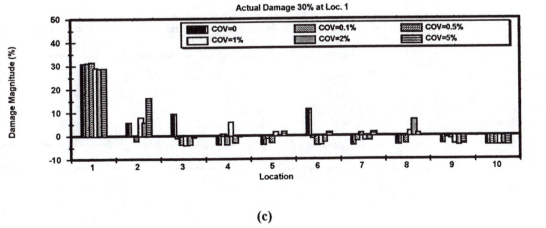

(c)

Figure 10.   Summary of Predicted Damage Magnitudes at Location 1 of Actual Beam. (a) Damage of 2%, (b) Damage of of 10%, and (c) Damage of 30%.

87

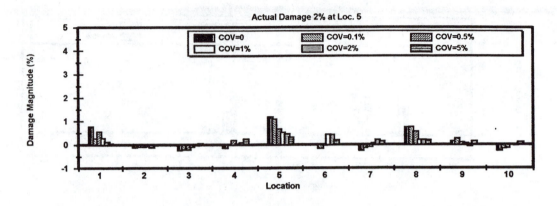

(a)

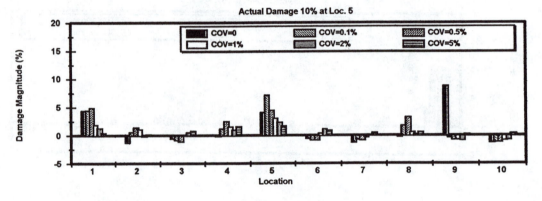

(b)

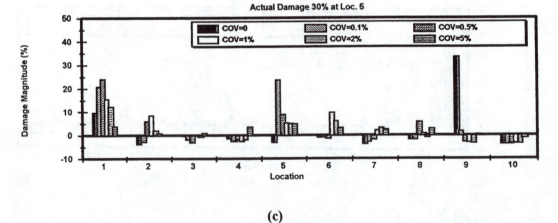

(c)

Figure 11.   Summary of Predicted Damage Magnitudes at Location 5 of Actual Beam.
(a) Damage of 2%, (b) Damage of 10% and (c) Damage of 30%.

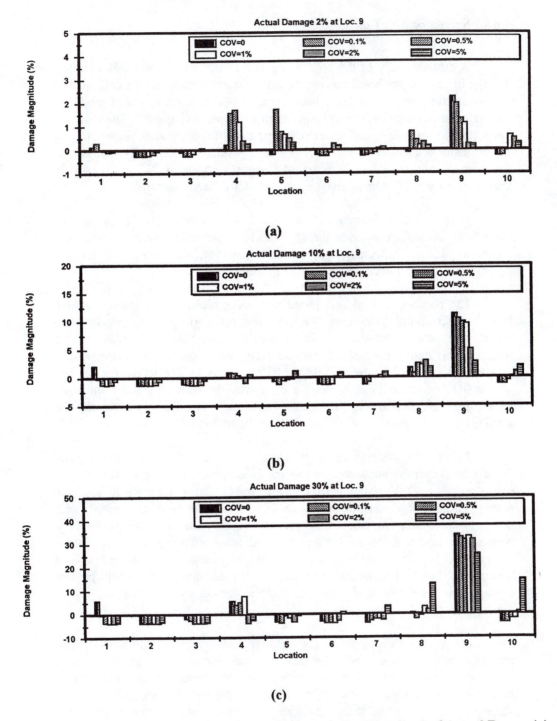

Figure 12. **Summary of Predicted Damage Magnitudes at Location 9 of Actual Beam.** **(a)**
Damage of 2%, (b) Damage of 10% and (c) Damage of 30%.

4.6   Summary And Conclusions

A detailed study of the capabilities of artificial neural networks to detect damage in a cantilever beam was conducted. The study included the definition of the architecture for a three layer backpropagation neural network that processes the resonant frequencies of a damage beam to locate and quantify the damage. The network was trained and tested with deterministic and random information of the resonant frequencies of the damage beam generated analytically, and it was also tested with experimentally measured resonant frequencies. Several sensitivity tests were conducted at three levels of damage for different locations.

Overall, the performance of the neural network was satisfactory, and its predictions of damage provide the same level of accuracy given by analytical sensitivity damage detection approaches. However, the processing time is significantly reduced once the network is trained.

The network trained and tested with deterministic data showed a high level of detectability. However, the same network performs very poorly when tested with data contaminated with random uncertainties. According to the results of this study, this problem may be overcome by training the network with data with uncertainties. Nevertheless this solution is limited to the use of data with a COV of up to 2%. It was not clear why the network trained with data with a COV of 5% performed less accurate. It might be necessary to modify the architecture of the network when the COV of the training data is high.

All the networks exhibited some degree of detectability when experimental measurements were processed. In general, the networks trained with data containing COVs ranging from 0.1% to 1% had a tendency to give the correct location and magnitude of the damage. The network trained with deterministic data gave more false predictions than the other networks. The networks trained with high COV values exhibited relatively good detectability, but considerably underpredicted the magnitude of the damage. Furthermore, it was observed that all networks performed much better for the 10 and 30 percent damage, and for detecting the damage near the support and near the free end of the cantilever.

It is believed that a neural network-based methodology similar to the one presented here could be applied for detecting and assessing damage for complex and realistic structures. However, instead of considering the training data to consist of only resonant frequencies, the training data should include modal shape responses or complete frequency response functions at several points of the structure. This research is currently being conducted by the authors; preliminary results from training neural networks with mode shape data look promising.

4.7 Acknowledgements

This study was sponsored in part by the NASA Johnson Space Center, under contract NAG 9-483, and by the Material Research Center of Excellence at The University of Texas at El Paso. The enormous cooperation of Angel Urbina, Adolfo Aguilera, Alex Barron and Ernesto Avila during this study is greatly appreciated.

4.8 References

Elkordy, M.F., Chang, K.C. and Lee, G.C. (1993). "Neural Networks trained by analytically simulated damage states*," Journal of Computing in Civil Engineering*, Vol. 7, No.2, ASCE, pp. 130-145.

Osegueda, R.A., Vila, M., Mahajan, S.K. (1990). "A Modal Analysis Method for Locating Stiffness and Mass Changes in Structures", in *Developments in Theoretical and Applied Mechanics*, Eds. S.V. Hanagud, M.P. Kamat & C.E. Ueng, Georgia Institute of Technology, Atlanta, Georgia, pp. 333-340.

Stephenson, T.W. (1993). "Probabilistic Evaluation of a Vibrational NDE Damage Detection and Reliability Assessment Method for Aerospace Structures", Master of Science Thesis, Department of Civil Engineering, The University of Texas at El Paso, El Paso, Texas, August.

Stubbs, N.S. (1985). "A General Theory of Nondestructive Damage Detection in Structures". In *Structural Control Proc. of the 2nd Int. Symposium on Structural Control*, University of Waterloo, pp. 694-713.

Stubbs, N., and Osegueda, R.A. (1990), "Global Damage Detection in Solids -- Experimental Verification", *International Journal of Analytical and Experimental Modal Analysis*, Vol 5, No. 2, pp. 81-97, April.

Szewczyk Z.P., and Hajela, P.(1992). "Neural Networks Based Damage Detection in Structures," *Computing in Civil Engineering*, B.J. Goodno and J.R. Wright (Eds.), ASCE, pp. 1163-1170.

Wu, X., Ghaboussi, J. and Garret J.H. (1992). "Use of Neural Networks in Detection of Structural Damage," *Computers and Structures*, Vo.42, No.4,pp. 649-659.

Yao, J.T.P. (1984). *Safety and Reliability of Existing Structures*. Pitman, 1984.

Chapter-5

Neural Network for Identification and Control of Civil Engineering Structures

G.Z. Qi[1], J.C.S. Yang[1], and F. Amini[2]

Abstract: In dynamic model identification and control of civil engineering structures, the main characteristics which causes difficulty are the complexity and uncertainty of structures, control systems and their interactions. The capability to learn, the ability to generalize to new inputs, the robustness to noise, the inherent ability to handle nonlinear systems, and the ability to perform fast computations are the major advantages in the application of neural networks to solving these difficulties. The neural network models, including their architectures and training processes for structural dynamic identification and control developed based on the knowledge of dynamics of the structures, are presented in this chapter. The robustness to noise and the ability to generalize to new input of these neural network models were verified by applying them to the measured responses in a real 10- story building due to three earthquakes. The results showed great promise in the dynamic identification and control of civil engineering structures subjected to dynamic loadings by using neural network technique.

5.1 Introduction

In this chapter, the application of neural networks to the identification and modeling representing the dynamic behavior of civil engineering structures and to the active control for protecting civil engineering structures from the damaging effects of destructive environmental loadings is presented. Although neural networks have shown great promise in function mapping, pattern recognition, and image processing, the dynamic model identification and dynamic control for

---

[1]Robotics and Structural Dynamics Lab., Dept. of Mechanical Eng., Univ. of Maryland, College Park, MD 20742

[2]Dept. of Civil Eng.. Univ. of District of Columbia, 4200 Connecticut Ave., N.W. Washington DC 20008

complex dynamic systems are still challenging topics as neural network applications [Albus 1975, Bhat and McAvoy 1989, Cybenko 1989, Grossberg 1989, Hopfield 1979, Narendra and Parthasarthy 1990, Werbos 1988, Werbos 1990a, Werbos 1990b, Werbos 1992].

The identification and modeling of dynamic systems through the use of measured data is a problem of considerable importance in all areas of engineering. System identification may be classified into two categories: identification of system parameters in a deterministic manner and identification of system parameters in a statistical manner [Liu and Yao 1978, Ljung and Soderstor 1983, Qi et al. 1990, Shinozuka and Deodatis 1992, Shinozuka 1993, Udwadia 1987a, Udwadia 1987b]. Most of the existing identification techniques can only be successfully used for linear systems. Some nonlinear techniques are available, but just for simple cases. In model identification of civil engineering structures, the main characteristics which causes difficulty are their large sizes, the complexities of the structure, the interaction between the soil and structure, and the uncertainties arising from the noise in measured data. These uncertainties require the model for civil engineering structures to be identified essentially in a statistical manner, although some deterministic models have been used.

In structural engineering, one of the constant challenges has been to find new and improved means of designing new structures and strengthening existing structures so that they, together with their occupants and contents, can be sufficiently protected from the damaging effects of destructive forces such as earthquakes and tornadoes. Control is one means to protect civil engineering structures against environmental loadings and can be classified into passive and/or active control. In the passive control area, base isolation and a variety of mechanical energy dissipaters [Liu et al. 1990, Nagarajaih et al. 1993, Soong and Skinner 1981, Yang and Samali 1983] have been used. Research and development in active structural control technology has a more recent origin. In the United States, it appears that Yao's concept paper in 1972 [Yao, 1972] marked the beginning of active control research when he proposed an error-activated structural system whose behavior varies automatically in accordance with unpredictable variations in loading as well as environmental conditions and thereby produces desirable responses under all possible loading conditions. Significant progress has been made since 1972. Active structural control has now become an established area of research in which the motion of a structure is controlled or modified by a control system through some external energy supply. Recent United States activities in structural control may be grouped into the following three broad areas: basic research, laboratory experiments of scaled model structures, and full scale implementations [Chung et al. 1988, Chung et al. 1989, Housner et al. 1994, Kobori 1990, Kobori et al. 1991a, Kobori et al. 1991b, Masri et al. 1992, Rehak and Garret 1990, Soong and Skinner 1981, Yang and Soong 1988]. The control algorithms which have been utilized for the control of civil engineering structures subjected to environmental loadings include instantaneous optimal control [Soong and Skinner 1981, Yang et al. 1987, Yang et al. 1990, Yang and Samali 1983, Yang and Soong 1988, Yang et al. 1991], acceleration and velocity feedback control [Yang et al. 1991], adaptive control [Chung et al. 1988, Soong and Skinner 1981], fuzzy control [Subramaniam et al. 1992), feedback-feedforward control [Yang et al. 1991], and optimal placement control [Cheng et al. 1991, Cheng and Pantelides 1990, Cheng et al. 1992]. Due to the complexities of the structure to be controlled and the uncertainties arising from errors in the descriptive model and the measured data, stability and robustness of the currently available control algorithms are still critical issues of concern [Hackel et al. 1992, Soong and Skinner 1981].

A requirement for both the conventional identification and control of structures is the formulation of the mathematical model representing the dynamics of the structure and the interaction between the control system and the structures. Due to the complexity of civil engineering structures and the uncertain nature of their model, it is difficult to formulate these mathematical expressions. For example, at the present time, the models which can accurately describe the interaction between the soil and the structure are not available yet. One of the attributes of neural networks is the capability of learning from sampled data of systems without knowing the mathematical formulations, as long as the relationship to be learned is included in the sampled data [Albus 1975, Werbos 1988, Werbos 1990a, Werbos 1990b, Werbos 1992]. Therefore, neural networks is a powerful technique in dealing with the dynamic identification and control of civil engineering structures.

The uncertainties arising from the structural model errors, the environment loadings, and the control parameters are other factors which cause difficulties in the dynamic identification and control of civil engineering structures. The attributes of neural networks include the ability to generalize to new inputs and the robustness to noise which makes it suitable to solve these difficulties.

Finally, since the control goal is to protect civil engineering structures from the damaging effects of destructive environmental loadings, the timing is a very important factor in practice. The inherent parallelism and the simple mathematic operation involved in the network not only lead to fast computations but also provide the possibility for fast hardware implementations of the neural network [Rumelhart and McClellad 1986, Werbos 1988, Werbos 1990a, Werbos 1990b].

The capability to learn, the ability to generalize to new inputs, the robustness to noise, the inherent ability to handle nonlinear systems, and the ability to perform fast computations are the major advantages in the application of neural networks to the dynamic model identification and control of civil engineering structures. The results from the measured responses in a 10-story building presented in this chapter show great promise for these applications. Although no mathematical formulation for the system to be identified and/or controlled is required, one issue emphasized in this chapter is that the engineering knowledge regarding the dynamics of the system will be significant to the success of the neural network application. In addition, another issue to be addressed is that of the neural model network representing the dynamic behavior of the structures as a required component to be included in the neural control network. This is essential to ensure the success of the neural network training for structural control.

5.2 Neural Network For Identification And Control
Neural Network Structure
Backpropagation Neural Network

A number of neural network techniques, such as the backpropagation network, the Hopfield network, the Kohonen network, and the Cerebellar Model Articulation Controller (CMAC), have been used in the identification and control of systems [Albus 1975, Bhat and McAvoy 1989, Billings and Chen 1992, Hopfield 1979, Hunt and Sbarbaro 1992, Montague et. al. 1992, Wen et al. 1992, Werbos 1988, Werbos 1990a, Werbos 1990b, Zbikowski and Gawthrop 1992]. In this chapter, the most widely-used one, the backpropagation neural network is adapted for the dynamic model identification and control of civil engineering structures. The detail of the processing elements, the network topology, and the learning algorithm of the backpropagation neural network can be found in Chapter 2, Part 1. For convenience, a brief description of the backpropagation neural network is presented below.

The backpropagation neural work can be fully connected or partially connected between the nodes in the network. However, most researchers prefer to use layered networks in which all conncection weights are zero out except for those going from one layer to the next. Multi-layered networks are used in this chapter.

Figure 1 shows a typical 3-layer backpropagation neutral network: an input layer with l nodes, a hidden layer with m nodes, and an output layer with n nodes. Between the layers, there are weights, W_{hi} and W_{ho}, representing the strength of connections of the nodes, where the subscripts i, h, and o are integer number ranging from 1, 2, ... l, and 1, 2, ... m, and 1, 2, ... n, respectively. The first operation of a backpropagation neural network is called "feed forward", which is shown as solid lines with an arrow in Fig. 1. The input vector, I(t), is fed forward through the hidden layer to the output layer. The output of the node o in the output layer, $O_o(t)$, can be obtained from

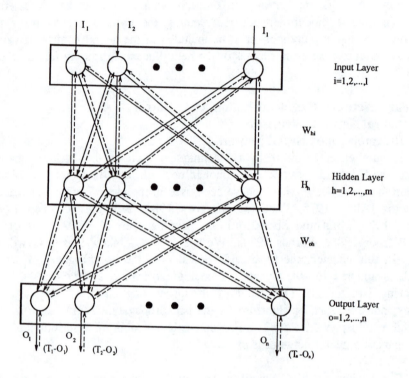

Fig 1: Typical 3-layer Backpropagation Neural Network.

$$O_o(t) = F\left(\sum_h W_{oh} \, F(\sum_i W_{hi} \, I_i(t))\right) \tag{1}$$

where $F(x)$ is the activation function which has to be differentiable and t represents the time at which the input time series and the output time series are sampled. Since the differentiable function is needed for the backpropagation network, the step-like, smooth sigmoid function,

$$F(x) = \frac{1}{1 + e^{-x}} \tag{2}$$

is chosen as the activation function in this chapter.

The second operation of a backpropagation neural network is called "error backpropagation", which is marked by dashed lines in Fig. 1. The error function, defined by the sum of the square of the differences between the known outputs, $T_0(t)$, and network outputs, $O_0(t)$, is

$$E(O) = \tfrac{1}{2} \sum_{t,o} \left(T_0(t) \quad O_0(t) \right)^2 \qquad (3)$$

For the hidden layer to the output layer connections, the adaptive rule of the weight, W_{oh}, can be determined as

$$\Delta W_{oh} = -\eta \sum_h \Delta_o(t) H_h(t) \qquad (4)$$

where $H_h(t)$ represents the output from the node h in the hidden layer and can be written as

$$H_h(t) = F \sum_i \left(W_{hi} \ I_i(t) \right) \qquad (5a)$$

and $D_0(t)$ represents the difference between the target and neural network output and is defined by

$$\Delta_o(t) = \frac{dF(\text{Net}_o)}{d\ Net_o} \left(T_o(t) - O_o(t) \right). \qquad (5b)$$

Net_0 represents the total input to the node o in the output layer. Similarly, the adaptive rule for the input layer to the hidden layer connections, W_{hi}, can be written as

$$\Delta W_{hi} = -\eta \sum_h \Delta_h(t) I_i(t) \qquad (6)$$

where

$$\Delta_t(t) = \frac{dF(\text{Net}_h)}{d\ Net_h} \sum_o W_{ho} (\Delta_o(t) \qquad (7)$$

and Net_h represents the total input to the node h in the hidden layer. The coefficient in equations (4) and (6) is called the learning rate. The learning rate is an important factor which controls the learning process. Generally speaking, a small learning rate can ensure the reduction of the error function but may slow the convergent process, while a large learning rate can speed the learning process but may cause divergence. Therefore, careful selection and appropriate adjustments of the learning rate are necessary to successfully train the backpropagation neural network. Applying the differentiation process successively, the error backpropagation rules can be expanded to the networks with any number of hidden layers. Their weights will be continuously adjusted until the inputs and outputs reach the desired relationship. The network shown in Fig. 1 is the basic unit of neural network structures used for the dynamic model identification and control in this chapter.

Dynamics of Structures

To demonstrate how to successfully use the knowledge of structural dynamics in neural network application, the general concept of structural dynamics is briefly discussed in this section. The responses of a structure subjected to ground acceleration, $\ddot{G}(t)$, and external force, u(t), can be described by the equation

$$M\ddot{Z}(t) + C\dot{Z}(t) + KZ(t) = M\ddot{G}(t) + Du(t) \qquad (8)$$

where M, C and K are the mass, damping and stiffness matrices respectively, and Z(t) is the displacement with respect to the ground. The equation can be re-written in the state equation as

$$\dot{X}(t) = AX(t) + Bu)\dot{y}(t) + Ff(t) \qquad (9)$$

$$X(t) = \begin{bmatrix} Z(t) \\ \dot{Z}(t) \end{bmatrix} \qquad (10)$$

where the matrices A, B, F and f in the state equation can be determined as follows,

$$A = \begin{bmatrix} -\mathbf{M}^{-1}C & -\mathbf{M}^{-1}K \\ I & O \end{bmatrix} \qquad (11)$$

$$B = \begin{bmatrix} -\mathbf{M}^{-1}D \\ O \end{bmatrix} \qquad (12)$$

$$F = \begin{bmatrix} I \\ O \end{bmatrix} \qquad (13)$$

$$f(t) = \ddot{G}(t). \qquad (14)$$

Furthermore, equation (9) can be written in the discrete form,

$$X(k+1) = \Phi X(k) + \Gamma u(k) + Hf(k) \qquad (15)$$

$$\Phi = e^{A\Delta t} \qquad (16)$$
$$\Gamma = \Phi B \qquad (17)$$
$$H = \Phi F \qquad (18)$$

where k is an integer number, k = 0, 1, 2, . . . , N, X(k) is the response at time t = k t, and t is the sampling period. For a nonlinear system, a representative form of the equation of motion can be expressed in the form

$$M\ddot{Z}(t) + \psi(Z(t), \dot{Z}(t), Z((t-1), \dot{Z}(t-1),..., Z(t-1), \dot{Z}(t-1) = M\ddot{G}(t) + Du(t) \quad (19)$$

where ψ is called the function vector and represents the nonlinear function of the vectors Z(t), $\dot{Z}(t), Z((t-1), \dot{Z}(t-1),..., Z(t-1)$ and $\dot{Z}(t-1)$ with M components, namely $\psi = (\psi_1, \psi_2, ..., \psi_M)^T$. M is the number of degrees of freedom and l is the number of time lags which characterizes the nature of the nonlinear stress-strain hysterestic loop. The corresponding state equation becomes

$$\dot{X}(t) = \gamma(X(t), \dot{X}(t-1), ..., X(t-l)) + \dot{X}(t-l) + Bu(t) + Ff(t) \qquad (20)$$

where γ represents a nonlinear function vector with M components.

Generally speaking, the conventional technique for system identification is to determine the system parameters M, C, and K/(A and G) or ψ / γ from the measured structural responses, $Z(t)$, $\dot{Z}(t)$ and $\ddot{Z}(t)$, using equation (8)/(9) or (19)/(20). The uncertainty for nonlinear system identification is raised from not only the difficulty to determine the nonlinear function vector ψ or γ, but also the difficulty to solve the nonlinear parameters from equation (19) or (20) using the least square method even if the form of ψ or γ is given.

Neural Network Architecture for Identification

In general, the backpropagation neural network can be used to empirically map any function using measured experimental data [Cybenko 1989]. However, dynamic function mapping is still a challenging topic in neural network applications [Narendra and Parthasarathy 1990, Hunt et al. 1992, Werbos 1990c]. To avoid the difficulties encountered in structural dynamic model identification, Masri and his co-workers recently developed two types of approaches for identification of nonlinear dynamic systems using neural networks [Masri et al. 1992, Masri et al. 1993]. One of these approaches is to identify the internal forces from the system responses using neural networks first and then to include the identified internal forces into the equation of motion of the system, solving the equation using conventional computational schemes (Runge-Kutta) [Masri et al. 1993]. It is clear that in this approach, the neural network is included as part of the equation of motion and used only to perform the static function mapping. Another approach developed by Masri et al. is to involve the dynamic differential equation into each of the neural network processing elements to create a new type of neuron called the dynamic neuron [Masri et al. 1992]. The dynamic neuron approach is also proposed by other investigators [Chassiakos et al. 1990, Kosmatopoulos et al. 1990, Zbikowski and Gawthrop 1992]. Since differential equations are involved, these two approaches cannot take full advantage of the neural network operation. In this chapter, "the dynamic model identification of structures using neural network" is defined as follows: (1) in the neural model, only simple operations shown in equation (1) are involved; (2) the dynamic behavior of the structure is represented completely by the trained neural model itself, namely, given the initial conditions, $Z(1)$, for linear structures in equation (15) or the initial conditions, $X(1)$, $X(0)$, $X(-1)$, . . . , $X(1-l)$, for nonlinear structures in equation (20), as well as the excitation force, $f(t)$, and/or the applied force, u(t), the time histories of the structural responses are completely predicted from only the trained neural model. From this definition and the dynamics of structures characterized by equation (15) or (20), the neural network architecture for structural dynamic model identification can be determined.

Equation (15) shows that given the state variables, X(k), including the displacement, Z(k), the velocity, $\dot{Z}(k)$, the dynamic loading, f(k), and/or applied loading, u(k), the response of the structure at the next time step, X(k+1), can be completely determined. Therefore, given initial state variables, X(1), the excitation force, f(1), and/or the applied loading, u(1), X(2) will be determined. By applying the recursive process, the time histories of the responses, X(2), . . . , X(N), will be computed successively from equation (15). Here N is the total number of time steps of the structural responses.

A neural network which can be trained to represent this recursive dynamic behavior of a structure described by equation (15) has to have an external feed-back recurrent architecture. As shown in Fig. 2, in addition to the excitation input, f(t+1), the output of the neural network, $X_m(k+1)$, will be fed back as the new input to the neural network at the next time step. If the outputs of the neural network, $X_m(k+1)$, converge to the structural responses, $X_s(k+1)$ for k=1, 2, . . . , N-1, through training, the neural network model will represent the dynamic behavior of the structure and can be used to predict the response time history, X(2), X(3), . . . , X(N), of the structure subjected to new excitation inputs if the initial conditions, X(1), is given. Comparing equations (20) and (15), it can be expected that for nonlinear systems, the architecture of the neural network model will be the same as that shown in Fig. 2 except that the inputs of state variables should be with time lags, e.g. X_m, $X_m(k+1),...,X_m(k-l)$.

Neural Network Architecture for Control

As shown in Fig. 3, the function of the neural network for structural control is based on the input vector, inmcluding the state variables $X_s(k)$ for linear systems and $X_s(k)$, $X_s(k-1),...,X_s(k-l)$ for nonlinear systems to produce a series of control commands, u(k), so that the responses of the structure, $X_s(k+1)$, subjected to the dynamic loadings, f(k), and control command, u(k), will follow the desired responses, $X_d(k+1)$.

Therefore, for structural control, the control targets are the structural state variables, $X_s(k+1)$. However, the output of the neural action network is the control command, u(k), acting on the structure. To adjust the weights of the action network in terms of the error function, E_c, the relationship between the control command, u(k), and the structural variables, $X_s(k)$, needs to be formulated first. This relationship includes the dynamics of the structure and the control system as well as the interactions between the structure and the control system. As discussed earlier, due to the complexities and uncertainties of the structure, and the control system and their interactions, it is difficult to formulate this relationship. Fortunately, this relationship can be represented by the neural model network shown in Fig. 2.

The structure of the neural network for the active control of civil engineering structures shown in Fig. 4 consists of two components. The first component is the neural model network which represents the dynamic behavior of the structure to be controlled, and the second component is the neural action network which produces the control commands.

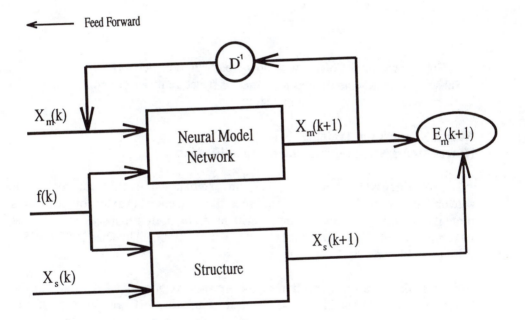

Fig 2: Neural Network Architecture for Structural Dynamic Model Identification. D^{-1} represents one time step delay; subscripts s and m represent structural and neural model outputs, respectively.

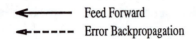

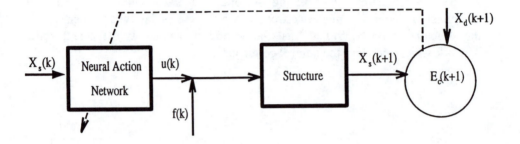

Fig 3: Structural Control with only Neural Action Network.
Subscript d represents desired responses of structure under control
command u.

Neural Network for Training
Neural Model Network Training for Identification

As discussed in Section 2.1.1, an external feed-back recurrent neural network shown in Fig. 2, can represent the dynamic behavior of structures through training. A number of algorithms have been proposed to train the recurrent neural network [Pineda 1987, 1988, 1989, Almeida 1987, 1988, Billings and Chen 1992].

However, since the error function of the neural network output depends on the history of the weights in the network, it is usually difficult for a recurrent network, representing a complex system, to be trained converging to a stable state. In this chapter, an alternative process, shown in Fig. 5, is adapted to train the neural model network. Instead of feeding back the neural model network outputs, $X_m(k+1)$, shown in Fig. 2, the measured responses in the structure, $X_s(k)$ for k=1, 2, . . . , N, are used as inputs to the network during the entire training process. The weights in the network are initialized with small random numbers. By feeding forward the input vector, $I_i(k)$, including $X_s(k)$ and f(k) where k = 0, 1, 2, . . . , N, through the network, the outputs, $X_m(k+1)$, are then computed from equation (1). The error function, $E_m(k + 1)$, is calculated from the difference between the outputs of the neural network, $X_m(k + 1)$, and the outputs of the structure, $X_s(k+1)$. Backpropagating the error function, $E_m(k + 1)$, to adjust the weights according to equations (4) and (6), the outputs of the neural model network can be trained to reach the desired accuracy with respect to the structural responses. This training process can be done by adjusting the weights once, either according to the error function determined from equation (3) after the entire N number of time steps has been fed through the network, or according to the error determined after each time step.

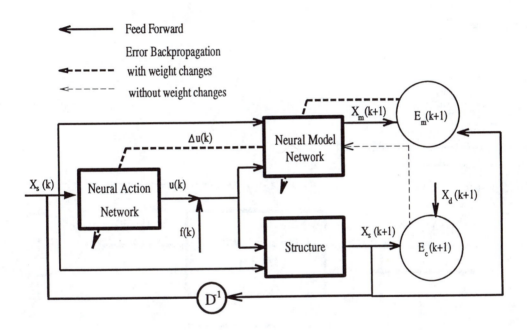

Fig 4: Architecture and Training of Neural Network for Control.

Fast convergence may be the main advantage of this alternative training process. The question is whether the trained neural model in Fig. 5 converges to the external feed-back network in Fig. 2. Theoretically, if the error functions, E_m, are trained to be zero, both of the neural model networks shown in Figs. 2 and 5 should be exactly the same. Both models are still equivalent if the differences between the outputs of the structure and the neural network are small enough and randomly distributed. In order to successfully train the neural network model, we have to understand the process of two neural model networks physically and mathematically. As discussed in Section 2.1.1, the neural model shown in Fig. 2 can represent the dynamic equation (15) or (20) through training. Since equation (15) or (20) is the discrete form of the corresponding equation of motion of the system, the smaller sampling time step is better able to satisfy the requirement of equation (15) and the neural model shown in Fig. 2. Physically, the neural model has to be trained to represent the effect of the excitation, $f(k)$ and/or $u(k)$, on the structural responses, $X(k+1)$. However, if the sampling time step is too small, the neural model shown in Fig. 5 may ignore the effect of the excitation input, $f(k)$, and learn only the extrapolation of $x(k)$ to reach the required accuracy of $X(k+1)$. Therefore, appropriate selection of the sampling step to fit the requirements of both the discrete differentiation and the alternative training process is important to the success of the neural model network training.

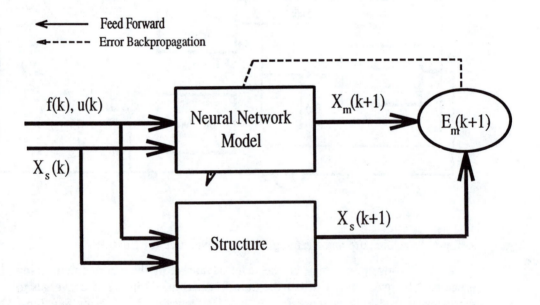

Fig 5: Training Process of Neural Network for Structural Dynamic Model Identification.

Other factors which affect the neural model network training are the length of the trained data set and the size of the neural network. Since the theory of neural networks is still in its infancy and no analytic results are available to quantitatively define these factors, they can only be given in a quantitative manner from the knowledge of structural dynamics and from limited experience. The pattern is an often used terminology characterizing the complexity of the signal to be treated. However, in structural engineering, the number of modes, the modal frequencies, and the modal dampings are usually used to describe the nature of the structural dynamics and responses. In general, in order to successfully train the neural model network, the resolution of the data set in frequency domain has to be high enough to characterize the model properties including the natural frequencies and dampings. Increasing the size of the network is likely to improve the representative capabilities of the network for the data set used in the training. However, network overfitting not only increases the training time, but it may also lose the generalization to the new inputs. Since the number of the nodes in the input and output layers is determined by the state variables of the system, only the size of the hidden layer needs to be determined in practice.

Neural Action Network Training for Control

After the neural model network is obtained, then the neural action network can be trained. The weights of the neural action network are filled with small random numbers as initial guesses. The training process of the neural action network is shown in Fig. 4. By sending the input vector, $X(k)$, to the neural action network, the control command, $u(k)$, is produced as its output. Applying the computed control command to the structure subjected to the dynamic loading, $f(k)$, the modified response, $X_s(k + 1)$, can be observed. The error function, $E_c(k + 1)$, can then be formulated as

$$E_c(k + 1) = \frac{1}{2} \sum_o \left(X_d^o(k + 1) - X_s^o(k + 1) \right)^2 \qquad (21)$$

where the $X_d(k + 1)$ is the desired responses of the structure to be controlled. The superscript o represents the component o of the vector, X_d and X_s. The adjustment of the weights, W_{ij}^A, in the neural action network in terms of the error function, E_c, can be mathematically expressed as

$$\Delta W_{ij}^A = -\eta \frac{\partial E_c}{\partial W_{ij}^A} \qquad (22)$$

$$= -\eta \sum_k \left(\frac{\partial E_c}{\partial u_k} \right) \left(\frac{\partial u_k}{\partial W_{ij}^A} \right) \qquad (23)$$

where h is the learning rate to be assigned during the training, and u_k is the component k of the control command, u. Equation (23) shows that the adjustment of the weight, W_{ij}^A , during the training process is split into two steps. First, by backpropagating the error function, E_C , through the pre-trained neural model network without any changes in the weights, W_{ij}^M , the corresponding error of the control command, u, is calculated. Then, by backpropagating the error, Du, through the neural action network, the weights, W_{ij}^A , can be adjusted.

The process of computing u from the error function, E_C , can be explained using a typical 3-layer neural model network, shown in Fig. 1. First, the changes, DH_h , of the node h's output, H_h , in the hidden layer is calculated as

$$\Delta H_h = -\eta_1 \frac{\partial E_c}{\partial H_h} \tag{24}$$

$$= -\eta_1 \sum_o \Delta_o(k + 1) \, W_{oh}^M \tag{25}$$

where

$$\Delta_o = \frac{dF(Net_o)}{dNet_o} \left(X_d^o (k + 1) - X_s^o (k + 1) \right). \tag{26}$$

Here W_{oh}^M is the weight connecting node o in the output layer and node h in the hidden layer of the neural model network; Net_o represents the input to the node o in the output layer from the hidden layer; and h_1 is a constant.

In the next step, the corresponding changes, u_i , can be determined as

$$\Delta u_i = -\eta_2 \frac{\partial H_h}{\partial u_i} \tag{27}$$

$$= -\eta_2 \frac{dF(Net_h)}{d \, Net_h} \sum_h W_{hi}^M \Delta H_h \tag{28}$$

where W_{hi}^M is the weight connecting node h in the hidden layer and node i in the input layer of the neural model network; Net_h represents the input to the node h in the hidden layer from the input layer; and h_2 is a constant. Du(k) is then backpropagated to adjust the weights, W_{ij}^A , of the neural action network. This training process is repeated until the structural responses reach the desired responses within the pre-determined tolerance over the total time, T where T = ND t.

In principle, as shown in Fig. 4, the on-line training of the neural model network and the neural action network can be achieved simultaneously by successively turning the switches of the error functions, E_m and E_c , on and off. However, due to the slow convergence, it is difficult to perform the on-line training. In practice, the convergence of a backpropagation neural network can be sped up for the on-line training if the off-line pre-trained network is used as the initial model of the backpropagation neural network. During off-line training of the neural action network, the pre-trained neural model network is also used to replace the real structure, shown in Fig. 4, to produce the structural responses due to both the dynamic loading, $f(t)$, and the control command, $u(t)$.

5.3 Application Of Neural Networks To Real Structure
Structure to be Controlled

To demonstrate the performance of the neural network in the identification and control of a structure under dynamic loadings, a 10-story apartment building in San Jose, California is chosen as the structure to be identified and controlled. As shown in Fig. 6, there are 13 acceleration sensors installed on the ground floor, the 6th floor, and the roof.

Three real earthquake responses recorded in the building are used in these studies. They are the April 24, 1984 Morgan Hill, with a magnitude of 6.2, the March 31, 1986 Mt. Lewis, with a magnitude of 5.8, and the October 17, 1989 Loma Prieta, with a magnitude of 7.0, earthquakes. The seismic data, including displacement, velocity, and acceleration, were processed by the California Strong Motion Instrumentation Program (CSMIP), Division of Mines and Geology, California, having a uniform time interval of 0.02 seconds and a total of 2,000 points (40.0 seconds) [Tape Morgan Hill 1984, Tape Mt. Lewis 1986, Disk Loma Prieta 1989].

Neural Network Training for Building
Neural Model Network Training

The neural model network, shown in Fig. 5, is constructed with a 4-node input layer, a 4-node hidden layer, and a 1-node output layer. In addition to the excitation force, $f(k)$, and/or the control command, $u(k)$, the input vector of the neural model network consists of the sae variables, $X(K)$, for linear structure and state variables with time lags, $X_x(k), \ldots, X_x(k-1)$, for nonlinear structure. The velocity information included in the state variables can be implied in the displacements with time lags. Previous studies showed that only weak nonlinearity was observed in this apartment building during these three earthquakes [Nisar et al. 1992]. Therefore, only the displacements of the East component on the roof with 3 time lags, namely $Z_s(k)$, $Z_x(k-1)$, and $Z_s(k-2)$ (channel No. 6 in Fig. 6), are chosen as the inputs to the neural model network, and the East component of the acceleration on the ground floor, $G(k)$ (channel No. 12 in Fig. 6), representing the ground motion excitation force, $f(k)$, are chosen as the other input. The output of the network is the displacement on the roof at the next time step, $Z_m(k+1)$. The error function, $E_m(k+1)$, is calculated from the differences between), for nonlinear r the calculated output, $Z_m(k+1)$, and the measured structural responses on the roof, $Z_s(k+1)$.

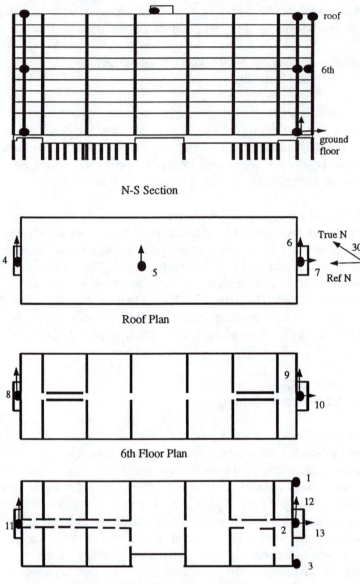

Fig 6: San Jose Apartment building (↑ ,. represents sensor locations and directions of recorded responses, · also represents the normal direction of paper plane).

The data set, used for training the model network, is the first 1,000 points taken from the 2,000 point record of the Morgan Hill earthquake. The weights are adjusted based on the error function, E_m , with the learning rate of $= 0.7$. The whole off-line training process takes 59,200 cycles, and the root-mean-square error of the displacement is reduced to 0.000474(cm).

Figure 7 is the comparison of the responses recorded on the roof of the structure to the generated responses from the trained model network. This figure shows that the trained model network represents the real structure very well, not only in the first 1,000 points used for training, but also in the remaining 1,000 points not used in training. The root-mean-square error of the generated responses from the model network reaches 0.0065(cm) ($Z_{max} = 0.63$ cm).

In training the neural model network presented here, the weights are adjusted once according to the errors calculated after each time step. As mentioned above, the weights can also be adjusted according to the error computed from equation (3) after the entire 1,000 time steps have been fed through the network. The later training process also performed well. Other factors that affect the neural model network training include the sampling time step, the length of the trained data set, the size of the neural network and the learning rate. At the present time, no analytic results are available to quantitatively define these factor. The principles for the determination of theses factors have been discussed in Section 2.2.1. Empirically, taking 10-20 data samples for each cycle in the time domain and including at least 5 points for each modal peak in the frequency domain are suitable to satisfy the requirement of the resolutions in both domains for the success of training; for the apartment building model, the size of the hidden layer with different nodes including 3 node, 6 and 8 nodes as well as the size of the two hidden layer with 3 and 4 nodes in each layer were also tried; again, empirically, one hidden layer with 3 nodes may be enough to handle the response of the structures with only one mode, and if two modes are involved, at least 4 nodes in the hidden layer are required. For nonlinear systems with more that 5 time lags, use of two hidden layers with less nodes in each layer is better than only one hidden layers with more nodes; for learning rate, though the optimization technique has been proposed [Billings and Chen 1992], on-line adjustments are still important in the success of training.

Neural Action Network Training for the Building

After the neural model network is trained, as shown in Fig. 4, then the neural action network is trained. The neural action network is modeled as a three layer network: a 3-node input layer, a 4-node hidden layer, and a 1-node output layer. The inputs of the action network are the displacements on the roof of the building with 3 time lags, $Z_s(k)$, $Z_s(k - 1)$ and $Z_s(k-2)$, and the output is the control command, $u(k)$. The first 1,000 points of the Morgan Hill earthquake record are chosen as the training data for the neural action network. In the off-line training of the neural action network, the structure in Fig. 4 is replaced by the trained neural model network to generate the responses, $Z_s(k + 1)$, of the structure due to the loadings of both the control command and the base acceleration. The output, $Z_s(k + 1)$, from the model network is fed back to update the inputs to both the model and the action networks in order to compute their outputs at the next time step. The weights of the action network are adjusted based on the control command errors computed from equations (24) and (26) which backpropagate E_c through the model network without weight changes. The training process takes 4,960 cycles and the root-mean-square error displacement and the maximum error displacement on the roof of the building are reduced to 0.000485(cm).

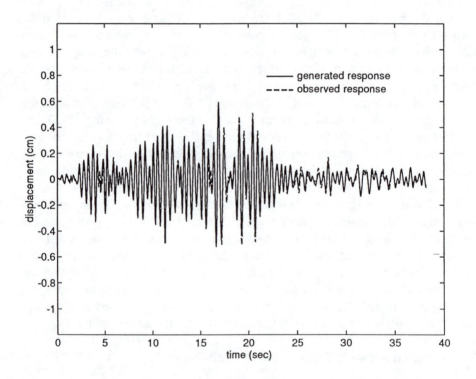

Fig 7:   Comparison of the Generated and Observed Responses
of the Structure Subjected to the Morgan Hill Earthquake.

Figure 8 shows the comparison of the responses on the roof of the structure due to the dynamic loadings of the Morgan Hill earthquake before and after the neural control network is applied. It can be seen that the trained neural action network performs very well, not only in the first 1,000 points used for the training, but also in the remaining 1,000 points not used in the training.

Generalization and Robustness of Trained Network

The main attributes of the neural network are its robustness to noise data and its ability to generalize to new inputs. In other words, a trained network is capable of providing sensible output when presented with input data that has not been used during training. To examine the robustness and generalization of the trained model network and action network for the apartment building, the responses recorded in the building during the Loma Prieta, with a magnitude of 7.0, and the Mt. Lewis, with a magnitude of 5.8, earthquakes were used as the input data to the neural model network and neural action network.

Figures 9 show the Fourier spectra of the input data due to the Morgan Hill, the Loma Prieta and the Mt. Lewis earthquakes. It can be observed that there exist extreme differences in the noise and the frequency contents of these three earthquakes.

Neural Model Network

Given the entire time series of the acceleration in the ground level representing the excitation force, and the initial conditions of the responses on the roof in the apartment building, the entire response on the roof for a total time of $T=40$ sec due to the Loma Prieta and the Mt. Lewis earthquakes were generated from the neural model network trained by using the data records in the same building due to the Morgan Hill earthquake.

The comparison between the observed responses on the roof of the apartment building and the generated responses from the trained model network due to the Loma Prieta and Mt. Lewis earthquakes are shown in Figs. 10 and 11 respectively. The root-mean-square differences between the observed responses in the building and the generated responses from the neural model network are 0.015 cm ($Z_{max}=1.02$cm) for the Loma Prieta earthquake and 0.0052 cm ($Z_{max}=0.38$ cm) for the Mt. Lewis earthquake. From Figs. 7, 10, and 11, it is observed that the neural model network trained by a part of the responses due to one earthquake can predict all of the responses for the building for the three earthquakes extremely well. These results show great promise for the trained neural model network in the robustness to noise and the ability to generalize to different inputs.

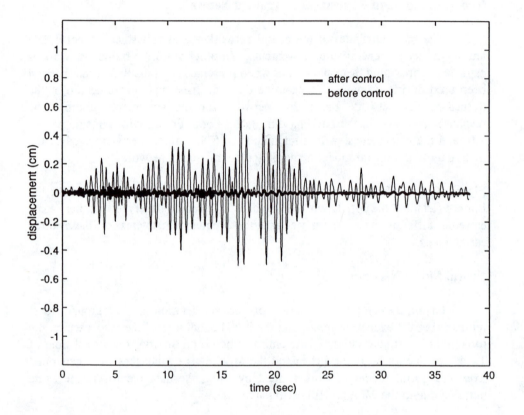

Fig 8: Comparison of the Responses of the Structure Subjected to the
Morgan Hill Earthquake Before and After the Controller is Applied.

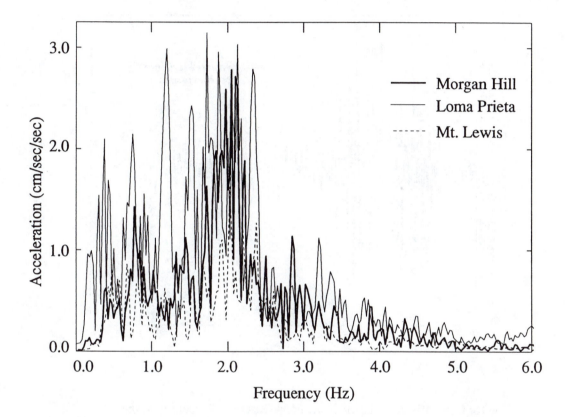

Fig 9: Acceleration Spectra on Roof of Building due to Morgan Hill,
Loma Prieta and Mt. Lewis Earthquakes.

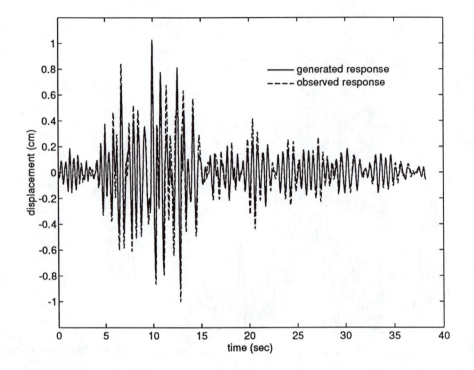

Fig 10: Comparison of the Generated and Observed Responses of the

Structure Subjected to the Loma Prieta Earthquake.

Neural Action Network

Figures 12 and 13 show the comparisons of the responses in the structure subjected to the Loma Prieta and the Mt. Lewis earthquakes before and after the controller is applied.
It is observed that although there are differences in the input data shown in Fig. 9, the performance of the neural action network trained using the recorded data due to the Morgan Hill earthquake also worked well for the Loma Prieta and Mt. Lewis earthquakes.

The control performance of the neural network is shown in Table 1. The maximum displacements for the three earthquakes are reduced to less than 15% of the measured responses. The neural action network also illustrates the robustness to noise and the ability to generalize to different inputs.

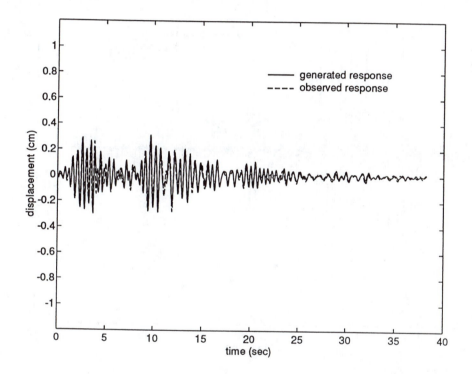

Fig 11: Comparison of the Generated and Observed Responses of the Structure Subjected to the Mt. Lewis Earthquake.

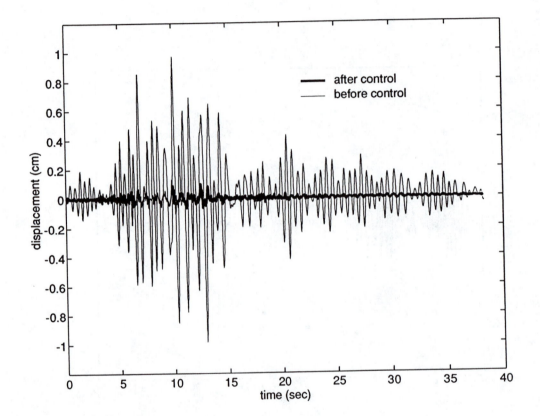

Fig 12: Comparison of the Responses of the Structure Subjected to
the Loma Prieta Earthquake Before and After the Controller is
Applied.

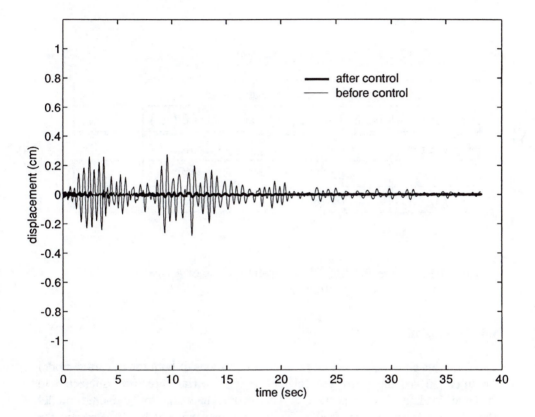

Fig 13: Comparison of the Responses of the Structure Subjected to
the Mt. Lewis Earthquake Before and After the Controller is Applied.

Max. Relative Displacement			
earthquake	before control (cm)	after control (cm)	ratio (%)
Loma Prieta	0.9997	0.1307	13
Mt. Lewis	0.2787	0.0327	12
Morgan Hill	0.5783	0.0422	7

Table 1:Maximum Relative Displacement on Top of Apartment
Building.

5.4 Conclusions

In this chapter, the neural network applications to both the dynamic model identification and the active control of civil engineering structures subjected to dynamic loadings are presented. The neural network for dynamic model identification is an external feed-back recurrent network which can represent the dynamic behaviors of both linear and nonlinear systems through training. The neural network for the active control of structures subjected to dynamic loadings has to have two components: the neural model network representing the dynamics of the structure to be controlled and the neural action network producing the control commands to the structure. The proposed neural network models for the identification and control have been verified by the results from the application of these models to: 1) the measured responses in a real apartment building due to the three earthquakes; 2) the simulated responses of the finite element structure models; and 3) the experimental tests of a 3-story steel frame model structure on a shake table. These results have shown great promise in the dynamic model identification and control of structures by using neural network technique. Due to page limitations, only the results from the real apartment building are presented in this chapter.

One issue to be addressed is that knowledge of structural dynamics is significant to the success of the neural network application in the dynamic model identification and the control of structures. In this chapter, the neural network architecture, the training process and the input and output vectors for structural identification and control were determined based on the general forms of the equations of motion for both linear and nonlinear structures. Information on the complexity of structural dynamics, characterized by the modal numbers, frequency span, the natural frequencies and the dampings involved in the structural responses, are also useful in the determination of the neural network size, the sampling time step, and the data set length used for training. Since the theory of neural networks is still in its infancy, these factors can only be determined in a quantitative manner from limited experience. Therefore, further study of these factors based on the information of structural dynamics is necessary in the neural network application to the dynamic model identification and control of civil engineering structures.

5.5 Acknowledgement

This research is supported by National Science Foundation under grant BCS- 9114047 and BCS-9202159. The support is gratefully acknowledgment. The authors are also grateful to Mr. H.M. Chen who is a Ph.D. candidate in the Mechanical Engineering Department of University of Maryland at College Park for his significant contributions in the completion of the NSF supported projects.

5.6 References

Albus, J. (1975). "A New Approach to Manipulator Control: The Cerebeller Model Articulation Control." Trans. of ASME, J. of Dynamics, Systems, Measurements and Control, 97:220-227.

Bhat, N.V., and McAvoy, T.J. (1989). "Use of Neural Nets for Dynamic Modeling and Control of Chemical Process Systems." Proc. of American Control Conference, pages 1336-1341, Pittsburgh, PA.

Billings S., and Chen S. (1992). "Neural Networks and System Identification." *Neural Networks for Control and Systems*, edited by Warivick, K., Irwin, G.W., and Hunt, K.J. 9:181-205.

Chameau, J., Reed, D.A., and Yao, J.T.P. (1991). "Intelligent Systems in Civil Engineering." *Proc. Int. Fuzzy Systems Assoc.*, Brussels, Belgium.

Chen, Y.H., Leitmann, G., and Xiong, Z.K. (1991). "Robust Control Design for Interconnected Systems with Time-varying Uncertainties." *Int. J. Control.* 54:1119.

Cheng, F.Y., and Pantelides, C. (1990). "Optimal Placement of Controller for Seismic Structures." *J. Eng. Struct.* 12:252-262.

Cheng, F.Y., Tian, P., and Suthiwong, S. (1992). "Generalized Optimal Active Control Algorithm of Seismic Structures and Related Soil-structure Formulation." K.P. Chong, S.C. Liu, and J.C. Li, editors, *Proc. U.S.-China Joint Symposium on Computational Mechanics*, Elsever, London.

Chung, L.L., Lin, R.C., Soong, T.T., and Reinhorn, A.M. (1989). "Experimental Study of Active Control of MDOF Seismic Structures." *Journal of Engineering Mechanics*, ASCE, 115(8):1609-1627.

Chung, L.L., Lin, R.C., Soong, T.T., and Reinhorn, A.M. (1988). "Experimental Study of Active Control of MDOF Structures Under Seismic Excitations." Technical report, NCEER, Technical Report NCEER-88-0025.

Cybenko, G. (1989). "Approximation by Superpositions of a Sigmoidal Functions." *Mathematics of Control, Signals and Systems*, 2:303-314.
Grossberg, S. (1989). "Competitive Learning: From Interactive Activation to Adaptive Resonance." *Cognitive Science*, 1:23-63.

Hackel, L., Cheng, A., Yang, C.Y., and Chajes, M.J. (1992). "Stability, Bifurcations and Chaos of Nonlinear Structural Control." *Proc. ASCE EMD Specialty Conference*.

Hopfield, J.J. (1979). "Neural Networks and Physical System with Emergent Collective Computational Abilities." *Pro. Natl. Accad. Sci. USA*, 2554-2558.

Housner, G.W., Soong, T.T., and Masri, S.F. (1994). "Second Generation of Active Structural Control in Civil Engineering." *presented at First World Conference on Structural Control*, Los Angeles, California, U.S.A., August 3-5.

Hunt, K.J., and Sbarbaro, D. (1992). "Studies in Neural Network Based Control." *Neural `Network for Control and Systems,* edited by Warivick, K., Irwin, G.W., and Hunt, K.J. 6:94-111.

Kobori, T. (1990). "Technology Development and Forecast of Dynamical Intelligent Building (D.I.B.)." K.P. Chong, S.C. Liu, and J.C. Li, editors, *Intelligent Structure*, pages 42-59. Elsever Applied Science.

Kobori, T., Koshika, N., Yamada, K., and Ikeda, Y. (1991). "Seismic Response Controlled Structure with Active Mass Driver System. Part 1: Design." *Earthquake Engineering   and Structural Dynamics*, 20:133-149.

Kobori, T., Koshika, N., Yamada, K., and Ikeda, Y. (1991). "Seismic Response Controlled Structure with Active Mass Driver System. Part 2: Verification." *Earthquake Engineering and Structural Dynamics*, 20:151-166.

Liu, S.C., Lagorio, H.J., and Chong, K.P. (1990). "Status of U.S. Research on Structural Control Systems." *Proc. of Workshop on Research Needs in Intelligent Control Systems*, pages 1-5. NSFEPRI.

Liu, S.C., and Yao, J.T.P. (1987). "Structural Identification Concept." *J. of the Structural Div.* ASCE, ST12, 104:1845-1858.

Ljung, L., and Soderstorm, T. (1983). *Theory and Practice of Recursive Identification.*
MIT Press, Cambridge, MA.

Masri, S.F., Chassiakos, A.G., and Caughey, T.K. (1992). "Structure-Unknown Non-linear Dynamic Systems: Identification Through Neural Networks." *Smart Structure*, 1:45-56.

Nagarajaih, S., Feng, M.Q., and Shinozuka, M. (1993). "Control of Structures with Friction Controllable Sliding Isolation Bearings." *Soil Dynamics and Earthquake Engineering*, 12:103.

Narendra, K.S., and Parthasarathy, K. (1990). "Identification and Control of Dynamical System Using Neural Networks." *IEEE Trans. on Neural Networks,* 1:4-27.

Nisar A., Werner S.D., and Beck J.L. (1992). "Assessment of UBC Seismic Design Provisions Using Recorded Building Motions." *Proc. of Tenth World conference on Earthquake Engineering.* Balkema, Rotterdam, pages 5723-5728.

Qi, G.Z., Yang, J.C.S., and Kan, C.D. (1990). "A New System Identification Technique for On-line Nondestructive Evaluation." *Intelligent Structure-2*, pages 147-161. Elsever Applied Science.

Rehak, D.R., and Garrett, G.H., Jr. (1990). "Intelligent Structure Control Using Neural Networks." K.P. Chong, S.C. Liu, and J.C. Li, editors, *Intelligent Structure*, pages 368-387. Elsever Applied Science.

Rumelhart, D.E., and McClellad, J.L. (1986). *Parallel Distributed Processing, Volume 1: Foundations*. MIT Press, Cambridge, MA.

Shinozuka, M. and Deodatis, G. (1991). "Simulation of Stochastic Processes by Spectral Representation." *Applied Mechanics Reviews*, 44:191.
Shinozuka, M. (1993). "Summary - Distribution Systems." *Applied Mechanics Review*, 46:187.

Soong, T.T., and Skinner, G.T. (1981). "Experimental Study of Active Structural Control." *Active Structural Control*, pages 1057-1067, Dec. 1981.

Subramaniam, R., Reinhorn, A.M., and Nagarajaih, S. (1992). "Application of Fuzzy Set Theory to the Active Control of Base Isolated Structure." *Proc. US/China/Japan Trilateral Workshop on Structural Control,* Shanghai, China, pages 153-159.

Udwadia, F.E. (1987). "Response of Uncertain Dynamic System I." *Applied Mathematics and Computation*, 22:115-150.
Udwadia, F.E. (1987). "Response of Uncertain Dynamic System II." *Applied Mathematics and Computation*, 22:151-187.

Wen, Y.K., Ghaboussi, J., Venini, P., and Nik, K. (1992). "Control of Structures Using Neural Networks." *Proc. of the U.S./Italy/Japan Workshop on Intelligent Structures,* Sorrento, Italy, pages 232-251.

Werbos, P. (1988). "Backpropagation: Past and Future." *Proceeding of the IEEE International Conference on Neural Networks, Volume 1*, pages 343-353.

Werbos, P. (1990). "Neurocontrol - A Status Report." *Proc. of the Sixth Yale Workshop in Adaptive and Learning Control.* Yale University.

Werbos, P. (1990). "Neurocontrol and Related Techniques." A.J. Maren, editor, *Handbook of Neural Computing Application*, chapter 22, page 345. Academic Press,
New York, NY.

Werbos, P. (1992). "Neurocontrol and Supervised Learning: An Overview and Evaluation." *Handbook of Neural Computing Application,* pages 65-89. Van Nostrand Reinhold, New York, NY.

Yang, J.N., Akbarpour, A., and Ghaemmaghami, P. (1987). "New Optimal Control Algorithm for Structure Control." *Journal of Engineer Mechanics*, 113:1369-1386.

Yang, J.N., Danielians, A., and Liu, S.C. (1990). "Aseismis Hybrid Control System for Building Structure Under Strong Earthquake." K.P. Chong, S. C. Liu, and J. C. Li, editors, *Intelligent Structure*, pages 179-195. Elsever Applied Science.

Yang, J.N., Li, Z., and Liu, S.C. (1991). "Instantaneous Optimal Control with Acceleration and Velocity Feedback." *Journal of Probabilities Engineering Mechanics*, 23.

Yang, J.N., and Samali, B. (1983). "Control of Tall Buildings in Along-wind Motion." *Journal of Structural Engineering*, ASCE, 109(1):50-68.

Yang, J.N., and Soong, T.T. (1988). "Recent Advancement in Active Control of Civil Engineering Structures." *Journal of Probabilities Engineering Mechanics*, 3(4):179-188.
Yao, J.T.P. (1972). "Concepts of Structural Control", ASCE J. Structural Div., 98(7), 1567-1574.

Zbikowski, R., and Gawthrop, P.J. (1992). "A Survey of Neural Network for Control." *Neural Network for Control and Systems*, edited by Warivick, K., Irwin, G.W., and Hunt, K.J. 3:31-50.

Loma Prieta Earthquake of October 17, 1989. "Strong-Motion Data, San Jose - 10 - Story Residential Bldg." CSMIP California Department of Conservation, Division of Mines and Geology, Office of Strong Motion Studies.

Morgan Hill Earthquake of April 24, 1984. "Structure-Response Records. Tape: MORGANHILL84-S." California Department of Conservation, Division of Mines and Geology, Office of Strong Motion Studies.

Mt. Lewis Earthquake of March 31, 1986. "Structure-Response Records. Tape: MTLEWIS86." California Department of Conservation, Division of Mines and Geology, Office of Strong Motion Studies.

Chapter-6

Application Of Neural Networks To Owner-Contractor Prequalification

Awad S. Hanna[1], Jeffrey S. Russell[2] ,Mahmoud A. Taha[3] and Sang C. Park[4]

Abstract: The purpose of this chapter is to introduce the capabilities of neural networks in solving problems related to the area of Construction Engineering and Management. This is illustrated by the development of a neural network application to assist a project owner in selecting the most appropriate bidders for a particular project. The neural network system for the prequalification of construction contractors has an input vector of 8 components and an output vector of 1 component (binary). The variables included in the input vector were: (1) contractor's experience, (2) contractor's financial stability, (3) contractor's capacity to accept new projects, (4) contractor's safety procedures, (5) reference evaluation of candidate contractor, (6) contractor's project management capabilities, (7) percentage of work subcontracted to minority business enterprises, and (8) contractor's experience in fixed mechanization. The output vector represents whether a contractor is qualified or not qualified to submit a bid on a project. Brainmaker, a commercially available neural network simulator, was used in the training of the neural network model. The training is accomplished by using 80 prequalification cases collected from previous prequalification efforts by the United States Postal Service. Testing the neural network model performance is conducted by cross-validation experiments to estimate the true error rate. The experimentation results estimated that the error rate of the model on unseen cases is 8.0%.

---

[1] Assistant Professor, Dept. of Civil and Environment Eng., University of Wisconsin-Madison, Madison, WI 53706.

[2] Assistant Professor, Dept. of Civil and Environment Eng., University of Wisconsin-Madison, Madison, WI 53706.

[3] Research Associate, Department of Agriculture Engineering, University of Wisconsin-Madison, Madison, WI 53706.

[4] Assistant Professor, School of Business, University of Wisconsin-Madison, Madison, WI 53706.

6.1 Introduction

Neural networks, which are capable of learning relationships from data, represent a class of robust, non-linear models inspired by the neural architecture of the human brain. Theoretical advances, as well as hardware and software innovations, have made them available to a wide variety of problems (Salchenberger 1992). One such problem that occurs frequently in the construction industry is owner-contractor prequalification. Recently, there has been considerable interest in the development of neural network applications for solving a variety of construction problems. This is because of their parallel and distributed structure along with their capabilities of generalization, fault tolerance, and adaptive performance. Also, their generalization capabilities enable them to produce meaningful solutions to problems in which the input data are noisy and uncertain. Among those applications are process optimization (Flood 1990), selecting vertical formwork systems (Kamarthi et al. 1992), selecting horizontal formwork systems (Hanna 1994), estimating construction productivity (Chao and Skibniewski 1994), and construction modularization (Murtaza and Fisher 1994).

The main purpose of this chapter is to describe how to design and train neural networks to simulate construction problems. This is illustrated by the development of a neural network application to assist a project owner in selecting the most appropriate bidders for a particular project. The application is intended to mimic the prequalification procedures used by the United States Postal Service. The neural network paradigm selected for developing the contractor prequalification model is a feedforward network based upon the backpropagation training algorithm (Rumelhart, Hinton, and Williams 1986) that has proven its utility and power in handling problems requiring pattern matching, classification, or prediction (Pao 1989; Weiss and Kulikowski 1991; Hegazy and Moselhi 1994).

6.2 Model development

The following methodology has been used to illustrate the development of the present model. It includes three main phases: (1) problem definition and structuring, (2) model implementation, and (3) running the model for direct problem solving. Each of these phases is described in the following.

6.2.1 Problem definition and structuring

The prequalification of a construction contractor is the process of determining his/her competence and ability to meet specific project requirements prior to issuing the project plans and specifications for bidding (Russell and Skibniewski 1990). The prequalification process reduces the large number of prospective contractors to those who have demonstrated their ability to perform consistently with acceptable standards of quality and reliability. If properly used, prequalification can reduce the risk of poor contractor performance. The decision to qualify or not to qualify a contractor is highly dependent on the decision-maker's experience in performing the prequalification task.

The contractor prequalification problem has been treated by researchers in various ways. Diekmann (1981) applied multiattribute utility theory to a case study in the evaluation and selection of contractors for cost plus contracts; Nguyen (1985) applied fuzzy set theory to evaluate contractors according to a number of decision factors; Russell and Skibniewski (1990) developed Qualifier-1, a computerized tool that employs a linear model to rank contractors based on subjective weighting factors provided by the user; Russell, Skibniewski, and Cozier (1990) developed Qualifier-2, a prototype knowledge-based expert system, to select the most appropriate bidders; and Jaselskis and Ashley (1991) used discrete choice modeling and logistic regression to develop three models to determine the most promising contractor to meet the owner's project goals during the final selection process. The work presented here provides an alternative approach that utilizes the adaptivity of feedforward neural networks.

Feedforward neural network models can fit the contractor prequalification problem because of their adaptivity owing to their structure. This is because the existence of hidden units and the non-linear activation function in their structure permits them to make reasonable generalization (Salchenberger 1992). This important property of feedforward neural network models might enable the performance of complex multiattribute, nonlinear mapping for contractor prequalification.

Since the prequalification process depends largely on the owner characteristics, several public owners' prequalification procedures were closely examined. It was found that the prequalification procedure used by the United States Postal Service (USPS) was the most comprehensive. Therefore, this procedure was selected as a basis for the development of the present neural network model.

Based on the USPS prequalification procedure, eight factors were identified (Taha 1994). Each of these factors has four possible values, excellent, good, fair, or poor. A description of these factors is given in Table 1.

Accordingly, a direct structure for the contractor prequalification problem is clearly one network having all identified factors as inputs. Since the prequalification decision in the collected cases belongs to the binary classification (qualified vs. not qualified), only a single output node is used. Therefore, the network output can be interpreted as follows:

IF	Outcome-Value	>	0.5	THEN	Qualified
ELSE IF	Outcome-Value	<=	0.5	THEN	Not Qualified

Table 1. Description of Input Attributes

Input Attribute (1)	Importance (2)	Range (3)
Construction Experience	An assessment of the past experience of contractor that demonstrates his/her ability to perform the project requirements.	1-4
Financial Stability	To ensure that the candidate contractor has the financial capabilities to handle the exposure to risk that he/she will be taking.	1-4
Contractor's Capacity	To assess his/her ability to assume and subsequently successfully perform the project under consideration.	1-4
Safety Procedures	An assessment of the effectiveness of the construction contractor's safety procedures.	1-4
Reference Evaluation	Comments of contractor's business associates about candidate contractor's recent performance and reputation can be used by project owner to obtain an assessment of contractor future performance.	1-4
Management Capabilities	An assessment of the ability of the candidate contractor to plan, schedule, and control field operations to complete the work associated with the project within time and resource constraints.	1-4
Percentage Awarded to MBE	The USPS, as a public entity, requires each candidate contractor to subcontract a percentage of his/her work to minority business enterprises	1-4
Experience in Fixed Mechanization	Mechanization cost in USPS projects usually ranges from 0% to 63% of total project cost. Therefore, the assessment of contractor experience in fixed mechanization is used as a prequalification criterion.	1-4

6.2.2 Model implementation

The implementation phase of a neural network model comprises four main aspects: (1) gathering training examples, (2) development tool, (3) determining network structure, and (4) training and testing (validating) the network. Each of these aspects is described in the following sections.

Gathering Training Examples

Training examples represent the most important ingredient in the development of a neural network model. They consist of all the input and output data used by the neural network's learning algorithm. Without those examples, the network will not be able to learn anything about the problem. A given training example consists of two components: (1) a data case consisting of a set of attributes, each with an assigned value, and (2) the corresponding correct class membership or the classification decision made by a domain expert according to the given data case. These examples can be assembled in several ways: (1) they may come from an existing database that forms a history of observations; (2) they may be a carefully culled set of tutorial examples prepared by a domain expert(s); (3) they may be obtained from simulation results; or (4) they may be hypothesized results (Baily and Thompson 1990).

The examples used for training and testing the present neural network model were compiled from actual contractor prequalification statements submitted to the United States Postal Service. The cases (46 qualified and 34 not qualified) were related to seven projects initiated between 1988 and 1992. Each case is described in terms of eight attributes plus the prequalification decision made by the domain expert given as *qualified* or *not qualified*. The attributes included in the model are shown in Table 1. During the example preparation efforts, we found that about 30% of the training examples did not have values for one or more attributes. Accordingly, we asked the experts at USPS to complete these examples to the best of their abilities. Therefore, although the collected training examples are complete in terms of information, we can not guarantee that they are free of noise. However, they provide a good training environment that represents the current industry practice. A sample of the training examples containing the input values and the corresponding expert decision is given in Table 2.

Development Tool

A number of languages and tools are currently available for building neural network models. These tools can be categorized into two groups. The first group includes the traditional programming languages such as FORTRAN and C. Traditional programming languages provide maximum flexibility, but require an experienced programmer to minimize training time. The second group consists of network simulators such as Brainmaker and Neuralworks. Neural network simulators require no programming skills and often come with special hardware to minimize training time.

The commercially available neural network simulator Brainmaker was used for the development of the proposed neural network application. The brainmaker package forms a complete system for designing, building, training, testing, and running neural networks on IBM personal computers and compatibles. The brainmaker package contains two programs: Netmaker and Brainmaker. Netmaker and Brainmaker are completely menu driven with full color and mouse support.

Determining the Network Structure

Following the data collection phase, a feedforward neural network model is developed to mimic the complex mapping function between the inputs and output. The backpropagation learning algorithm is used to perform the training requirements. This is because the contractor prequalification problem requires a learning paradigm that can determine the correct relationship between the contractor characteristics and owner needs. The determination of the network structure is a very difficult step as it involves many variables including learning rate parameters, number of hidden layers, and the number of hidden units per hidden layer.

The learning rate parameter plays a critical role in the convergence of the network to the true solution. For a given network and an infinitesimal learning rate, the weights that yield the minimum error can be found. However, they may not be found in a reasonable span of time. Use of a large learning rate will proceed much faster but may produce oscillations between relatively poor solutions. However, high-dimensional spaces (with many weights) have relatively few local minima (Rumelhart, Hinton, and Williams 1986).

The number of hidden layers and the number of neurodes per hidden layer determine the number of connections which represent the "brain" of the network. With too few connections, the network can not learn much. There are a number of rules of thumb that have evolved for selection of the number of hidden units. A widely used approach is to assume the number of hidden units to be 75 percent of the number of input units (Salchenberger 1992). Another approach suggests that the number of hidden units can be calculated using the following equation (Lin and Lin 1993):

$$j = \frac{me}{n+z} \quad\text{..} \quad (1)$$

Where: $j \equiv$ the number of hidden units; $m \equiv$ the number of training examples, $e \equiv$ allowable error in percent; $n \equiv$ the number of input units; and $z \equiv$ the number of output units. A third approach suggests that the number of hidden units should be between the average and the sum of the nodes in input and output layers (Berke and Hajela 1991).

Table 2. A sample of Training Examples

Construction Experience (1)	Financial Stability (2)	Contarctor's Capacity (3)	Safety Procedures (4)	Reference Evaluation (5)	Management Capabilities (6)	% Awarded to MBE (7)	Mechanization Experience (8)	Final Outcome (9)
Excellent	Excellent	Excellent	Good	Good	Excellent	Excellent	Fair	Qualified
Good	Excellent	Excellent	Good	Good	Excellent	Excellent	Good	Qualified
Good	Excellent	Excellent	Excellent	Good	Excellent	Excellent	Excellent	Qualified
Good	Excellent	Excellent	Excellent	Excellent	Excellent	Excellent	Good	Qualified
Good	Excellent	Excellent	Good	Excellent	Excellent	Excellent	Excellent	Qualified
Poor	Fair	Excellent	Fair	Good	Fair	Poor	Fair	Qualified
Good	Poor	Excellent	Good	Excellent	Good	Poor	Poor	Qualified
Poor	Poor	Poor	Poor	Good	Poor	Poor	Poor	Notqualified
Poor	Fair	Poor	Fair	Good	Good	Excellent	Poor	Notqualified
Poor	Excellent	Excellent	Good	Fair	Poor	Poor	Poor	Notqualified
Fair	Good	Excellent	Poor	Fair	Fair	Fair	Poor	Notqualified
Poor	Fair	Poor	Good	Good	Good	Excellent	Poor	Notqualified
Good	Excellent	Excellent	Good	Good	Excellent	Excellent	Fair	Notqualified
Good	Good	Excellent	Excellent	Good	Excellent	Excellent	Good	Notqualified

The net result of poor parameter settings will be slow convergence and/or poor performance of the model (Pao 1989; Weiss and Kulikowski 1991). The hill climbing approach is used in this work to set the network parameters for this problem. It is an iterative method that consists of testing the potential improvement to be gained by incremental changes to each parameter under consideration. The process is repeated until no potential change yields an appreciable improvement. The only drawback of this approach is that it is time consuming. But with good initial conditions, the hill we climb may not be the tallest one around.

The use of Brainmaker in training and testing the contractor prequalification model has assisted in overcoming the difficulties of this step. Brainmaker, like any other simulator, has training and testing defaults for the value of learning rate, number of hidden layers and number of units per hidden layer, and the error tolerance. These defaults were taken as a starting values in our search. The structure of the network pertaining to the contractor prequalification problem is as discussed in the following section.

Training and Validating the Neural Network

To perform the network training, several experiments were conducted to select the optimum network configuration. A learning rate of 1.0 was used in all the experiments without encountering any problem of local minima. These experiments were repeated for networks having 6, 8, 10, 12 and 14 hidden nodes (in a single layer). During the training, the following general guidelines were considered:

- A fully connected neural network was considered.
- Sigmoid transfer function.
- Patterns (training examples) were presented sequentially during each training session.
- Updating network weights was performed after each training pattern was presented to the network.
- Each run was repeated five times with a different random starting state to make sure the solution obtained was not a local minimum.
- The stopping criteria were set such that the maximum error (absolute difference between output actual value and its desired value) for each pattern in the training set does not exceed 0.1, and the total number of iterations does not exceed 50,000 epochs, or a 0.0001 root-mean-square (RMS) difference, whichever comes first.

The performance of each neural network model is tested by conducting 10-fold cross-validation (Stone 1974) experiments. In these experiments, the available contractor prequalification cases were divided randomly into 10 mutually exclusive test partitions of 8 cases. For each set, a model was constructed using the training set (72 cases) and its performance was tested using the corresponding test set (8 cases). The cases not found in each test partition were independently used for training, and the resulting model was tested using the corresponding test set. Then, the average error rate over the 10 unseen test sets would be a good predictor of the error rate of a model built from all the data. Each train-and-test experiment was repeated five times with a different random starting state to make sure that the solution obtained was not a local minimum. Network configuration and training were conducted on a powerful DX2-66 MHz IBM compatible. Training took 20 minutes on average for each run. A total of 250 runs were used to find out the best network configuration. Table 3 summarizes the results of the two categories of examples (training and testing) on the network's estimation errors averaged over all the examples used for each of the cross-validation experiments.

The final results of these experiments revealed that the network with 12 hidden units had a better ability to decrease the system error rate (error rate due to training is 5.0%) and provided a better prediction ability (error rate due to testing on unseen cases is 8.0%) than other configurations tried despite noise inherent in the data of these examples. Accordingly, the neural network model with 8 input units, 12 hidden units in a single layer and 1 output unit was considered. After establishing an estimation of the system true error, the complete data set (80 cases) was used to develop the interconnection weights for this model.

6.2.3 Running the model for direct problem solving

The obtained neural network is just a set of interconnection weights that are simple real numbers. The end user can use this network in two ways:
1 If the user owns a copy of the Brainmaker simulator, he/she can use it to run this network and use it to predict new cases.
2 For a user who does not own a copy of this simulator, a query-and-answer program was developed, using LEVEL5 OBJECT©, to help the end user to run the neural network model. The program will first prompt the user to input the rating for each prequalification factor as excellent, good, fair, or poor. The program then will propagate these inputs through the neural network with the obtained interconnection weights and prompt the end user with the final recommendation.

Table 3. Percent Error Rate for Cross-Validation Experiments for a Single Hidden Layer Network

$$\% \text{ Error} = \frac{\left| X_a^{1} - X_d^{2} \right|}{X_d} \times 100$$

Run Number	(8 6 1)[3]		(8 8 1)		(8 10 1)		(8 12 1)		(8 14 1)	
	Train	Test	Train	Test	Train	Test	Train	Test	Train	Test
(1)	(2)	(3)	(4)	(5)	(6)	(7)	(8)	(9)	(10)	(11)
1	8.95[4]	16.00	8.36	16.20	7.42	9.40	6.48	9.10	3.87	19.20
2	9.59	27.30	8.83	12.30	7.93	18.00	6.71	16.60	5.00	20.60
3	8.54	15.90	9.11	19.80	7.21	17.50	0.62	0.00	0.53	0.00
4	9.75	15.80	8.06	15.90	6.71	9.20	4.69	6.90	4.58	18.00
5	8.83	29.00	8.25	10.00	6.40	9.40	5.38	13.80	3.16	16.00
6	9.33	26.10	7.68	9.00	7.21	26.70	5.29	9.90	3.32	25.70
7	9.11	34.50	9.38	20.40	7.41	26.60	5.83	0.00	4.12	5.30
8	9.95	30.00	8.06	7.60	7.00	10.00	5.56	7.80	4.36	24.60
9	10.00	24.80	8.00	21.50	6.32	16.80	4.47	7.30	4.58	9.60
10	8.66	22.80	0.00	15.80	0.00	34.10	0.00	5.80	0.00	28.70
Average Error	9.256	24.33	8.46	13.90	7.16	15.85	5.07	8.01	3.62	16.18

1 Actual output value as calculated by the neural network model.
2 Desired output value.
3 Network architecture.
4 Each value is the average of five repeated runs with different initial conditions.

6.3 Summary and conclusion

The focus of this work was to introduce the capabilities of neural networks as a promising tool for problems related to the construction industry. To illustrate this, we have described the development of a neural network based approach to prequalify construction contractors. Real contractor prequalification cases, compiled from actual contractor prequalification efforts by the United States Postal Service, were used to train and validate the developed neural network model. Our example shows that neural networks are able to model the complex relationship between the contractor characteristics and owner needs and achieve an acceptable accuracy. The presented approach agrees well with the way in which a project owner makes an intuitive classification based on accumulated experience.

This work also indicated that the use of cross-validation has a great potential in estimating the true error rate on unseen cases. The randomly selected train-and-test experiments are a direct simulation of exactly what we wish to measure: performance on new cases. The great advantage of using the cross-validation is that all the cases in the available data sample are used for training and testing the model. Using the entire data sample in both training and testing means that the available information was utilized for both training and testing, which leads to a more accurate model and unbiased error rate.

The approach described herein could be applied to other problems for which solutions are generated based on analogy with previous cases rather than deduction and deep reasoning.

6.4 References

Bailey, D.L., and Thompson, D.M. (1990). "Developing Neural Network Applications," *AI EXPERT* (September), pp. 34-41.

Berke, L. and Hajela, P. (1991). "Application of Neural Networks in Structural Optimization," NATO/AGARD Advanced Study Institute, Vol. 23(I-II), 731-745.

California Scientific Software (1992), Getting Started With Brainmaker (User's Guide and Reference Manual), California Scientific Software, Nevada City, CA.

Chao, L.C., and Skibniewski, M.J. (1994). "Estimating Productivity: Neural-Network-Based Approach," *Journal of Computing in Civil Engineering*, Vol. 8, No. 2, pp. 234-251.

Diekmann, J.E. (1981). "Cost Plus Contractor Selection: A Case Study," *Journal of Technical Councils of ASCE*, Vol. 107, No. TC1, pp. 13-25.

Flood, I. (1990). "Simulating the Construction Process Using Neural Networks," *Proc. of the 7th International Symposium on Automation and Robotics in Construction*, ISARC, Bristol Polytechnic, Bristol, UK.

Gallant S. (1988). "Connectionist Expert Systems," *Communication of the ACM*, Vol. 31, No. 2, pp. 152-169.

Hanna, A.S. (1994). "Neural Network Development for Selection of Horizontal Formwork Systems," *American Concrete Institute Monograph* (under publication).

Hegazy, T. and Moselhi, O. (1994). "Analogy-Based Solution To Markup Estimation Problem," *Journal of Computing in Civil Engineering*, Vol. 8, No. 1, pp. 72-87.

Jaselskis, E.J. and Ashley, D.B. (1991). "Optimal Allocation of Project Management Resources for Achieving Success," ," *Journal of Construction Engineering and Management*, ASCE, Vol. 117, No. 2, 321-340.

Kamarthi, S.V., Sanvido, V.E., and Kumara, S.R.T. (1992). "NEUROFORM - Neural Network System for Vertical Formwork Selection," *Journal of Computing in Civil Engineering, ASCE*, Vol. 6, No. 2, pp. 178-199.

Lin, F.C. and Lin, M. (1993). "Analysis of Financial Data Using Neural Networks," *AI EXPERT* (February), 36-41.

Moselhi, O., Hegazy, T. and Fazio, P. (1991). "Neural Networks as Tools in Construction," *Journal of Construction Engineering and Management,* ASCE, Vol. 117, No. 4, pp. 606-625.

Murtaza, M.B., and Fisher, D.J. (1994). "NEUROMODEX--Neural Network System for Modular Construction Decision Making," *Journal of Computing in Civil Engineering*, Vol. 8, No. 2, pp. 221-233.

Nguyen, V.U. (1985). "Tender Evaluation by Fuzzy Sets," *Journal of Construction Engineering and Management*, ASCE, Vol. 111, No. 3, pp. 231-243.

Pao, Y.H. (1989). *Adaptive Pattern Recognition and Neural Networks*. Addison-Wesley Publishing Co., Reading, Mass.

Rumelhart, D.E., Hinton, G.E., and Williams, R.J. (1986). "Learning Internal Presentations by Error Propagation." In D.E. Rumelhart and J.L. McClelland (Eds.), Parallel *Distributed Processing: Explorations in the Micro structures of cognition,* Vol. 1: Foundation*s*, MIT Press, Cambridge, MA, pp. 318-362.

Russell, J.S. and Skibniewski, M.J. (1990). "Qualifier-1: Contractor Prequalification Model," *Journal of Computing in Civil Engineering*, ASCE, Vol. 4, No. 1, pp. 77-90.

Russell, J.S., Skibniewski, M.J., and Cozier, D.R. (1990). "QUALIFIER-2: Knowledge-based System for Contractor Prequalification," *Journal of Construction Engineering and Management,* ASCE, Vol. 116, No. 1, pp. 155-169.

Salchenberger, L.M., Cinar, E.M., and Lash, N.A. (1992). "Neural Networks: A New Tool for Predicting Thrift Failures," *Decision Science*, Vol. 23, pp. 899-916.

Stone, M. (1974). "Cross-Validatory Choice and Assessment of Statistical Predictions." *Journal of the Royal Statistical Society*. Vol. 36. 111-147.

Taha, M. A. (1994). "Applying Distributed Artificial Intelligence to the Prequalification of Construction Contractors," thesis presented to University of Wisconsin at Madison, in partial fulfillment of the requirements for the degree of Doctor of Philosophy.

Weiss, S.M. and Kulikowski, C.A. (1991). *Computer Systems That Learn*, Morgan Kaufmann Publishers, Inc, San Mateo, CA.

Chapter-7

Neural Network Applications In Transportation Engineering

Ardeshir Faghri[1], Member, David Martinelli[2], Member and Michael J. Demetsky[3], Member, ASCE

Abstract: Recent research has demonstrated that (Artificial) Neural Networks offer promising applications in the field of transportation engineering. In this chapter, we first describe the problem areas that are conducive to utilizing a neural network approach within transportation engineering. As is common with new computing paradigms, there are many misunderstandings as to when neural networks are applicable to a particular problem. Next, we discuss the advantages of Neural Networks for solving transportation problems over conventional tools (e.g., regression analysis) as well as other computing paradigms (e.g., expert systems).

This chapter continues with a thorough literature review of the more successful applications of neural networks. The review identifies those efforts currently in the research stage as well as those that have been applied successfully in practice. The literature are grouped into four basic areas of transportation engineering: transportation planning, traffic control and operations, construction and maintenance, and facilities management. Design is not included due to the lack of neural network research in the design area.

Following the literature review, we identify the primary research needs for neural networks in transportation engineering. We focus primarily on those areas where applications of neural networks are promising but have not yet seen significant activity. Finally, we discuss advances in basic neural

[1] Assistant Professor, Dept. of Civil Eng., University of Delaware, Newark, DE 19716

[2] Assistant Professor, Dept. of Civ. and Env. Eng., West Virginia Uni., Morgantown, WV 26505.

[3] Professor, Dept. of Civil Eng., University of Virginia, Charlottesville, VA 22903.

network research that will prove most useful to transportation engineering, including how expected advances in the technology will likely be utilized for transportation engineering.

7.1 Introduction

The first application of neural networks in transportation engineering appeared in (Nakatsuji 1989): "Application of Neural Network Models to Traffic Engineering Problems" in the Proceedings of Infrastructure Planning. The same authors published "Development of a Self-Organizing Traffic Control System Using Neural Network Models (1991)," the first direct neural network application to a transportation engineering problem in the US. They used a multilayer neural network model to develop a self-organizing traffic control system and reported that the neural network model gave a satisfactory performance when compared with traditional analytical methods. During the same year, Ritchie et. al. (1991) reported on a non-contact, non-destructive pavement evaluation system, using a novel artificial intelligence (AI)-based approach. In addition to conventional algorithmic and modeling techniques, their approach integrated three technologies: computer vision, neural networks, and knowledge-based expert systems. They demonstrated the feasibility of a neural network approach in a case study application using a multilayer perceptron and a backpropagation learning rule.

Fix and Armstrong (1990) were among the first to consider the application of neural networks to automated vehicle control. They applied neural networks to the task of driving a vehicle within a simulation environment and demonstrated a favorable similarity to the characteristics obtained of the subject driver.

These initial applications demonstrated the potential applicability and apparent success of neural networks in transportation engineering. In addition, government, private research, business and industry showed increased interest in neural networks. These two conditions were the primary motivating factors for the transportation engineering research community to begin neural networks research. Neural networks also seemed to be a particularly interesting and useful research and development tool because of the many general application areas in transportation that posess the types of nonlinearities that justify advanced analytial techniques. These application areas included control, forecasting/prediction, classification, noise filtering, image processing, and others. Previously, many of these application areas had been utilized in transportation engineering by conventional methods such as regression analysis, simulation, and expert systems.

7.1.1 Characteristics of Neural Networks as Related to Transportation Engineering

Faghri and Hua (1992) described the architectures of 12 different types of neural network paradigms and identified the most applicable problems in transportation that would lend themselves to a neural network-based solution.

Tables 1 and 2 represent the application evaluation of different neural network models to transportation engineering. Within a transportation engineering context, neural networks can be categorized as either belonging to the forecasting/prediction group or to the classification groups as most problems fall within these two groups. Examples of forecasting and prediction problems are trip generation forecasting of a particular landuse or determination of travel demand for a particular air route for an airline. Classification problems include roadway seasonal classification based on permanent traffic counters. Both groups of problems have been traditionally solved by mathematical and statistical methods such as regression analysis and cluster analysis.

Although neural networks can be applied to problems that have been solved by conventional mathematical and statistical methods, the success of a neural network-based solution compared to conventional solutions seems to depend on the specific problem being solved.

In a general sense, neural networks offer the following advantages over conventional mathematical and statistical approaches (Zhang et. al. 1993):

* Neural network schemes can perform highly non-linear mapping between input and output spaces, thus having the potential of capturing the non-linear, dynamic features of traffic flow systems.

* Neural networks have highly parallel connections between processing elements which allows faster processing speed. This feature seems especially useful for analyzing large transportation networks for real-time traffic control as well as other ITS technologies.

* Neural networks have a greater degree of robustness than many conventional schemes because the computation is distributed among many processing elements.

Table 1: Application Evaluation of ANN Models
Source: (Faghri, A., and Hua, J., 1992)

Model \ Category	Mada /Ada	ART	BAM	Hopf	Boltz Mach	Back Prop	BSB	Coun Prop	Lin. Asso	Learn Mat.	Koho	GMDH
Recognition	●			●	●	●		○				
Control	◉	◉	◉	◉		●					○	
Forecasting /Prediction	●					●						
Classi-fication		●				●	◉	◉			●	
Diagnosis		◉				◉	●					
Optimization				●	◉	●						●
Noise Filtering	◉					●						
Image Processing	◉	◉	◉	◉	◉	◉	◉					
Association			◉	●	○		○		○	◉		
Decision Making		◉						●				
Temporal Processing	◉	◉				●						

Key: Strong Applicability   ●

       Moderate Applicability   ◉

       Applicable   ○

       Difficult to Evaluate   □

Table 2. ANN Models Related to Transportation Applications
Source: (Faghri, A., and Hua, J., 1992)

Applications	neural network models							
	Boltz. Mach.	Ada./ Mada.	Back prop.	Hop. net.	ART1	ART2	Cauchy Mach.	Neo-cognitron
trip generation		X						
OD distribution			X					
splits optimization			X				X	
traffic pattern classification				X	X	X		
TSP optimization	X			X				
license plate number recognition			X					X
road pavement distresses detection			X					
road mark classification			X	X				
design supporting systems		X	X					

* Neural network approaches are non-parametric and makes no assumption about the functional form of the underlying distribution of the input data. Consequently, many of the linear regression models of the trip generation equations in the Trip Generation Handbook (ITE 1985) that suffer from poor fits low R-squares may be good candidates for a neural network-based solution.

* Neural networks have a noise filtering feature. The noisy nature of many transportation databases, such as volume counts or vehicle classifications from permanent traffic recorders, could benefit from this feature for applications in planning, design and management.

7.1.2 Neural Networks Versus Expert Systems

Heuristic computing problem applications such as traffic control around work zones and designing highway noise barriers have been appressed by expert systems. Although neural networks and expert systems share certain similarities in their operation (e.g. knowledge storage and learning processes) each has its own characteristics. Therefore, neural networks will enhance and complement-- not replace--expert systems. Some of the major differences between neural networks and expert systems in regard to their applications to transportation engineering are as follows (Faghri and Hua, 1992):

* Neural networks and expert systems differ in the method of developing an intelligent system. The expert system approach uses a domain expert to identify the explicit heuristics used to solve the problem, whereas the neural network approach assumes the problem-solving steps are derived without direct attention as to how a human actually performs the task. Thus, expert systems attempt to determine how the human mind is working; neural networks mimic the most primitive mechanisms of the brain and allows the external input and output to designate the proper functioning.

* Neural networks are flexible with knowledge. The knowledge stored in expert systems is restricted to the human knowledge domain. In contrast, neural networks can be trained with data acquired in the past for the particular problems to be solved; the data may not even need to be a type of knowledge. For some problems, it is not necessary to understand the knowledge about the data. Neural networks give answers according to their own internal criteria.

* Neural networks have different ways of learning. The learning of expert systems is designed to store knowledge in the system. The learning of neural networks is to adjust the strengths of the connections between the processing units. The knowledge in a neural network is more like a function than a content. Some neural networks could have a self-learning capability.

* Neural networks have different ways of computing. The results from an expert system depends on how the knowledge has been represented. On the other hand, the computation method used by a neural network is determined by its architecture, and the results depend on how the network is structured.

In a multilayer neural network, if the number of hidden units is changed, the accuracy of the results will be different.

* Once a neural network is developed, no more programming is required. The only requirement is to feed data to the neural network and train it. However, in expert systems, programming may be required if additional knowledge is to be introduced to the system.

Neural networks and expert systems can cooperate with each other for some common applications. Once integrated, it is expected that they will enable artificial intelligence to cover a much wider variety of applications.

7.2 Neural Network Applications in Transportation Engineering

7.2.1 Overview

In the last five years, neural network applications have been proposed in many areas of transportation engineering. The diverse applications of neural networks in this field represent the usefulness of neural networks and the necessity for further research. Thus far, multi-layered, perceptron-type neural networks with backpropagation (BP) learning algorithms seem to be the major paradigm for transportation use. The attention of the transportation engineering research community to the BP network is somewhat over-concentrated and over-emphasized. Most of the applications of neural networks in transportation engineering are utilizations of existing neural network models, especially BP. Therefore, transportation problem-oriented development of neural network variations or even new neural network paradigms will be in great demand in the future.

This section describes neural network applications in different transportation engineering areas. The literature discussed is grouped into four basic areas of transportation engineering: planning, traffic control and operations, construction and maintenance, and infrastructure management. Following a general description, two neural network applications are summarized as examples for each area.

7.2.2 Planning

Planning is defined as "identifying a set of actions that will lead to the achievement of given objectives in the future" (Yeh, et al., 1985). In general, transportation planning deals with defining the transportation problem, collecting appropriate set(s) of data, analyzing and deducing the data, evaluating the alternative solution strategies, and recommending the one alternative that solves the problem consistent with defined criteria and constraints (Garber et al., 1986).

Some of the essential tasks involved in the transportation planning process are the following:

- forecasts of future traffic demand
- evaluation of the impacts of transportation facilities on land use and the environment
- evaluation of the impacts of new land uses and developments on the transportation network

The large number of parameters in transportation planning necessitates an intensive modeling processes. In general, current or previous modeling processes have been based on historic or statistical data. This process matches the training essence of some neural network paradigms, for example, BP. Consequently, neural networks should give reasonable performance in cause-effect expressions mostly reflected in demand forecasting and impact studies in the transportation planning area.

Examples of Neural Network Applications in Tranportation Planning

1. *Artificial Neural Network Approach for Evaluating Transportation Network Improvements*

To develop a model to select the best combination of improvement projects and schedules for a multiperiod network design, Wei and Schonfeld (1993) evaluated numerous network improvement alternatives in several time periods. The neural network model (a perceptron with a BP training method) was used to estimate total travel times corresponding to various project selection scheduling decisions over a multiperiod planning horizon. When the benefits or costs of those projects are interdependent, the selection and timing of improvement projects is a problem. Because most existing models neglect the interdependence of projects and their impacts during intermediate periods of a planning horizon, they fail to identify the optimal improvement program. In addition, a conceptual multiperiod network design model for programming transportation network improvement projects was included.

The Calvert County highway system in southern Maryland was used to illustrate and evaluate the neural network model. In this particular case, a single hidden layer neural network was preferred due to its improved computability and prediction accuracy. In addition, restricting the activation function to linear output ranges saved training time and yielded accurate predictions. The authors also reported that larger step size between the input and hidden and output layers may improve training efficiency.

2. A Neural Network Approach to the Identification of Real-Time Origin-Destination Flows from Traffic Counts

Real-time origin-destination (O-D) flows through intersections or in a road network are important for efficient on-line traffic planning, management, and control on congested transportation systems. This information can be obtained from the time-sequence of traffic counts, which are available from vehicle detectors. Several dynamic methods have been proposed recently for the purpose of estimation based on prediction error minimization, recursive least squares, and Kalman filtering techniques. As traffic flows through a transportation facility, it is treated as a dynamic process in which the sequence of short time exiting counts depend on causal relationships upon the time-varying sequences of entering counts. Therefore, sufficient data can be obtained from the traffic counts at the entrances and exits to identify O-D flow patterns without further a priori information. These methods are especially suitable for on-line applications at the site of data collection.

By representing a transportation facility such as a road intersection in the form of a simple two-layered neural network, Yang et. al. (1992) developed a method based on the error BP learning algorithm of neural networks for the on-line estimation problem. In the learning process, the distribution of output traffic counts over time intervals is assumed to have an approximate normal distribution and is transformed into a standard one. The transformed data are then normalized into values between 0 and 1 using a logistic type function. The entering traffic counts are not normalized. Hence, the O-D flow rates correspond to the connection weights in the neural network. Therefore, the O-D flow pattern will be updated successively from the time-sequences of entering and exiting counts with the error BP learning algorithm.

The neural network model can be applied to the dynamic estimation of turning movements in a typical four-way intersection, in which two cases with constant and time-varying turning flow rates are then simulated. The method compares favorably with conventional static estimators using actual freeway traffic count data.

7.2.3 Traffic Control and Operations

In transportation engineering, the area of control and operations includes problems such as traffic congestion diagnosis and control, hazardous material transportation, traffic control through work zones, air traffic control, and ground traffic signal timing control. The control or operation can also be seen as a process that reacts to external stimuli. Nearly all neural networks are in an input-output form, where the output is a representation of a reaction to the stimulus. The output of a neural network is made based on the fuction formed in its architecture and, ocassionally, the contents stored in its architecture. This mechanism is natural for the control and operation as defined above. With hardware implementations, neural networks can provide significant advantages in transportation control and operations.

Examples of Neural Network Applications in Transportation Control and Operations

1. Self-Organizing Traffic Control System

Nakatsuji and Kaku (1991) developed an optimizing split traffic control system using a four-layer neural network based on the following two assumptions: (a) cycle length is common over the road network and does not vary with time, and (b) there are no offsets between adjacent intersections. Their research estimated optimal splits of signal phases using neural network technology. The inputs to the neural network are control variables: split lengths of signal phases and the traffic volumes on inflow links; the outputs from the neural network are the measures of effectiveness such as queue lengths and the performance index. The authors reported that their system was effective in adjusting the synaptic weights in the training process and was able to improve the convergence into global minimum, thus achieving solutions which were in accord with analytical solutions.

2. Macroscopic Modeling of a Freeway Traffic Using a Neural Network

In their paper, Zhang, Ritchie, and Lo (1993) presented the development of a multilayer feed-forward neural network model to address the freeway traffic system identification problem. This problem must be solved in order to build an improved freeway traffic flow model for the purpose of developing real-time predictive control strategies for dynamic traffic systems. To study the initial feasibility of the approach, a three layer feed forward neural network model was developed to emulate an improved version of a well known higher-order continuum traffic model. Simulation results show that the traffic dynamics of this model correlate quite closely.

7.2.4 Construction and Maintenance

Transportation construction involves all aspects of the construction process, including preparation of the surface, placing the pavement material, and preparation of the roadway for use by traffic (Garber et al., 1986). Maintenance begins after the construction and involves all the work required to keep the facility operational. Maintenance work on highways involves patching, painting, surface treatment, and other related tasks.

Examples of Neural Network Applications in Transportation Maintenance

1. Neural-Network-Based Procedure for Condition Assessment of Utility Cuts in Flexible Pavements

Utility companies often dig up sections of pavement to install or inspect utility services. These locations, called "Utility Cuts," introduce discontinuities, weaken pavements, and cause localized distress. To evaluate their condition, a small-area investigation must be completed. No specific guidelines exist for these investigations. A procedure for investigation of utility cuts and a rating index called the Utility Cut Condition Index (UCCI) was developed by Pant, et al., (1993). A survey of utility cuts in Cincinnati was performed using the Delphi method. Field data were used to develop a back propagation neural network for predicting UCCI on the basis of the type and severity of distress. The model was trained and tested for its accuracy. The UCCI predicted by the neural network can be used to identify conditions of the utility cuts and to assign priorities for their maintenance.

2. Intelligent System for Automated Pavement Evaluation

The intelligent system for automated pavement evaluation was developed by Ritche, et al. (1991). The research focused on the development of an advanced sensor-processing capability using neural network technology to determine the type, severity, and extent of distress from digitized video image representations of the pavement surface acquired in real time. The potential of using three-layer neural networks for distress classification of pavement images as part of the innovative noncontact intelligent pavement maintenance system was demonstrated.

7.2.5 Infrastructure Management

Transportation facilities include guideways, terminals, and stations. The different problems included in the area of transportation infrastructure management include congestion response and management, accident response and management, toll booth infrastructure management, and terminal facilities management. Similar to a general request-response process, neural networks can be used for detection, reaction selection, and routine procedure computerization. In detection, the classification capability of neural networks are most frequently utilized for differentiating states of transportation facilities (e.g., whether a normal or congested traffic condition is taking place on a roadway network). Applications of neural networks in this area reflect the unique power of neural

147

networks, namely, to provide satisfactory output for a set of input data never seen before.

Example of Neural Network Applications in Transportation Infrastructure Management

1. Use of Neural Networks to Recognize and Predict Traffic Congestion

Dougherty et al. (1993) demonstrated an application of neural networks to recognize and predict congestion patterns on traffic networks. Two main problems that occur in all automatic traffic control systems are the following:

- recognizing that the road system is in a particular state (e.g.,that links are 'congested' or that link occupancy or queue lengths have risen above certain thresholds), and
- short-term forecasting to anticipate upcoming congestion

To show how neural networks can assist in these types of pattern recognition problems, they described the main features of a neural network approach, the trials of its application to a congestion recognition problem, and the trials of short-term forecasting of flows on an urban network. The authors also discuss the possibility of training neural networks to infer parameters that are not usually directly measurable on the field.

2. Freeway Incident Detection Using Neural Networks

In the past several decades, a number of conventional incident detection algorithms have been developed, with mixed success in their performance. In their paper, Ritchie et al. (1992) demonstrate the application of a neural network approach for freeway incident detection. Multi-Layer feed-forward neural networks have been applied to a freeway section of approximately 1 mile in Orange County, California, to classify traffic into incident or incident-free conditions. Fourteen such networks have been trained with data consisting of hundreds of incidents, obtained from a microscopic freeway traffic simulation model. The neural network with the best training results was compared with the "California Algorithm" currently being applied in the freeway system in the Los Angeles basin of Southern California. Results based on an independently simulated data set show that the neural network model produces a significant improvement in detection rate, false alarm rate and a reduction in time-to-time detection of incidents.

7.3 Advances In Neural Network Research

Studies of neural networks have rapidly expanded. In summary, recent neural network research are reflected in the following categories:

- Applications
- Variations of existing paradigms
- Development of new paradigms
- Training/Learning Algorithms
- Optimization of architectures

In the applications area, the studies made of neural network applications are, perhaps, the largest proportion of current neural network research activities. Because neural networks seem to be problem-dependent in terms of their architectures, in most cases, for a different purpose or objective, the neural network architecture will be different. This characteristic of neural networks leads to a significant effort to examine the compatability of the problem and the paradigm. Validating the neural network paradigm selected is frequently a necessary part of the work. In the past, comparative analysis of neural networks vs other conventional methods has been a major undertaking in neural network application research.(Jin et al.,1991, and Chiu et al., 1991). In transportation engineering, such phenomena has been especially obvious(Hajek, et al. 1993). These application studies are expected to expose the nature of neural networks and the associated problems of implementing them to solve engineering problems.

In the second category, because of its problem-dependent characteristics, the creation and investigation of variations of existing neural network paradigms has grown. Many researchers are interested in solving similar problems with variations of different paradigms (Monrocq 1993 and Ishibuchi 1991).

Among the existing paradigms, the variation studies of BP have been the most successful. Because it is a multipurpose application including modeling, control, classification, and recognition, the BP has been well examined (Cheng, et al., 1991, and Azimi-Sadjadi, et al. 1991). The properties of BP explored even shadowed that of other paradigms. The diversity of studying neural networks for transportation engineering should be recommended.

Transportation systems are highly dynamic, on a large-scale, complex, and multi-purpose. In the third category-- new paradigms which can better suit transportation problems are expected. New neural network paradigms must be dynamic, hybrid, and interface neural network architectures and other technologies (Ae, T., et al. 1991, and Atkins, M. 1991).

In the fourth category--techniques for efficient training/learninghave been developed (Pandya,A.S., et al., 1991). Self-learning processes are considered effective and efficient means to achieve reasonable architectures. Efficient and on-line learning processes will be especially useful in solving dynamic, management problems which are often seen in transportation systems.

Finally, in order to determine the best architecture for a specific problem, directly affects the performance of a neural network. Many issues that are important to the successful performance of neural networks are still unsolved. For instance, two issues that need to be solved include how to determine the optimal number of hidden processing units and how to escape from local minima traps.

In summary, neural networks research is currently very active and many preliminary results are indicating a great potential for applying neural networks to transportation engineering. Advanced neural network study will benefit transportation engineering.

7.4 Primary Research Needs

Considering the highly dynamic, large scale, complex, and uncertain nature of many transportation systems, neural networks are recognized as effective tools in solving numerous transportation problems. Neural networks have not yet reached their theoretical maturity. Many neural network applications are still in the conceptual stage. For transportation engineering purposes, there are several priority areas for further research.

7.4.1 Modeling Properties

Neural network modeling is an acceptable substitute for conventional mathematical modeling. Many transportation problems are solved using regression analysis. With historical data for building the model that describes some cause-effect relations such as trip generation and traffic volume prediction. Viewing modeling as a "curve fitting" process, the relationship between inputs and outputs can be represented by a BP model being trained with the historical database. Properties gained from BP modeling are: a multi-inputs/multi-outputs system that can be easily modeled; fewer pre-modeling processes are necesary in terms of identifying the basic type of mathematical equation needed; and in some special cases, mathematical drawbacks such as differentiability can be overcome (Hua, et al., 1994). Although the BP can only give a heuristic solution for the output, uncertainty normally exists in transportation systems anyway, and well problem-adapted and well trained neural network models should maintain satisfactory accuracy. An intensive study of neural network modeling should be made utilizing the properties of neural networks in transportation modeling.

7.4.2 Control Logic

Control logic, the relation between stimulus to a system and the reaction of a systemis a key point in the control process. Conventionally, control logic was best expressed in mathematical form, however in advanced control studies, artificial intelligence such as expert systems have been impressively applied. Neural networks can also be used as substitutes for conventional mathematical formulas to represent the control logic. The advantage of neural network control is primarily the flexibility of control logic formulation. For instance, a neural network based controller may be very sensitive to a specific range of a continuous stimulus while maintaining normal sensitivity to other stimulus signals exceeding that range. This process normally causes more effort in building conventional mathematical control logic and, sometimes makes it even impossible. To investigate applicability of neural networks in transportation control systems, more research must be directed towards specific problems.

7.4.3 Information Processing

Neural network information processing is defined as all informative processes such as image processing, knowledge processing, data processing, data acquisition, data compression, and recognitive performance. Transportation engineering is characterized by large databases and diverse, collective, uncertain, abstract, and incomplete information types. To deal with large amounts of complex transportation information, multi-methods are required. Neural networks have been proven to be good performers at numerous information processing tasks. Exploring the power of neural networks in processing transportation information may produce effective tools for simplifying or solving transportation information processing problems (Hua et. al. 1994).

7.4.4 Intelligent Transportation Systems

Lastly, Intelligent Transportation Systems (ITS) is a new research area for the near future. As a branch of artificial intelligence, neural networks are expected to provide a software-base for hardware implementation of IVHS. A study examining the application potential of neural networks to IVHS has identified neural network applicability(Hua, j. et al., 1994).Figures 1-3 present the results of this study. The next step should produce real hardware implementations.

7.5 Concluding Remarks

This paper presents an overview of the potential applicability of neural networks in the transportation engineering field. The overview is based on literature survey both in transportation engineering and in neural networks. Results indicate that because of their basic characteristics neural networks have already played and will continue to play an important role in transportation engineering research.

The following additional concluding remarks are offered:

- Neural networks are powerful stand-alone and/or supplementary techniques to conventional methods. They will play an important role in those transportation engineering problems with cause-effect relationship.

- Neural networks have already been successfully demonstrated in the major areas within transportation engineering including planning, control and operations, construction and maintenance, and facilities management. Their application potentials in the area of design should be investigated as well.

IVHS Elements / Technical Requirements	ATMS	ADIS	AVCS	CVO
prediction	●	●		●
classification	●			
control	●		●	●
pattern recognition	●	●	●	
optimization	●			
noise cancellation	●	●	●	
image processing			●	
knowledge processing	●	●		
signal processing			●	
data compression		●		
natural language processing			●	●
speech recognition			●	●

Useful technique for the corresponding IVHS element
Figure 1. Technical Requirements of IVHS
Source; (Hua, J., and Faghri, A., 1994)

- studies on the variations of existing neural network paradigms and development of new paradigms are recommended for solving specific problems in transportation engineering, especially those that have been unsuccessfully tried by conventional means or even standard neural network architectures.

ANN paradigms \ ANN Applications	control logic modeling	pattern recognition	prediction	noise reduction
(M)ADALINE	●		●	●
Backpropagation	●	●	●	
ART	●			
Hopfield Network	●	●		
Boltzman Machine		●		
Neocognitron/ Cognitron		●		
Counter- propagation				
Kohonen Net.				
Neural GMDH				
BSB				
LVQ	●			
BAM	●			

Figure 2. ANN Application Domains
Source: (Hua, J., and Faghri, A., 1994)

- Parallel processing combined with hardware implementation will provide a great deal of benefit in terms of computation speed. This feature should be utilized more in the future because of the highly dynamic and data processing-intensive nature of many transportation problems.

Figure 2. (Cont'd)

ANN Applications / ANN paradigms	knowledge processing	classification	image processing	optimization
(M)ADALINE			●	
Backpropagation	●		●	●
ART	●	●	●	
Hopfield Network		●	●	
Boltzman Machine	●		●	●
Neocognitron/ Cognitron			●	
Counter-propagation		●		
Kohonen Net.		●		
Neural GMDH				●
BSB	●	●	●	
LVQ			●	●
BAM			●	

154

ANN Applications Domains / IVHS Applications	control logic modeling	pattern recognition	prediction	noise reduction
route guidance			●	
vehicle identification		●		
neural suspension	●			
obstacle detection		●		
driving control	●			
navigation				●
collision avoidance	●			●
traffic control		●	●	●
incident detection		●		
traffic information			●	●

Figure 3. Potential Applications of ANN
Source: (Hua, J., and Faghri, A., 1994)

- Researchers in the new area of Intelligent Transportation Systems should look into neural networks for many of the problems that they face. The enhanced image processing capabilities, enhanced modeling of complex systems, and other neural network features, could support the components of ITS.

Figure 3 (Cont'd)

ANN techniques / IVHS Applications	temporal pattern recognition	classification	image processing	speech & language
route guidance				
vehicle identification			●	
neural suspension				
obstacle detection			●	
driving control			●	●
navigation				
collision avoidance				
traffic control	●	●		
incident detection		●	●	
traffic information				

7.6 References

Ae, T., Aibara, R., and Nishioka, Y. (1991). "A memory-based artificial neural network." *IEEE International Joint Conference on Neural Networks*, 614-619.

Atkins, Mark, A. (1991). "Oscillatron-1: A Connectionist Unified Theory of Cognition." *IEEE International Joint Conference on Neural Networks*, 60-65.

Azimi-Sadjadi, M. R., and Sheedrash, S. (1991). "Recursive node Creation in back-propagation neural networks using orthogonal projection method." *IEEE Proceedings of the International Conference on Acoustics, Speech, and Signal Processing*, 2181-2184.

Cheng, L. M., Mak, H. L., and Cheng L. L. (1991). "Structured backpropagation network." *IEEE International Joint Conference on Neural Networks*, 1641-1646.

Chiu, C., Norcio, A. F., and Petrucci, K. E. (1991). "Using Neural networks and expert systems to model users in an object-oriented environment." *Conference Proceedings of IEEE International Conference on Systems, Man and Cybernetics*, 1943-1948.

Dougherty, M. S., Kirby, H. R., and Boyle, R. D. (1993). "Use of Neural Networks to recognize and predict traffic congestion." *Traffic Engineering and Control Volume 34*, Number 6, 311-314.

Faghri, A., and Hua, J.(1992). "Evaluation of Artificial Neural Network Applications in Transportation Engineering." *Transportation Research Record 1358*, TRB, National Research Council, Washington, D.C.

Fix, E. and Armstrong, H. G. (1990). "Modelling human performance with neural networks." *Proceedings of the International Joint Conference on Neural Networks*, San Diego, CA, 1, 247-252.

Garber, N., and Hoel, L.(1986). *Transportation and Traffic Engineering*. West Publishing Company. St. Paul, Minnesota.

Hajek, J. J., and Hurdal, B.(1993). "Comparison of Rue-Based and Neural network solutions for a structured selection problem." *Transportation Research Record 1399*, TRB, National Research Council, Washington, D.C., 1-7.

Hertz, J., Krogh, A., and Palmer, G. R. (1991). Introduction to the Theory of Neural Computing, Addison-Wesley, Redwood City, CA.

Hua, J. and Faghri, A. (1994). " Applications of ANNs to IVHS." *73rd Annual Meeting, Transportation Research Board, National Research Council,* Washington, D.C.

Ishibuchi, H., and Tanaka, H. (1991). "An Extension of the BP-algorithm to interval input vectors-Learning from numerical data and expert's knowledge." *IEEE International Joint Conference on Neural Networks*, 1588-1593.

Jin, Y. C., and Pipe, T. (1991). "Neuralnet versus control theory." *IEEE International Joint Conference on Neural Networks*, 1548-1553.

Monorocq, C. (1993). "Probabilistic Approach which provides a modular and adaptive neural network architecture for discrimination." *IEEE, 3rd International Conference on Artificial Neural Networks*, 252-255.

Nakatsuji, T., and Kaku, T. (1989). "Application of Neural Network models to traffic engineering problems." *Proceedings of the Infrastructure Planning*, Volume 12, 297-304.

Nakatsuji, T., and Kaku, T.(1991). "Development of a self-organizing traffic control system using neural network models." *Transportation Research Record 1324*, TRB, National Research Council, Washington, D.C., 137-145.

Pandya, A. S., and Szabo, R. (1991). "A fast learning algorithm for neural network applications." *Proceedings of the 1991 IEEE International Conference on Systems, Man, and Cybernetics*, 1569-1573.

Pant, P. D., Zhou, X., Arudi, R. S., Bodocsi, A., and Aktan, A. E. (1993). "NeuraL-Network-Based procedure for condition assessment of utility cuts in flexible pavements." *Transportation Research Record 1399*, TRB, National Research Council, Washington, D.C., 8-13.

Ritche, S. G., Kaseko, M. and Bavarian, B. (1991). "Development of an intelligent system for automated pavement evaluation." *Transportation Research Record 1311*, TRB, National Research Council, Washington, D.C., 112-119.

Ritche, S. G., Cheu, R. L., and Recker, W. W. (1992). "Freeway incident detection using artificial neural networks." *International Conference on Artificial Intelligence Applications in Transportation Engineering*, San Buenaventura, California, 215-234.

Wei, C-H., and Schonfeld, P. M. (1993). "An Artificial Neural Network Approach for Estimating Multiperiod Travel Times in Transportation Networks. *72nd Annual Meeting, Transportation Research Board*, Washington, D.C.

Yang, H., Akiyama, T., and Sasaki, T. (1992). : A Neural network approach to the identification of real time origin-destination flows from traffic counts." *International Conference on Artificial Intelligence Applications in Transportation Engineering, San Buenaventura*, California, 253-269.

Yeh, C-I., and Ritchie, S. G. (1986). "Knowledge-Based Expert Systems in Transportation Planning and Research." *65th Annual Meeting, Transportation Research Board*, Washington, D.C.

Zhang, H., Ritchie, S. G., and Lo, Z-P. (1993). " Macroscopic modeling of freeway traffic using an artificial neural network." 72nd Annual Meeting, *Transportation Research Board*, Washington D.C.

Chapter 8

Geomaterial Modeling Using Artificial Neural Networks

Dayakar Penumadu[1] and Chameau Jean-Lou[2]

Abstract: The approach of modeling the soil behavior within a unified environment based on the artificial neural network architecture is presented. The concept of feed back network is introduced for representing the behavior of sand and clay type soil. Test data obtained from CIUC triaxial stress path on mortar sand with different grain size distributions were used for training and testing the neural network sand model. Stress-Strain data obtained from a series of undrained tests performed on cubic soil samples under pressuremeter stress path in a true triaxial testing device was used as the data base for training and testing the neural network clay model. Issues related to the size of the network and learning algorithm are addressed. The problems related to "overtraining" a network during training phase and the importance of convergence criteria on the self-generalizing capabilities of the trained neural network clay model are shown. A method of choosing appropriate learning rate and momentum factors is also suggested. A well trained neural net model for a specified soil type and stress path can then be combined along with the finite element method, for solving complex boundary value problems. This research could see valuable applications in other related fields of engineering.

8.1 Introduction

The objective of numerical methods in geomechanics is to apply the developments in the theory of geomaterial behavior to provide reliable procedures to the analysis and design of geotechnical structures. Significant amount of research effort has been devoted to constitutive modeling in

---

[1] Assistant Professor, Dept. of Civil and Environmental Eng., Clarkson University, Box: 5710, Potsdam, NY

[2] President, Golder Associates, 3730 Chamblee Tucker Road, Atlanta, GA 30341.

geomechanics over past 40 years. At the third workshop on constitutive equations for granular non-cohesive soils, Scott (1988) says: "*In the course of the second of our workshops at Villard-De-Lans, models were presented that had 25 constants ... and, in the present meeting we have a model that can contain up to 40 constants. Obviously, by this stage, if even the experienced inventor of this model were to be given the description of a sand, he would be hard put to give you a quantitative opinion of the coefficients in general ... constants are growing in numbers at a compounded annual rate of about 12 % ; If they were an investment, it would be a good one*". This statement reflects the limited success achieved in the past, in modeling cohesionless soil using conventional elasticity/plasticity based approach.

On the other hand, the strength and deformation behavior of cohesive soil is governed by both plastic and viscous effects. The viscous properties introduce a dependency of the states of stress and strain on time, and the plastic behavior is dictated by the dependency of these states on the loading path. In the past, several stress-strain-time models have been developed (Roscoe et. al., 1963 ; Schofield and Wroth, 1968 ; Dafalias, 1982 ; Kavazanjian and Mitchell, 1980 ; Hsieh et. al., 1990) based on specific assumption or for a given loading path and their generic applicability is often questioned because of the assumptions they are based on. In addition, it is often difficult for the user to understand and correctly use these complex models even for simplified stress paths. It is proposed herein to approach this problem of modelling soil behavior from a fundamentally different angle using artificial neural networks. The potential of modeling the material behavior using artificial neural networks was first proposed by Ghaboussi et al., 1991. Since then a large body of ANN knowledge has been introduced in geotechnical related civil engineering publications (Ellis et al., 1992, Meier and Rix, 1993, Penumadu et al., 1992 and 1994). The approach proposed herein is to represent the stress-strain behavior of isotropic or anisotropically consolidated soils within a unified environment based on the neural network architecture. The soil behavior network is built from experimental data using the organizing capabilities of the neural network architecture, i.e the network is presented with the experimental data and is trained to learn the relationship between stresses and strains for varying controlling factors. The validity of the soil model is then tested at the end of training by making predictions on test data not previously seen by the neural net.

8.2 Soil Modeling using Neural Networks

A neural network model for predicting the stress strain characteristics of soil will be useful if it is properly trained for the variables that are often encountered in the practical applications of interest. One of the most important aspect in such neuromorphic models is the training phase. The data set must be as large as needed for the trained network to capture (i.e. learn and model) the relevant characteristics of the soil behavior. However, it is desirable to limit its size to control the size of the network and the computational effort needed for such a network. It is thus critical to select the optimum data set in training, as it will dictate the neural net predictive ability to a large extent. The issues related to type of the network to be used for stress-strain modeling, network topology, type of the learning algorithm and convergence criteria largely dictate the size of the optimum data set used in the training phase.

8.3 Type of Neural Network

A different type of network called feed back neural network was used by the authors for modeling the stress-strain behavior of soil. The idea is similar to the recurrent network proposed by Jordan (McClelland and Rumelhart, 1988). The network has two sets of input neurons called plan units and current-state units. These input units feed into a set of hidden units, which in turn feed into a set of output or next state units. At the initial phase of the training, a pattern is input to the plan units and zero input to the current-state units. Feed forward process occurs as in standard back propagation, producing the first output pattern. This output pattern is then copied back to the current-state units for the next feed forward sweep. The current-state units capture the prior history of activation in the network. From plasticity theory of soil, it is well known that current state of stress and strain have important influence on the next state of stress and strain. It is thus essential to use feed back neural network concept for simulating stress-strain curves of soil. This also ensures that the training phase of the soil model is in line with testing phase, where the neural network has to build the stress-strain curve incrementally based on the predictions for the loading conditions at the previous step.

Neural Net based Sand model under Triaxial (CIUC) Stress Path

Database: A series of undrained triaxial tests were performed in accordance with established procedures on eight mortar sands with different grain size distributions (Yao, 1993; Ellis et al., 1995). Table 1 indicates the summary of the laboratory test data. The grain shape was sub-rounded with smooth grain surface texture and the x-ray diffraction results indicate predominantly quartz as the mineral. Using these sands, 46 isotropically consolidated undrained triaxial compression tests (CIUC) were conducted with pore pressure measurements. The density of the samples ranged from loose to dense. Three levels of confining pressure (70, 210, and 350 kPa) were used and the samples were consolidated to an over-consolidation ratio in the range of 1 to 5.

8.4 Simulation of Stress-Strain Curves

Neural networks incorporating the effects of stress history and grain size distribution were used to simulate CIUC stress-strain behavior of sands. A sequential network with the architecture of 7x10x2 (Figure 1) was trained on 38 triaxial test results. Of the 7 inputs, $\sigma_{1,i}'$, u_i and $\varepsilon_{1,i}$ describe the current stress and strain state; σ_{3c}' and D_r are the confining pressure and initial relative density; OCR reflects the previous stress history; and C_u is the coefficient of uniformity, which characterizes the grain size distribution of sand. A constant small value of 0.0405% is used for the axial strain increment, $\Delta\varepsilon_1$. The two outputs are $\sigma_{1,i+1}'$ and u_{i+1}. The current-state units are $\sigma_{1,i}'$ and u_i. Thus, their value is equal to the output from the network's forward computation of the last iteration. The number of processing elements (PE's) in the hidden layer was determined through a trial and error procedure.

The ANN simulations associated with the experimental results used in the training phase are shown in Figures 2(a) and 2(b). For different sands, the trained network can account for the effects of D_r, σ_{3c}' and OCR on the stress-strain relations. This point, of course, merely reflects the power of ANN's in memorization. To demonstrate the predictive ability of the trained ANN sand model, the network was used to calculate stress-strain curves for a testing set of 7 tests which were not a part of the training set. The seven tests were chosen from seven different sands. It can be seen from Figures 3(a) and Fig. 3(b) that the trained network can predict the results reasonably well.

The ANN predicted the deviator stress $(\sigma_1-\sigma_3)$ versus axial strain ε_1 well. The worst prediction had a 20% relative error. Comparatively, the prediction for pore water pressure u is not as good as that for the stress-strain relation. However, it is interesting to note that the ANN prediction of u versus ε_1 is in good agreement with the general variation. To examine further the predictive capabilities of the trained network, the network was used to show systematically the effects of D_r, σ_{3c}' and C_u on stress-strain behavior and pore pressure development.

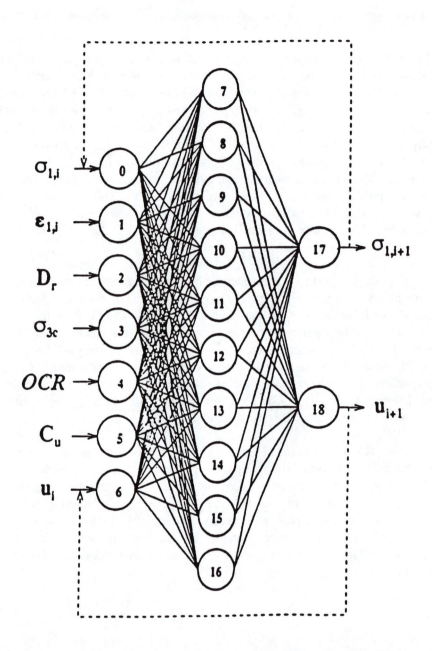

Figure 1 A 7x10x2 Sequential Neural Network Used to Simulate Effects of D_r, σ_{vo}' and OCR and Grain Size Distribution on the Stress-Strain Relationship of Mortar Sand

Table 1: Summary of CIUC Triaxial Tests

Sand	Test	D_r	$\sigma_x{}'$(psi.)	OCR	Sand	Test	D_r	$\sigma_x{}'$(psi.)	OCR
No.1	P30	0.42	50	1	No.10	P56	0.93	20	1
"	P34	0.55	50	1	No.22	P57	0.55	50	1
"	P35	0.37	30	1	"	P58	0.66	10	1
"	P36	0.40	10	1	"	P60	0.83	10	4
No.17	P37	0.53	50	1	No.23	P62	0.63	50	1
"	P38	0.29	10	3	"	P63	0.62	20	2
"	P39	0.02	10	1	"	P65	0.44	50	1
"	P40	0.14	10	5	"	P66	0.69	50	1
"	P41	0.55	30	2	"	P67	0.82	10	5
"	P42	0.32	10	1	"	P68	0.77	30	2
"	P43	0.60	50	1	"	P69	0.63	30	2
"	P44	0.72	30	2	"	P70	0.36	30	2
No.6	P45	0.58	50	1	"	P71	0.20	10	1
"	P46	0.32	30	1	No.21	P72	0.49	50	1
"	P47	0.67	10	5	"	P73	0.27	30	2
"	P48	0.17	10	5	"	P74	0.48	50	1
"	P49	0.12	50	1	"	P75	0.40	30	2
"	P50	0.06	30	2	"	P76	0.64	50	1
No.10	P51	0:86	10	1	No.25	P78	0.69	30	1
"	P52	0.82	30	2	"	P79	0.82	50	1
"	P53	1.0	50	1	"	P80	0.71	10	4
"	P54	0.74	50	2	"	P81	0.22	10	1
"	P55	0.58	10	4	"	P82	0.36	50	1

For example, to investigate the effect of one parameter such as D_r, all other parameters were held constant while D_r was allowed to change and the trends predicted by the neural network model agree with the laboratory observations. An attempt was also made to model the stress-strain curves with unload-reload loops using artificial neural networks and the details are presented by Ellis et al., 1995.

Neural net based clay model under pressuremeter stress path

Database: A series of undrained tests were performed on 100 mm cubic samples in a true triaxial testing device using pressuremeter stress path (Skandarajah et. al., 1991, Skandarajah, 1992). Floating flexible boundary conditions were used in the testing to minimize the edge effects. Two types of soils Kaolinite (LL=63 and PL=33) and fine crushed Silica (Sil-Co-Sil # 270) were used in the investigation. The soil samples were obtained from slurry consolidation to assure homogeneity. The soil samples were made of 100 % Kaolin or from a mix of 50 % Kaolin - 50 % Silica. All the specimens were consolidated to the same state of stress under K_O conditions and sheared undrained, using pressuremeter stress path in the true triaxial testing device. The undrained shear tests were performed at various rates of loading to evaluate the strain rate effects in pressuremeter testing. Since all the tests were performed under controlled laboratory conditions for the same consolidation stress, it was selected as an initial data base for evaluating the potential of neural networks for modeling the clay behavior for a specified (pressuremeter) stress path. The nonlinear elasto-plastic time dependent behavior observed for the Kaolin and Kaolin-Silica soil for varying strain rates, was transformed to patterns of data to be used for training and testing the neural net. The stress-strain response for Kaolin-Silica was strain hardening and that for Kaolin was strain softening. Investigating the ability of neural networks for modeling soil behavior using this data base would thus encompass the general variation of stress-strain curves encountered for cohesive soil.

Topology of the network: In neuromorphic models, one of the important aspects of using neural networks to solve a given problem depends on choosing the appropriate topography. This involves arriving at the number of input, hidden and output neurons for either three or four layered neural networks. Unfortunately, for many neural net applications (examples include pattern recognition, robotics control, artificial visualization), the topography, including the number of hidden neurons, is rarely based on physical considerations. An attempt was made to approach the problem of evaluating the topography by setting the number of equations equal to the number of unknowns, as shown below.

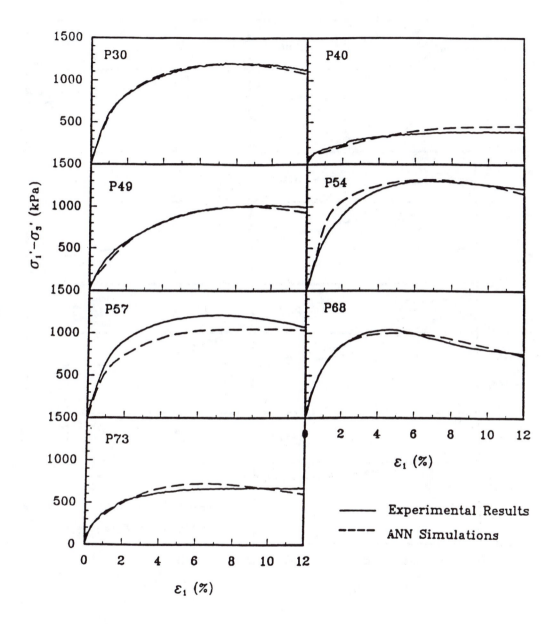

Figure 2(a) Neural Network Simulation of Stress-Strain Relationship for Different Sands with Varied D_r, σ_{vo}' and OCR Compared with Training Data

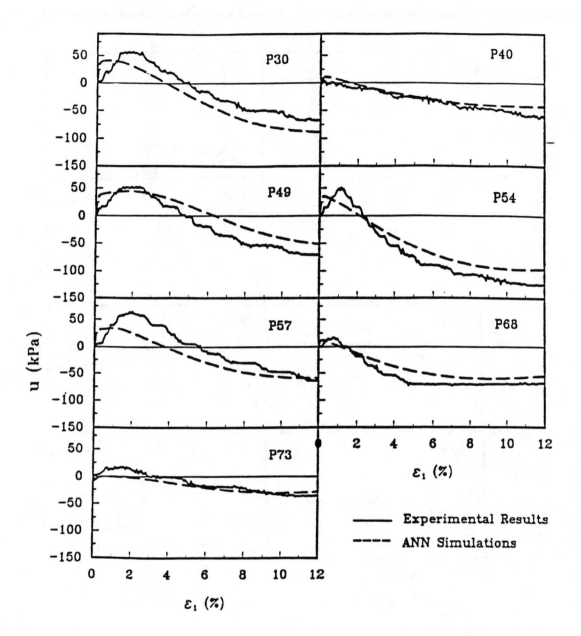

Figure 2(b) Neural Network Simulation of the Development of Pore Water Pressure in Undrained Triaxial Compression Tests for Different Sands with Varied D_r, σ_{vo}' and OCR Compared with Training Data

The objective of the training phase for the neural net soil model is to evaluate the connection strengths between neurons of layer1-layer2 and layer2-layer3 (for a three layered feed forward net) and the threshold levels of hidden and output neurons, i.e for neurons in layers two and three. With these connection strengths and threshold levels, the trained neural net soil model would then be in a position to model the soil behavior.

Number of equations = $(N_o)(N_p)$
Number of unknowns = $(N_i)(N_h) + (N_h)(N_o) + (N_h + N_o)$
N_i = Number of input neurons
N_h = Number of hidden neurons
N_o = Number of output neurons
N_p = Number of patterns of data used in training phase

The number of unknowns include the values of the connection weights between input-hidden and hidden-output layers, and the threshold values of the hidden and output neurons. Input and output neurons were decided based on inferences from plasticity theory for soils. The number of hidden neurons were calculated using the above procedure for a given number of patterns of data to be used during training. Thus a 4X10X1 (Figure 4) network was obtained for training and prediction of both Kaolin and Kaolin-Silica behavior. It is a norm to stop the iterative training phase when the global error reaches a minimum value on the normalized input-output data set. Using the connection weights and threshold levels obtained at the end of the training phase (when the error reached a global minima), predictions were made to evaluate the self-generalizing capabilities of the neural net clay model. For the initial phase of the research, minimum value of TSSR (total sum of the square of residuals) was used as the convergence criteria.

For kaolin-silica soil, the stress-strain curves for strain rate equal to 0.01 %/min and 1 %/min was used in the training phase. Figure 5(a) shows the test data and neural network predictions after the training was completed. It is important to recognize that the neural network has not seen the stress-strain data set for kaolin-silica corresponding to 0.1 %/min at the end of training stage. To evaluate the self-generalizing capability of this trained net, predictions were made for strain rate = 0.1 %/min. The comparison of test data set versus neural network predictions is shown in Figure 5(b). It is encouraging to note that despite small data set used in the training phase (effect of only two strain rates were shown to the network and the order of strain rate was varying by a factor of 100), the neural net model has learned the general trend but the predictions are poor.

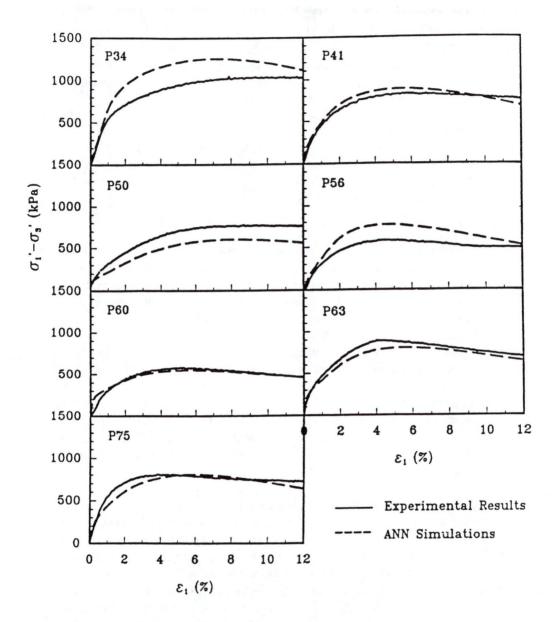

Figure 3(a) Neural Network   Simulation of Stress-Strain Relationship for Different Sands with Varied D_r, σ_{vo}' and OCR Compared with Testing Data

For kaolin soil whose stress-strain response is more complex (strain softening feature), a similar topography of 4X10X1 was used (Figure 4(b)), using the criteria described above. The stress-strain curves corresponding to strain rates of 0.01 %/min and 5 %/min were used in the training phase using the feedback network. At the end of training phase, simulations were made for the same strain rates and good agreement was obtained with the training data (Figure 6(a)). The stress-strain curve for strain rate equal to 0.1 %/min was now predicted using the trained neural net and comparisons with the lab test data are shown in Figure 6(b). It is clear that the neural net learned the general trend of variation but there was 24% error in predicting the undrained strength (peak value). It is important to recognize that the increase in undrained shear strength per log cycle of strain rate was approximately 14.3 % for kaolin and 15.3 % for Kaolin-Silica mixture. The neural network clay model performed poorly to learn and self-generalize the stress-strain variation of clays for the pressuremeter stress path because of the proximity of the stress-strain curves for large variation of strain rate and the limited data base used in the training phase (only two out of the three available data sets). This raises an important issue that large size training data sets are needed for developing reliable neural network based soil models.

8.5 Convergence Criteria for the Neural Net Clay Model

In order to investigate the effects of convergence criteria on the ability of the neural net clay model, all the three available data set (stress-strain curves corresponding to strain rates of 0.01, 0.1 and 1 %/min.) for kaolin soil were used in the training phase. The neural net was now used to simulate the stress-strain curves corresponding to strain rates of 0.05 and 0.5 %/min. It is important to realize that the laboratory test data for these two strain rates is not available for comparison purposes. The objective of the testing phase is to evaluate the qualitative simulation capabilities of the trained neural net clay model. In the first case, the convergence criteria during the training phase was based on the minimum value of the total sum of the square of residuals, TSSR. Though the simulations on the trained data set are excellent (Figure 7), the network did not learn the effects of strain rate correctly (e.g. curve corresponding to 0.5 %/min) when tested for self-generalizing capability (Figure 8). This is because of the "overtraining" problems. During the training phase, network initially configure's itself in accordance with the general statistical trends of the data, but after it has learned those trends it will set about learning any spurious patterns in the training data which deviate from those trends.

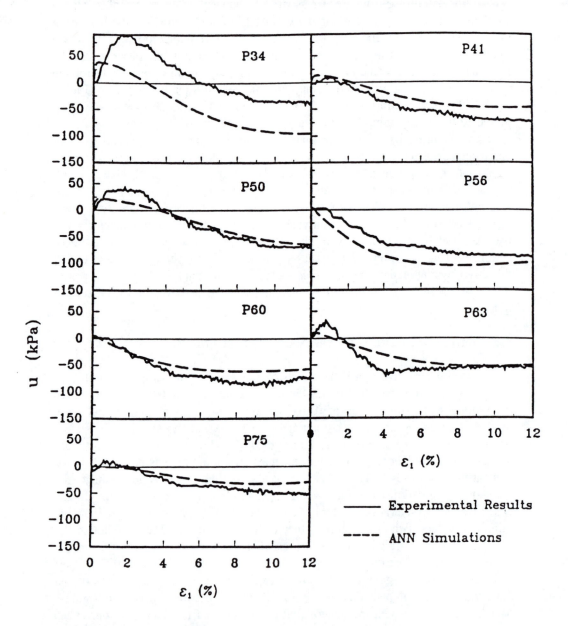

Figure 3(b) Neural Network Simulation of the Development of Pore Water Pressure in Undrained Triaxial Compression Tests for Different Sands with Varied D_r, σ_{vo}' and OCR Compared with Testing Data

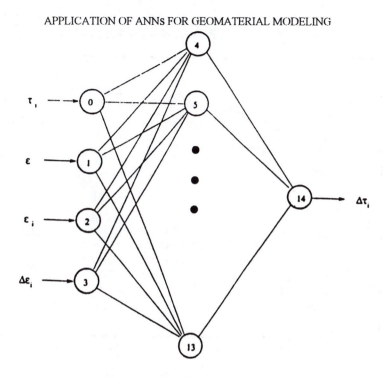

Figure 4 (a) : Neural Network Architecture for Kaolin - Silica

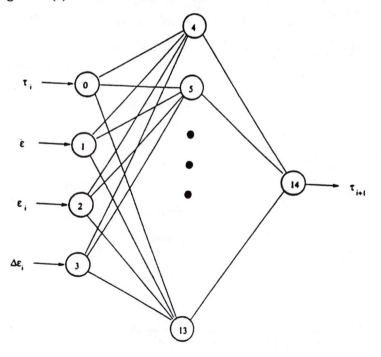

Figure 4 (b) : Neural Network Architecture for Kaolin

Neural Network Predictions on Trained Data Set

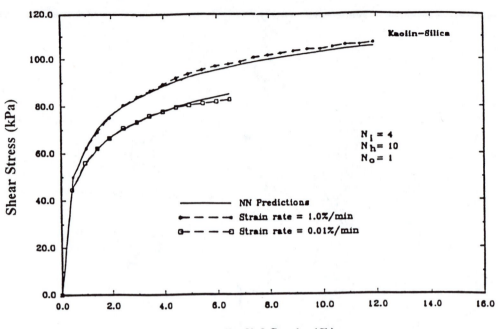

Figure 5 (a)

Neural Network Predictions on Test Data Set

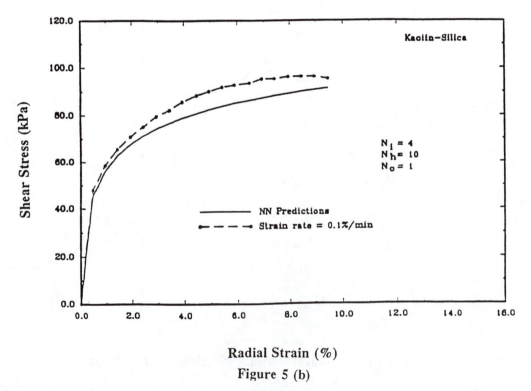

Radial Strain (%)

Figure 5 (b)

Thus there is a point in training phase where the performance on the test data will start to deteriorate whereas on the training set performance will improve until it has learned the correct responses to all the input. Using the same network topography (i.e. 4X10X1), the network was now retrained for the stress-strain curves corresponding to the same strain rates (0.01, 0.1, 1.0 %/min). However, the convergence criteria was changed. The training phase was stopped when the TSSR reached a small value (0.004) and at the same time the simulations agreed qualitatively with the experimental observations for both training and testing data. These results are shown in Figures 9 and 10. The lesson learned was that use of minimum TSSR value as the convergence criteria in the neural net training phase does not ensure correct self-generalizing capabilities. However, the convergence criteria proposed in this paper has a drawback that it involves the judgement of the researcher associated with the training phase.

Size of the hidden layer:
In order to evaluate the benefits, if any, of arriving at the number of hidden neurons using the approach described above, a parametric study was performed for the above data base (i.e. Kaolin-Silica test data) by randomly changing the size of the network based on initial research, the size of the network was changed to 4X4X1 (i.e. four hidden neurons) and comparison with the simulation capabilities of the previously explained neural net model (4X10X1) were made. It was found that the 4X4X1 neural net had very similar simulation capabilities on training and testing data sets as compared to the 4X10X1 neural net clay model. This investigation confirmed that the number of hidden neurons calculated by equating number of equations equal to unknowns was not the minimum number. However, authors still encourage this approach of evaluating the hidden neurons as a beginning, for a novice user applying neural networks to solve engineering mechanics related problems. This investigation also confirmed the observation reported above related to using minimum TSSR value as the convergence criteria during the training phase. Similar parametric study was carried out for modeling the strain softening stress-strain variation of Kaolin soil and identical observations were found related to the size of the hidden layer and convergence criteria. Thus, for the above clay models when the network topography of 4X10X1 was changed to a new topography of 4X4X1 (i.e number of hidden neurons changed to 4), very similar self-generalizing capabilities were obtained. This aspect of choosing appropriate size of the hidden layer for the neural network needs further investigation and is critical for deciding the "comprehensive" training data set.

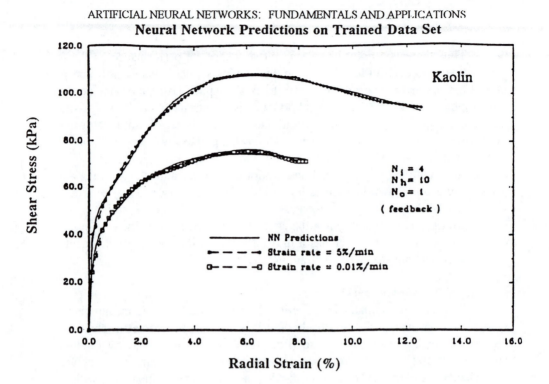

Figure 6 (a)

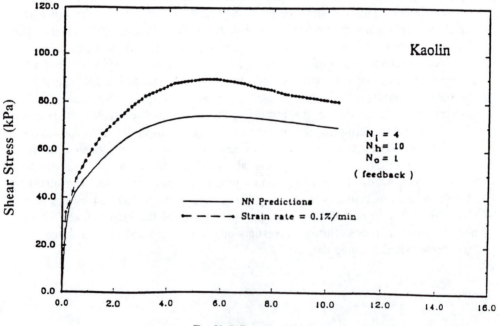

Figure 6 (b)

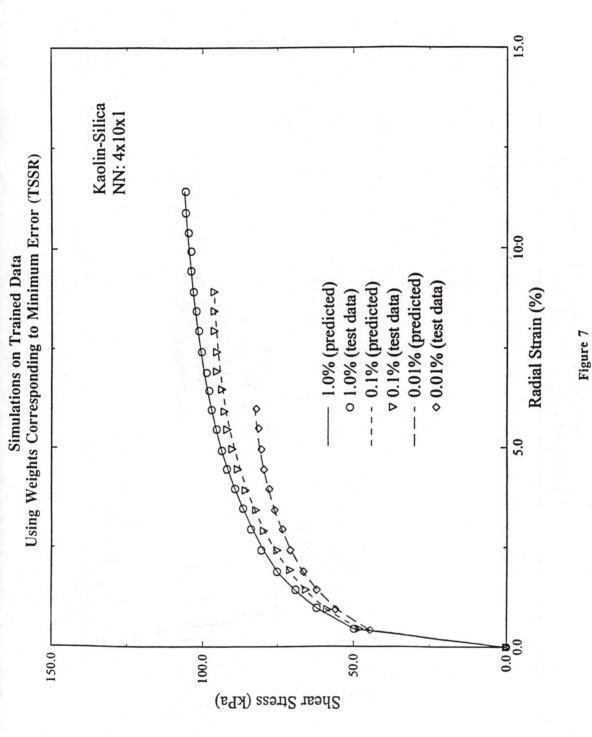

Figure 7

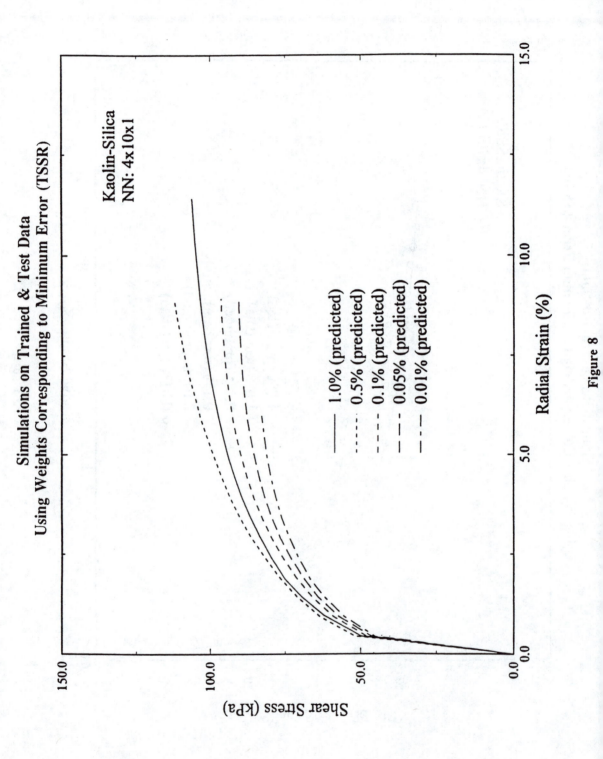

Simulations on Trained & Test Data
Using Weights Corresponding to Minimum Error (TSSR)

Kaolin-Silica
NN: 4x10x1

1.0% (predicted)
0.5% (predicted)
0.1% (predicted)
0.05% (predicted)
0.01% (predicted)

Shear Stress (kPa)

Radial Strain (%)

Figure 8

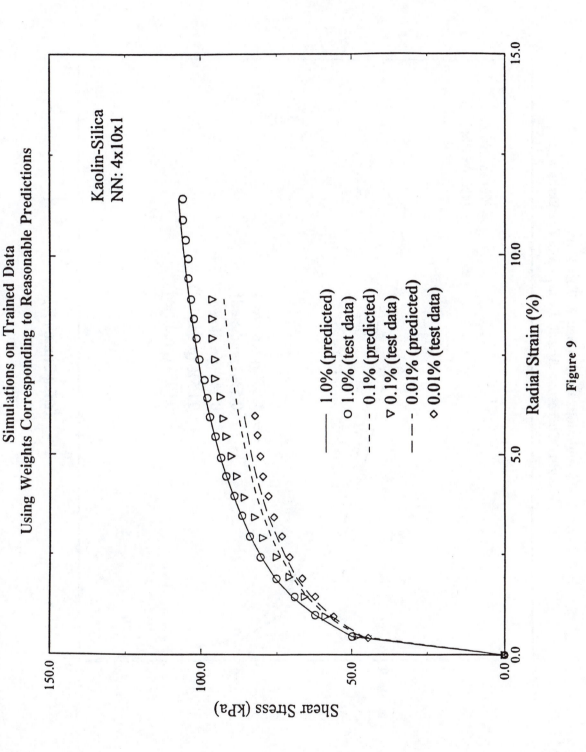

Figure 9

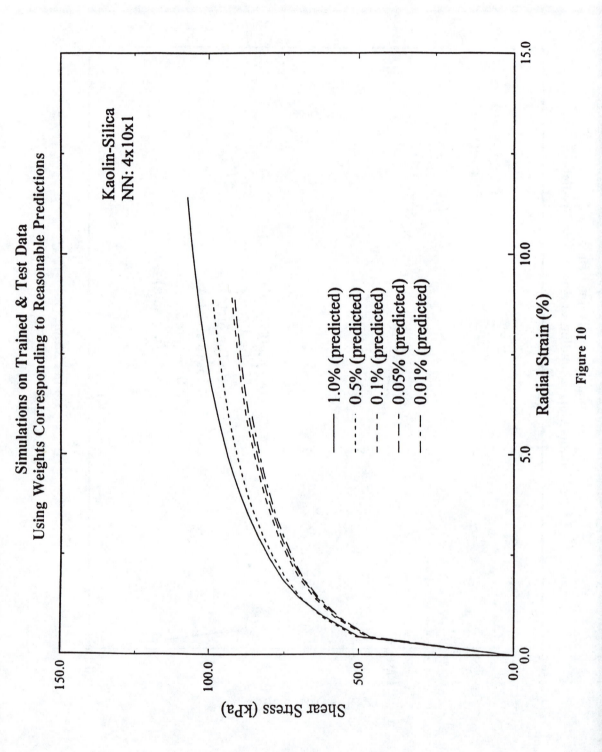

Figure 10

Issues related to back-propagation learning:

The predictive ability of a neural network soil model largely depends on the database used during training phase and also on the type of learning algorithm. For this research, back-propagation learning algorithm was used. The learning is accomplished through a sequence of epochs in which all pattern pairs are presented for one trial each during each epoch. The routine that performs change in weights can be called once per pattern or only once per epoch. The presentation is either sequential or random order. The important parameters that affect the back-propagation scheme that was used in this study are the learning rate and momentum factors. For the 4X4X1 neural net clay model, study was made to arrive at the appropriate values for the learning parameters and some of the results are shown in Table 2. The objective of this study was to choose proper combination of learning rate and momentum factors that converge to a small value of TSSR with minimum number of iterations. This reduces the training time in reaching the global minimum of the error domain. Based on authors experience, it is recommended that research be done for a given network topology and database in arriving at the proper learning parameters for the back-propagation algorithm before developing a comprehensive neural network based material model. These values seem to vary for different applications. For the two clay and sand models discussed above, a learning rate of 0.1 and momentum factor of 0.9 were used.

8.6 Summary and Conclusions

An attempt was made to develop neural network based soil models for modeling the stress-strain relationship of sand and clay type soil. Several issues related to comprehensive data set, training and testing procedures for the soil models were discussed. Discussion related to evaluating the neural network topography for material modeling was presented. Concept of feedback network was presented for simulating the soil behavior both at the training and testing phase. Based on this investigation, the following are concluded.

1. Feed-back networks instead of conventional feed-forward networks should be used for geo-material so that the training phase is in line with the simulation of the stress-strain curves in the testing phase.
2. The convergence criteria during the training phase should not be based on minimum global error (TSSR value). The connection weights and threshold levels of the network that correspond to a small TSSR value and give good predictions on the testing data set should be used. The chapter shows that "overtraining" problems can have important influence on the self-generalizing capabilities of the trained neural network soil models.
3. For developing reliable neural network based soil models, large size of the training data sets are needed.

Table 2: Effect of Learning Rate and Momentum Factor

Learning Rate	Momentum Factor	Iterations required to reach the indicated TSSR Value			
		TSSR=.01	TSSR=.002	TSSR=.0014	TSSR=.0012
1.0	1.0	365	451	812	1408
0.5	0.5	362	449	782	1355
0.1	0.9	347	434	733	1264
0.5	0.9	79	99	255	2730

The advantage of developing such neural network based soil models is that they can be continuously updated with new available data sets. A well trained neural net model for a specified soil type and stress path can then be combined along with the finite element method, for solving complex boundary value problems. This research could see valuable applications in other related fields of engineering.

8.7 References

Dafalias, Y. F. (1982), "Bounding Surface Elastoplasticity-Visco-Plasticity for Particulate Cohesive Media," *Deformation and Failure of Granular Materials,* A.A. Balkema, Pub., Rotterdam, 97-107.

Ellis, G.W., Yao, C. and Zhao, R. (1992), "Neural Network Modeling of the Mechanical Behavior of Sand," *Proc. of the Ninth Conf., ASCE Engineering Mechanics,* Texas, 421-424.

Ellis, G.W., Yao, C., Zhao, R. and Penumadu, D. (1995), "Stress-Strain Modeling of Sands Using Artificial Neural Networks," *Journal of Geotechnical Engineering, ASCE.,* Vol 121, No.5, 429-435.

Ghaboussi, J., Garrett Jr., J.H. and Wu, X. (1991), "Knowledge-Based Modeling of Material Behavior with Neural Networks," *J. of Engrg. Mech., ASCE,* Vol. 117, No. 1, 132-153.

Hsieh, H.S., Kavazanjian, E. Jr. and Borja, R.I. (1990), "Double-Yield-Surface Cam-Clay Plasticity Model. I," *Journal of Geotech. Eng., ASCE,* 116(9), 1381-1401.

Kavazanjian, E. Jr. and Mitchell, J.K. (1980), "Time-Dependent Deformation Behavior of Clays," *Journal of Geotech. Eng., ASCE,* 106(6), 611-630.

Lippmann, R. P. (1987), "An Introduction to Computing with Neural Nets," *IEEE ASSP Magazine,* Vol. 4, 4-27.

McClelland, J.L. and Rumelhart, D.E. (1988), *Explorations in Parallel Distributed Processing,* The MIT Press, Boston, MA.

McCulloch, W. S., and Pitts, W. (1943), "A Logical Calculus of the Ideas Immanent in Nervous Activity," *Bull. Math. Biophys.,* Vol 5.

Meier, R. W. and Rix, G. J. (1993), "An Initial Study of Surface Wave Inversion Using Artificial Neural Networks," *Geotechnical Testing Journal,* GTJODJ, Vol. 16, No. 4, 425-431.

Penumadu, D., Agrawal, G. and Chameau, J.-L. (1992), "Discussion of 'Knowledge-Based Modeling of Material Behavior with Neural Networks' by Ghaboussi et al.,"*J. of Engrg. Mech., ASCE,* Vol. 118, No. 5, 1057-1058.

Penumadu, D. (1993), "Strain Rate Effects in Pressuremeter Testing and Neural Network Approach For Soil Modeling," *Ph.D Thesis,* Georgia Institute of Technology, Atlanta, GA.

Penumadu, D., Jin-Nan, L., Chameau, J.-L. and Sandarajah, A. (1994), "Anisotropic Rate Dependent Behavior of Clays Using Neural Networks," , *Proc. of XIII ICSMFE,* New Delhi, Vol. 4, 1445-1448.

Rumelhart, D., Hinton, G., and Williams, R. (1986), "Learning Representations By Back-Propagating Errors," Nature, Vol. 323, 533-536.

Rumelhart, D. E., McClelland, J. L. and P. R. Group. (1986), *Parallel Distributed Processing Explorations in the Microstructure of Cognition,* 1 ed., Vol. 1, Cambridge, MA: Bradford Books/MIT Press.

Roscoe, K. H., Schofield, A.N. and Thurairajah, A. (1963), "Yielding of Clays in State Wetter Than Critical," *Geotechnique,* 13(3), 211-240.

Schofield, A.N. and Wroth, C.P.(1968), *Critical State Soil Mechanics,* McGraw Hill.

Scott, R. F. (1988), "Constitutive Relations for Soil: Present and Future," Constitutive Equations for Granular Non-Cohesive Soils, Saada & Bianchini (eds.), Rotterdam.

Skandarajah, A., Penumadu, D., and Chameau, J.L. (1991), "Strain Rate Effects in Pressuremeter Testing," *Eighth ASCE Engineering Mechanics Specialty Conference,* Colombus, OH, Vol.2, 1140-1145.

Skandarajah, A. (1992), "Strain Rate and Stress Relaxation In Simulated Pressuremeter Testing In Clays," *Ph.D Thesis,* Purdue University, W. Lafayette, IN.

Yao, C. (1993), "Artificial Neural Network Applications in Geotechnical Engineering," M.S Thesis, Clarkson University, Potsdam, NY.

Chapter 9

Assessing the Liquefaction Susceptibility at a site based on information from penetration testing

Girish Agrawal,[1] Associate Member, ASCE, Jean-Lou A. Chameau,[2] and Philippe L. Bourdeau,[3] Members, ASCE

Abstract: Assessing the liquefaction susceptibility of a site is a complex problem. We focus on the assessment of level-ground liquefaction potential based on field observations of performance of sites subjected to earthquakes in the past. Most applicable methods of evaluating the liquefaction susceptibility of a site remain empirical. Existing methods have an inherent either/or dichotomy in that they work by assigning a site to one of two classes. An associated probability of misclassification is sometimes provided in order to reflect the various uncertainties in data and procedures. We assert that liquefaction is a continuous (even ambiguous) event and it is not always appropriate to talk in terms of an either/or classification. Hence, the discussion and methodology presented in this chapter is in terms of a single behavior *viz.*, liquefaction, that each site displays to a certain degree. This continuous classification scheme is a natural consequence of the "neural-fuzzy" methodology presented. We prefer the term neural-fuzzy since we present ANNs trained such that they learn to recognize a pattern (the liquefaction event), and the classification produced by the network is interpreted as a "degree of belonging." This degree of belonging is also termed the "possibility of liquefaction" of the site under consideration and meshes with the terminology of fuzzy sets. A fuzzy sets interpretation also allows us to use the "fuzzy entropy measure" to assess a level of confidence for the classification produced by the network. We discuss some of the procedural, as well as mathematical drawbacks of the conventional methods used to assess the potential for liquefaction and how these may be overcome

---

[1] Staff Engineer, The Earth Technology Co., 2121 Alton Parkway, Suite100, Irvine, California.
[2] President, Golder Associates, Inc., Atlanta, Georgia.
[3] Associate Professor, School of Civil Engineering, Purdue University, West Lafayette, Indiana.

185

by the suggested neural-fuzzy methodology. We believe that our technique provides for a more realistic approach to the assessment of liquefaction potential. Throughout the chapter, our focus stays on the use of ANNs as practical engineering tools for assessing the possibility of liquefaction at a site. We use a feed-forward network with one hidden layer. The development/selection of the network topology and parameters is discussed. Data from sites around the world is used to demonstrate the training and testing of the particular ANNs developed for the problem. A "data enhancement" technique is presented which substantially improves the performance of the neural network by making use of our understanding of the physical processes involved in liquefaction. A small parametric study is also presented as a qualitative assessment of the success of network training. The approach to the problem is presented in sufficient detail that a reader would be able to understand, implement, and use the technique on a day to day basis without a major investment of time and resources.

9.1 Liquefaction

During a seismic event, agitation of saturated fine grained cohesionless soils can result in transient, but total, loss of intergranular stress due to a sudden rise in pressure in the water filling the intergranular voids of the soil mass. The result is a quicksand condition wherein a particular strata at the surface or at depth is temporarily transformed into a fluid state. This phenomenon is termed liquefaction and the resulting loss of strength commonly allows ground displacement or ground failure to occur. The National Research Council (1985) defines the phenomena as:

> The term liquefaction, as generally used, includes all phenomena involving excess deformations or movements as a result of transient or repeated disturbance of saturated cohesionless soils. This broad usage of the word liquefaction is endorsed by the great majority of engineers, although some would restrict use of the word to flow failures.

Liquefaction may also cause large horizontal movements as the ground-surface layers are decoupled from more rigid materials underlying the liquefied layer. Such decoupling reduces the vibrations but can cause severe damage to buildings, pipelines, and other structures due to large lateral deformations.

Some of the typical field observations which are taken as evidence of liquefaction are (Castro, 1987):

1) Ground settlement
2) Sand boils

3) Flow slides
4) Sinking of heavy buildings
5) Floating of light buildings
6) Slumping of slopes
7) Settlement of buildings
8) Lateral spreading

Even though all of these features may be observed during a shaking event and their physical mechanisms (and hazard levels) may be different, the term liquefaction is often used to refer to all of the phenomena, and hence, in the context of this chapter, the usage of the term liquefaction is broad and covers a range of phenomena that are not necessarily the same. It must also be kept in mind that our focus here is only on level-ground liquefaction.

9.2 Current Procedures for Liquefaction Potential Assessment

The assessment of the potential for liquefaction due to an earthquake at a site is a complex engineering problem. Many factors influence the mechanism of liquefaction. They include the magnitude and intensity of the earthquake, the distance from the source of the earthquake, the seismic attenuation characteristics of the bedrock between the source and the site, and most importantly, the site specific conditions such as: soil type and properties; initial confining pressure; and ground water level at the site.

Important advances have been made during the past two decades in understanding liquefaction and in developing tools to help assess safety against liquefaction, but numerous aspects of the problem remain uncertain and the most applicable methods of evaluating the liquefaction susceptibility of a site remain empirical. The many documented instances of liquefaction on level ground have been used to construct correlations involving the intensity of ground shaking, the depth of the water table, and the resistance of the soil.

Historically, geotechnical engineers have used earthquake magnitude and peak acceleration to characterize earthquakes. Acceleration and duration of strong ground motion, which are the parameters of primary interest in liquefaction investigations, have been correlated with magnitude and distance to the earthquake source (Seed, 1979a). "Since the Niigata earthquake, considerable field experience with liquefaction during actual earthquakes has been obtained and interpreted. This mass of data forms a basis for establishing empirical correlations relating the occurrence or nonoccurrence of liquefaction to the intensity of ground shaking and the principal characteristics of cohesionless soils" (National Research Council, 1985).

Theoretical analyses and laboratory tests have shown that the cyclic stress ratio is an appropriate measure of the liquefaction characteristics under level ground conditions. This is the ratio of the average cyclic shear stress ($\tau_h)_{av}$ (developed on horizontal sand layers as a result of the cyclic or earthquake loading) to the initial vertical effective overburden stress σ'_0. The penetration resistance N, evaluated by means of the standard penetration test (SPT), reflects various factors known from laboratory tests to affect susceptibility to liquefaction and is used as a measure of the resistance to liquefaction. Based on these considerations, empirical relationships have been suggested to identify the state which would trigger the development of liquefaction. The cyclic stress ratio may be computed from the estimated peak surface acceleration by a simple equation (Seed and Idriss, 1971) as follows:

$$\frac{(\tau_h)_{av}}{\sigma'_0} \cong 0.65 \frac{a_{max}}{g} \cdot \frac{\sigma_0}{\sigma'_0} \cdot r_d \tag{1}$$

where a_{max} is the maximum acceleration (usually estimated) at the ground surface; σ_0 equals the total overburden stress on the sand layer under consideration; and r_d equals a stress reduction factor that decreases from a value of 1 at the ground surface to a value of 0.9 at a depth of about 9.6 m ($\approx$30 ft). The number 0.65 in Eqn. 1 is a stress averaging factor which accounts approximately for the relative importance of the many different acceleration peaks in a typical ground motion record. The general form of this stress averaging factor is $0.1(M - 1)$, and the value 0.65 is used since the chart of Figure 1 was developed and refined by Seed and his co-workers for earthquakes with a Richter magnitude $M \approx 7.5$. When using Eqn. 1, the important effect of the duration of ground shaking (different for events of different magnitude) is taken into account by means of a correction related to the magnitude of the earthquake as explained in Seed and Idriss (1982). Since laboratory tests involve uniform cycles of loading only, and the time history of stress or strain during an earthquake is quite irregular, empirical methods for converting irregular cycles to equivalent regular cycles have been developed (Ishihara and Yasuda, 1975; Annaki and Lee, 1977; Haldar and Tang, 1981).

In Figure 1, the resistance of the soil is represented by the abscissa $(N1)60$, which is the recorded SPT blow count corrected to represent standard conditions as suggested by Seed et al. (1984). N1 results from a correction for overburden effects which is done by normalizing the recorded N value to a 96 kPa (1 tsf) overburden. $(N1)60$ is the N1 value normalized to an energy input to the top of the drill stem equal to that delivered by a standard SPT safety hammer (in use in the U.S.A.) operating at 60% efficiency. Both $\dfrac{\tau_{av}}{\sigma'_0}$ and $(N_1)_{60}$ can be evaluated at any number of depths in the deposit to determine the layer that is most critical from the standpoint of liquefaction.

The curves in Figure 1 are intended to divide zones corresponding to liquefaction and non-liquefaction. Each of the three curves corresponds to a different fines content (fines content is defined as the percentage of a given material that passes a #200 sieve) in soils. Each point on the chart corresponds to one of the boring records used to develop the curves. A new site would be evaluated by plotting a point corresponding to the blow count for the site and to the design earthquake ground motion. If the point plots on or above the curve, the site would be judged susceptible to liquefaction. If the point plots below the curve then a margin of safety has to be added before the site can be judged safe. There is no general agreement on the margin of safety.

Use of plots such as Figure 1 is regarded by many as the most applicable method available for assessing liquefaction susceptibility. This practice avoids the difficult problems and questions concerning undisturbed testing and sampling and makes direct use of actual experience during earthquakes; but there are drawbacks because of the uncertainties involved in estimating various parameters. Use of various correlations leads to a compounding of the uncertainties involved in each, and evaluating a rational measure of all these uncertainties is rarely possible.

Finally, there is some judgement involved in deciding where to locate the boundary curve separating liquefaction from non-liquefaction as can be seen from an examination of Figure 1. There have been various attempts to use statistical techniques to aid in choosing the most proper location for the boundary curve (e.g., Christian and Swiger, 1975).

9.3 A Suggested Neural-Fuzzy Methodology - looking at liquefaction as an ambiguous phenomena

Pattern Recognition (classification) is of fundamental importance in engineering as in any human activity, but it is often difficult to see that the task at hand is indeed a recognition problem. Assessing the potential for liquefaction at a site is currently seen as a problem of finding and making use of a method that, given the relevant measurements, allows assignment of any site to one of two classes: "liquefiable" or "non-liquefiable." The most commonly used procedure (Figure 1) does not provide any ready means of assessing the confidence that can be placed on the results. An associated probability of misclassification can be obtained when procedures based on statistical techniques such as linear discriminant analysis a straightforward extension of Bayes' rule are used (Christian and Swiger, 1975; Reyna, 1991). But an event is still forced to belong to one of two categories and the assumption is implicit that with perfect information all sites could be classified "correctly." These existing analyses simply do not have room for sites where the evidence for liquefaction is borderline.

189

Fuzziness is proposed as an alternative to randomness for describing the uncertainty associated with liquefaction. Fuzziness describes event *ambiguity*. It measures the degree to which an event occurs, not whether it occurs. Randomness describes the uncertainty of event occurrence. As Kosko (1992) says the issue concerns the occurring event: Is it uncertain in any way? Can we unambiguously distinguish the event from its opposite?

When we use available field data to predict liquefaction, the answer to the two questions above would be *yes* and *no*, respectively. Lack of surface manifestations such as sand boils or slumping/sinking of structures does not always imply the absence of liquefaction. There is always some uncertainty as liquefaction may have occurred in a thin layer at some depth, without causing any distress on the surface. The uncertainty in liquefaction is not simply that the event occurred, but the degree to which the event occurred. There is no such thing as 50% liquefaction. One may say that a given site will liquefy for 50% of the shaking events, or that 50% of the site area will undergo liquefaction, but this still leaves the question of degree unanswered. The event itself is ambiguous. Secondly, the physical phenomena of liquefaction can make a more or less smooth transition to its opposite (no liquefaction), making classification hard near the midpoint of the transition. The membership of any given site to the group of sites that liquefy is partial, graded, inexact, ambiguous, or uncertain.

Based on the preceding argument we assert that it is not appropriate to talk in terms of an either/or classification, rather, the available set of measurements (and observations) act as indicators of a single behavior, *viz.*, liquefaction which each site displays to a certain degree. What is needed is the ability to match a pattern: the particular combinations of parameters/conditions which would result (or not) in liquefaction, and to what degree.

The main philosophy behind the methodology used in the subsequent is that several geological phenomena have contributed to the uncertainties of each parameter being measured at the site and the problem is to find meaningful patterns of behavior when no sharp boundaries exist.

The output produced by a trained network can be represented as a *degree of belonging*, *i.e.*, each set of measurements (the input data-vector) is said to match the pattern representing liquefaction to a certain degree. This degree of belonging is also termed the *possibility* of liquefaction of the site under consideration. The possibility (the output, L, of the neural network) takes values in the range [0, 1] — the unit interval. The concept of degree of belonging comes from the theory of *fuzzy sets and systems* and hence we use the term *neural-fuzzy*. In the language of fuzzy sets, each site can be said to belong to a certain degree to the set representing the behavior liquefaction. Another reason to prefer the hybrid term neural-fuzzy is the fact that both techniques (fuzzy sets and artificial neural networks) can process inexact information, and process it without an explicit set of predefined rules. They also share more formal mathematical properties as detailed by Kosko (1992).

The *fuzzy entropy measure* (Appendix I) can be used to assess the confidence that can be placed on the output of the network. Entropy is a generic notion which provides a measure of the uncertainty of classification. We must recognize that the term possibility does not always mean the same as probability. Rather, probability is a special case of fuzziness when an event has no ambiguity. Since we claim that liquefaction is an ambiguous event, we will talk in terms of a possibility which accounts for the uncertainties associated with the parameters of the site. The remaining uncertainty is that associated with the magnitude and occurrence of the seismic event likely to impact the site and is properly accounted for by probability.

Assessing liquefaction should properly be treated as involving compound uncertainties: the randomness of earthquake magnitude and occurrence, reported as probabilities; and the ambiguity of liquefaction, measured in terms of a possibility. In other words, the probability of a fuzzy event. The following example makes this clear.

Say that a network trained to recognize the pattern "liquefaction" produces an output of 0.8 when presented with a certain set of values which include measurements of the input soil parameters and the information that an earthquake of magnitude 6.5 occurs at a fault zone at a known distance from the site. The output of the network, the number 0.8, can be taken to mean that given the level of information available, there is a 80% match between the event represented by the data-vector under consideration and the pattern representing liquefaction that is embedded in the trained network. It does not mean that there is a 80% chance that the site would liquefy for the given set of parameters. To assess the *chance* (the probability) that liquefaction occurs, we need to look at the probability of exceedance of an earthquake of magnitude 6.5 at the fault zone. If this probability is 0.7 over the next five years then we would say that there is a 70% chance that the site would experience, sometime within the next five years, an event which has an 80% match with our definition of liquefaction.

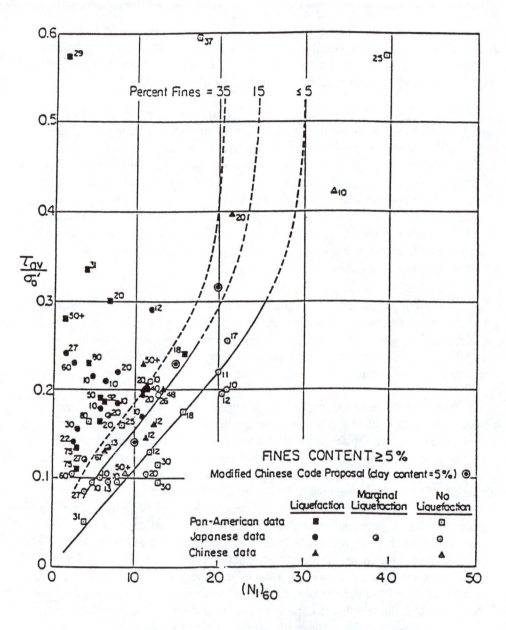

Figure 1. Relationship between stress ratios causing liquefaction and $(N_1)_{60}$ values for clean sands for magnitude 7.5 earthquakes. The curves divide zones of liquefaction from those of non-liquefaction (Source: Seed *et al.*, 1984)

We must learn to think of liquefaction at a site as an ambiguous event which occurs to a certain degree. We may even go so far as to say that liquefaction will always occur given that an earthquake occurs the degree to which it will occur is the factor that will control what we do about it. For instance a possibility of 0.2 would mean that the event shows very few if any features of sites that liquefy and 0.8 would mean that the event shows almost all of the features the network has learned to associate with the general phenomenon of liquefaction. Then it is entirely up to us to decide what label we wish to attach to the number. If one insists on an either/or classification, then possibility values between 0 and 0.5 could be called "No liquefaction" and those between 0.5 and 1 would be labelled "Liquefaction." Alternatively we could borrow techniques from the area of Decision Theory and Analysis and develop a range of labels (possibily linguistic) based on the judgement and knowledge of a number of experts. These labels could divide the range from 0 to 1 as follows:

0.0 to 0.2	——	Liquefaction *highly unlikely*
0.2 to 0.4	——	Liquefaction *unlikely*
0.4 to 0.6	——	Not enough information to decide
0.6 to 0.8	——	Liquefaction *likely*
0.8 to 1.0	——	Liquefaction *highly likely*

The middle range has maximum ambiguity (Entropy is greater than 0.66) and the extreme ranges have the least ambiguity (Entropy is less than 0.25).

9.4 SPT based Liquefaction Potential

The data for the liquefaction study has been taken from the published literature (Seed and Idriss, 1971; Christian and Swiger, 1975; and Law, Cao and He, 1990). Only actual field data is used. We have made an attempt to eliminate all data whose provenance was uncertain and/or we could not verify the original sources for some of the back calculated values. This reduced the data to the 31 sets listed in Table 1.

In existing techniques, a number of correlations need to be used in order to estimate the parameters for liquefaction assessment. A feed-forward artificial neural network, when properly trained, embodies a non-linear transformation that is effectively equivalent to the tasks performed by all such correlations. Since all procedures ultimately rely on measurements of the same basic data, the input data used for the network can be (and preferably should be) the most direct measurements available for the parameters of interest. After training the network using the available data sets, the relevant measurements for a new site can simply be presented to the input nodes of the network without any preprocessing—and the network will produce a number indicating the level of matching with the *pattern of liquefaction*. The fuzzy entropy can then be calculated to obtain a measure of how sure or ambiguous the classification is.

We apply the concept of *crossvalidation* as our principal device for analyzing the performance of the neural networks that we train. The basic idea is to use only a portion of the available database in training the network and to use the rest of the database in assessing the capacity of the network to generalize.

Crossvalidation is well-known within statistical pattern recognition. The choice of a network architecture amounts to a choice of parametrization for the input-output mapping that a network is supposed to learn (Hansen and Salamon, 1990), and crossvalidation is the standard tool in deciding between alternative choices of parametrization for a data set by statistical methods (Toussant, 1974).

A common mistake when developing a "model" of a physical process is to train a neural network using the complete database by minimizing the accumulated misclassifications of inputs in the data set. In the concluding section of this chapter, we discuss some of the problems associated with using all of the database for training and some common misconceptions about "modelling" with neural-networks.

Since our overall goal is not to minimize errors on the data set but rather to minimize misclassification on a much larger set of conceivable inputs, crossvalidation gives a much better measure of expected ability to generalize. Crossvalidation would also help avoid overtraining. An unbiased estimate of network performance can be obtained by bi-partitioning the database into specific training and test sets. Overtraining will then show up as poorer performance on the test set, *i.e.*, when crossvalidating.

Standard practice dictates that we perform some trials to find an acceptable architecture and parameters for the neural network and then trust all future classifications to the best network we find. We believe that it is preferable to keep a screened subset of the trial networks and run them all with an appropriate collective decision strategy. Such sets of neural networks are referred to as *ensembles* and the collective decision made by the ensemble is less likely to be in error than the decision made by any of the individual members (Hansen and Salamon, 1990; and Levin *et al.*, 1990). We use a limited version of the ensemble approach by restricting ourselves to two crossvalidated networks: one trained using all the odd numbered data sets from Table 1 (clear rows), that we call the 'odd' network; and an 'even' network trained using the data from the

15 even numbered sites of Table 1 (shaded rows). Both networks have an identical topography and starting parameters. Once training is complete, the average of their outputs for a given input data set is considered the ensemble output.

Input Parameter Selection is the first step in developing a trained network. We wish to make use of the most basic measurements available. Columns 4 through 8 of Table 1 were selected as the input parameters. The Richter Magnitude, M, and Hypocentral Distance, R, (columns 4 and 5 of Table 1) provide information about the seismic energy reaching the site. (The estimated peak surface acceleration, used to compute the resistance of a soil deposit in terms of the cyclic stress ratio in Eqn. 1, is usually computed from attenuation relationships based on M and R.) In the standard procedure, the depth to the critical sand layer and depth to water table (columns 6 and 7 of Table 1) are used in conjunction with density values to compute the overburden stress and the initial effective confining stress values. Since the estimated densities for the soils at all the sites in the database are roughly the same, we consider columns 6 and 7 sufficient to provide all stress information. The results show that we are justified in making this assumption. Lastly, we select the SPT-N value as the final input parameter. No corrections are applied to the recorded N value as reported in Table 1. The energy correction factor for all of the data points roughly works out to be the same value based on the suggestions contained in Seed *et al.* (1984), hence we do not need to make any correction for variations in the energy. The N values are not normalized for overburden effects as the overburden information is contained in the depth information as argued earlier. The output layer only needs to have a single node which represents the degree of liquefaction. Its expected value is given by Column 9 of Table 1.

The number of hidden layers and the number of nodes in each was decided by a trial and error procedure. This trial and error process is the most time consuming part in the entire development process as there are no definite rules for selecting a network topography for a particular task. We let our previous experience with geotechnical data analysis be our guide (Agrawal, 1992; Agrawal, Frost and Chameau, 1994; Agrawal, Weeraratne and Khilnani, 1994). The selection of the number of hidden nodes should also be based on the number of samples of data available. Some guidelines can be obtained from Fu (1990) and Sietsma and Dow (1991). For the present case, it was found that a network with six nodes in a single hidden layer works best in providing sufficient learning and generalization capability. In shorthand notation, the chosen network architecture is referred to as a 5-6-1 network, for obvious reasons.

Table 1. Data and Results for ANN based Assessment of Liquefaction Potential

Site No.	Earthquake	Year	Richter Magnitude (M)	Hypocentral Distance (km)	Depth to Critical Sand Layer (m)	Depth to Water Table (m)	Average SPT Resistance at Critical depth (N)	Field Behavior Liquefied (?) (YES=1;NO=0)	Case 6 Network Output ("Odd")	Case 5 Network Output ("Even")
(1)	(2)	(3)	(4)	(5)	(6)	(7)	(8)	(9)	(10)	(11)
1	Mino Owari	1891	8.4	51.4	6.09	2.43	16	1	0.90	0.93
2	Mino Owari	1891	8.4	51.7	13.71	0.91	17	1	0.97	0.96
3	Mino Owari	1891	8.4	51.4	9.14	1.82	10	1	0.99	0.98
4	Santa Barbara	1925	6.3	15.1	7.62	4.57	3	1	1.00	0.98
5	El Centro	1940	7.0	12.8	4.57	4.57	9	1	0.98	0.95
6	El Centro	1940	7.0	12.8	7.62	6.09	4	1	1.00	0.99
7	El Centro	1940	7.0	12.8	6.10	1.52	1	1	1.00	0.99
8	Tohnankai	1944	8.3	163.8	3.96	1.52	4	1	0.92	0.84
9	Tohnankai	1944	8.3	163.8	2.44	0.60	1	1	0.95	0.89
10	Fukui	1948	7.2	16.3	7.01	3.35	18	1	0.76	0.63
11	Fukui	1948	7.2	16.3	7.01	0.91	28	0	0.15	0.37
12	Fukui	1948	7.2	16.3	3.05	1.29	3	1	0.99	0.98
13	Fukui	1948	7.2	16.3	6.10	0.91	5	1	1.00	0.99
14	San Francisco	1957	5.5	11.9	3.05	2.43	7	1	0.87	0.81
15	Chile	1960	8.4	127.9	4.57	3.65	6	1	0.96	0.91
16	Chile	1960	8.4	127.9	4.57	3.65	6	1	0.96	0.91
17	Chile	1960	8.4	127.9	6.10	3.65	18	0	0.36	0.49
18	Niigata	1964	7.5	65.2	6.10	0.91	6	1	0.98	0.96
19	Niigata	1964	7.5	65.2	7.62	0.91	15	1	0.76	0.80
20	Alaska	1964	8.3	102.0	6.10	0.00	5	1	0.98	0.97
21	Alaska	1964	8.3	102.0	6.10	2.43	5	1	0.99	0.96
22	Alaska	1964	8.3	117.7	7.62	0.00	40	0	0.02	0.04
23	Alaska	1964	8.3	94.5	6.10	6.09	10	1	0.96	0.92
24	Alaska	1964	8.3	65.9	6.10	1.52	13	1	0.93	0.94
25	Caracas	1967	6.3	58.3	0.92	0.92	3	1	0.92	0.86
26	Ebino	1968	7.8	78.1	3.66	0.91	14	0	0.15	0.20
27	Ebino	1968	7.8	74.7	3.66	0.91	6	1	0.97	0.95
28	Ebino	1968	7.8	78.1	3.05	1.52	15	0	0.12	0.18
29	Ebino	1968	7.8	162.2	4.57	0.91	6	1	0.80	0.68
30	San Fernando	1971	6.6	11.6	6.10	4.58	2	1	1.00	0.98
31	San Fernando	1971	6.6	11.6	16.80	16.80	24	1	0.90	0.65
Test Site #1	Mino Owari	1891	8.4	51.4	7.62	1.82	19	0	0.80	0.89
Test Site #2	Niigata	1964	7.5	65.2	6.10	0.91	12	0	0.87	0.87
Test Site #3	Niigata	1964	7.5	65.2	7.62	3.65	6	0	0.99	0.96

Despite the fact that our ultimate objective is the ability to generalize, the objective for the initial tuning phase was kept at minimization of the sum of squared errors between the expected output for the training sets and the actual outputs produced by the network. Backpropagation being a standard technique and covered in detail in the first part of this monograph, we present only the details needed to make our experiments reproducible to some degree[4]. Besides the connection weights, the bias term for each node was also iterated by treating it as the connection weight from a node with a constant unit output. The initial bias weights and link weights were random values uniformly distributed on the interval 3 to -3, with the interval from 10^{-3} to -10^{-3} excluded to avoid numerical instabilities. The training algorithm used was a modified version of the back-propagation algorithm with the generalized delta rule (Rumelhart, Hinton and Williams, 1986), with a momentum term (α), a decay term (h) and a learning factor (η) inversely proportional to fan-in (where the fan-in of a unit is the number of units which are inputs to it). The change in w_{jim}, the connection weight between unit j on layer m and unit i on layer m-1, at iteration step t is given by

$$\Delta w_{jim}(t) = \frac{\eta}{n_{m-1}} \sum \delta_{jm} a_{i,m-1} + \alpha \Delta w_{jim}(t-1) - h w_{jim}(t-1) \qquad (2)$$

where the summation (of the errors) is carried out over the entire training set.

For the present work, the values of these parameters were selected based on the results of the tuning phase and are: the learning factor $\eta = 0.25$; the momentum coefficient $\alpha = 0.5$; and the decay factor $h = 10^{-5}$.

As the first step in developing and validating the final pair of trained networks, the initial 15 member 'even' data set (the shaded rows in Table 1, *i.e.*, sites 2,4,6,…,30) is used for training a network. This is called Case 1 in the following. A second network using the remaining 16 odd numbered sites is also trained. This is Case 2.

All data is normalized to lie between zero and one before being presented to the network. The normalization is done such that any input values (in test data) outside the ranges listed below would be set to 0 or 1. The choice of the normalization factors, and hence the normalization range, depends on a number of issues as discussed in the first part of this monograph. Based on our experience, we note that squeezing the available data into too narrow a range (say

---

[4] Depending on initial random generator, convergence criteria and precision of computations, the final weight values can be quite different for two networks—with the same topography, training algorithm, and training data—trained on different machines.

between 0.3 and 0.7) can prevent the network from converging, and when it does converge, it takes a much longer time. This is especially true of the input parameters. The range for an input parameter should just be wide enough to accommodate the range of values that one expects to encounter, for that particular parameter, in practice. We selected the following range:

Richter Magnitude M	5 to 9
Hypocentral distance R	5 to 200 km
Depth to critical sand layer	0 to 20 m
Depth to water table	0 to 20 m
SPT N-value	0 to 40 blows per foot

The expected output values are all zero or one and did not need to be scaled.

At each iteration, three forms of the output error are calculated: R.M.S. error, the square root of the mean of the squares of the individual errors; Average error, which is the mean of the absolute values of the individual errors; and the Maximum error, which is simply the largest output error (absolute value).

Figure 2(a) shows the error tracks for Cases 1 and 2 during training. The tracks show that after some initial iterations, the networks find some shallow local minima and settle into a gradual decline. We stop training at 1900 iterations. The Case 1 errors are: R.M.S. = 0.22; Average = 0.15; and Maximum = 0.60.

Errors for Case 2 are: R.M.S. = 0.33; Average = 0.22; and Maximum = 0.86. Both networks misclassify one or more sites (# 22 in Case 1, and #s 11 & 17 in Case 2). The generalization on the corresponding test sets (Case 2 data is the test set for Case 1 and vice versa) is poor. In both cases, the testing maximum error is 0.95 with the average error being about 0.3. We suspect that the reason for this poor performance is the inability of the available data to provide sufficient information for the network to be able to learn the relative importance of various input parameters and develop sufficient discriminating ability.

For the next step we *enhance* the data set by duplicating each data-vector and setting the earthquake magnitude and expected field behavior to zero (corresponding to columns 4 and 9 of Table 1) in the duplicated data vectors. This results in the *magnitude enhanced* database. Our intention is to provide the network with a training set which says that the magnitude of the seismic event is very important no earthquake means no liquefaction, irrespective of the values of any other parameter.[5]

The 'even' set now has 30 data-vectors and we label it Case 3. The 'odd' set now has 32 data-vectors and we label it Case 4. Figure 2(b) shows the error tracks during training.

The Case 3 network, as evidenced by error tracks, converges quite rapidly and we stop training at 1500 iterations when the final errors are: R.M.S. = 0.06; Average = 0.03; and Maximum = 0.17, which last occurs for the data of Site #26.[6] Testing this trained network with the Case 2 (original 16 member) data set we find that the errors are: R.M.S. = 0.26; Average = 0.15; and the Maximum = 0.75, which occurs for Site #11. One other site has a high error—the estimated possibility of liquefaction is 0.61 for Site #17 as against an expected value of zero.

Next we examine Case 4. The network rapidly locates a local minima but it takes a while before it finds a locally optimal minima such that the maximum error (corresponding to Site #17) falls below an acceptable level. The errors at end of 2500 iteration cycles are: R.M.S. = 0.09; Average = 0.05; and Maximum = 0.36. Cross-validation with the test set (the original 15 member Case 1 data set) produces an R.M.S. error of 0.11 with the average error being 0.08. The maximum error is 0.22 in the classification of Site #26.

These results are good[7] (better than the standard procedures) but we would like to improve them. We note that most of the convergence problems and the largest errors during training and testing occur for sites which were reported not to have displayed any evidence for liquefaction. That is, sites with an expected output value of zero. Enhancing the data set creates additional problems for these sites. The network is faced with input-output data-vectors which are identical in all respects, except for one input parameter. This creates a conflict and is the most probable cause of the problems and errors discussed above.

---

[5] Since the range for M has previously been selected as 5 to 9, all magnitudes less than or equal to 5 are normalized to 0, and magnitudes larger than 9 are normalized to 1.

[6] From the conventional two-valued viewpoint, the network performance for the training data is error free. All sites have a network output error less than 0.5 and are thus on the 'correct' side of the liquefaction/no-liquefaction boundary.

[7] The results are excellent when looked at in the conventional two-valued sense. The Case 3 network has success rates of 100% (30 out of 30) and 88% (14 out of 16) on its training data set and test set, respectively. The Case 4 network has a 100% success rate in both training and testing.

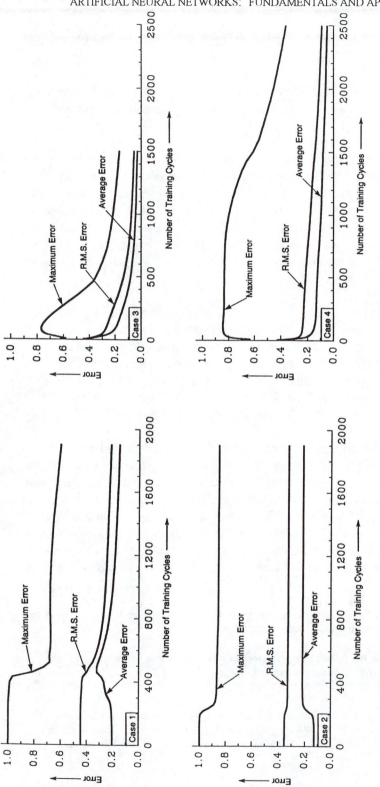

Figure 2. Error Traces During Trial Training: (a) Base Data; (b) "Magnitude Enhanced" Data

Hence, for enhancing the available data, we must only make use of data from sites which were reported to have liquefied. In other words, Sites 11, 17, 22, 26, and 28 are not used when enhancing the data set. Enhancing the data set by adding data vectors with a "no liquefaction" outcome is also reasonable since the field data is sparse for this category (probably because one rarely investigates cases where liquefaction does not occur).

As the final step, we enhance the data set by also adding data vectors which serve to provide information about the importance of the SPT N-value. We generate an additional copy of the original data vectors (only for sites that liquefied) by setting the N-value to 40 and the corresponding expected outputs to zero.[8] This is reasonable since a deposit with a penetration resistance of 40 blows per foot is considered highly unlikely to liquefy under any seismic loading.[9] The enhanced data set for the 'even' numbered data now consists of 39 data vectors (the original 15 + 12 "Magnitude Enhanced" + 12 "SPT N Enhanced" data-vectors), and is called Case 5. Case 6 has 44 sets (the original 16 'odd' numbered data vectors + 14 "Magnitude Enhanced" + 14 "SPT N Enhanced" data vectors).

Both networks were trained to 1500 iterations. The weights were recorded at the end of every 100 iterations. Each of these weight sets was used to test the performance of the networks on the corresponding test data (Case 2 data vectors, the original set of the 16 odd numbered sites, was used to test the Case 5 network. Data from the 15 even numbered sites comprising the Case 1 data vectors was used to test the Case 6 network). The optimal set of weights was considered to be the one which simultaneously minimized, as far as possible, the errors in estimation and errors in generalization. For Case 5 this was achieved with the weight set at end of 400 iterations and for Case 6 at 1000 iterations. The error tracks during training are plotted in Figure 3.

The Case 5 network converges smoothly and rapidly to a minima. The errors at the end of 400 iterations are: R.M.S. = 0.08; Average = 0.06; and Maximum = 0.20 (for Site #26). Testing was done using the Case 2 data set (the original 16 odd numbered data vectors). The errors for the test data are: R.M.S. = 0.15; Average = 0.15; and Maximum = 0.49 (for Site # 17). The results are presented in Table 1, where the Column 11 values in the shaded rows are the outputs of the network for the data used in training and those in the clear

---

[8] Any N-value greater than 40 is normalized to 1.

[9] This is not necessarily a firm upper limit. It is a somewhat arbitrary but generally acceptable upper limit in the authors' experience.

rows are the predicted possibilities of liquefaction for the odd numbered sites which were never seen by the Case 5 network.

The errors during training of the Case 6 network show that the network takes a longer time to find the best local minima but eventually the errors (and the generalization capability) become acceptable. At the end of 1000 iterations the maximum error is 0.36 which corresponds to Site #17. The R.M.S. error is 0.08 and the average error is 0.04. Testing was done using the Case 1 data set (the original 15 even numbered data vectors). The errors for the test data are: R.M.S. = 0.07; Average = 0.06; and Maximum = 0.24 (for Site # 10). The results are presented in Column 10 of Table 1, where the values in the clear rows are the outputs of the network for the data used in training and those in the shaded rows are the predicted possibilities of liquefaction for the sites which were never seen by the Case 6 network. The schematic in Figure 4 gives the final values of the bias terms and the connection weights used for both networks.

From this point on, both networks can be operated in parallel on a given input data-vector and the average of the two outputs (the ensemble output) is considered the estimated possibility of liquefaction of the site under consideration for the conditions represented by the data. It is also extremely easy to conduct parametric studies to evaluate conditions at a site. We present an example in the next section.

The relative importance of the various input parameters can be assessed by examining the connection weights of the final trained network using the methodology suggested by Garson (1991). We conducted this exercise for the Case 5 network using the connection weights at the end of 400 training cycles. The results are:

Richter Magnitude M	19.6%
Hypocentral distance R	29.3%
Depth to critical sand layer	13.3%
Depth to water table	11.4%
SPT N-value	26.5%

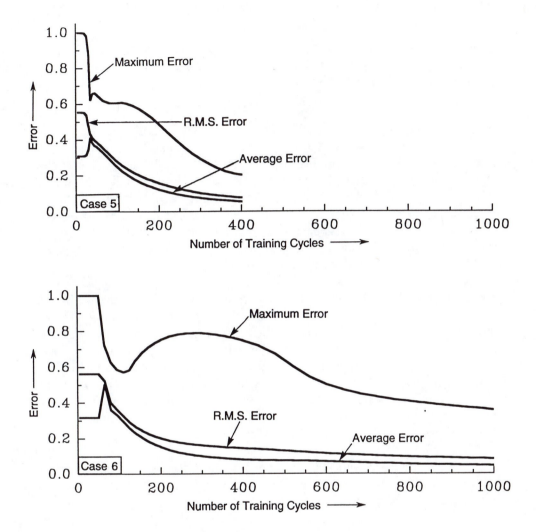

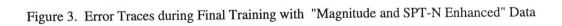

Figure 3. Error Traces during Final Training with "Magnitude and SPT-N Enhanced" Data

9.5 Parametric Study Using the Trained Network Ensemble

Three test sites are selected for this study where we suspect the reported N values are incorrect or that there was liquefaction but no surface evidence was found. These are listed as Test Site Nos. 1, 2 & 3 in Table 1.

Variation with SPT N-value: The first case studied was the change in the expected possibility of liquefaction with the SPT blow count. The results for all three test sites are shown in Figure 5. The thick solid line represents the ensemble output and should be considered when using the charts. Figure 5 shows that all other conditions being the same, the SPT N-value in each case should be much higher than in Table 1 for the sites to be considered unlikely to liquefy (possibility of liquefaction less than 0.4). The *minimum* N-values, with all other parameters staying the same, required to make the sites unlikely to liquefy must be 28, 20 and 22 for Test Sites 1, 2 and 3, respectively.

Variation with SPT N-value: The first case studied was the change in the expected possibility of liquefaction with the SPT blow count. The results for all three test sites are shown in Figure 5. The thick solid line represents the ensemble output and should be considered when using the charts. Figure 5 shows that all other conditions being the same, the SPT N-value in each case should be much higher than in Table 1 for the sites to be considered unlikely to liquefy (possibility of liquefaction less than 0.4). The *minimum* N-values, with all other parameters staying the same, required to make the sites unlikely to liquefy must be 28, 20 and 22 for Test Sites 1, 2 and 3, respectively.

When ground densification is done to mitigate the risk of liquefaction, a chart such as the one in Figure 5 can be very useful in determining the verification criteria.

Variation with Earthquake Magnitude: When we look at Figure 6, the first thing we notice is the gentler slope of the curves when compared with those in Figure 5 over the full range of the parameter being varied. Within the range of magnitudes considered, the transition from a site which is unlikely to liquefy (liquefaction possibility less than 0.4) to a site likely to liquefy (liquefaction possibility greater than 0.6) is very gradual for Test Sites 1 & 2. Test Site 1 is not likely to liquefy for events with a magnitude less than 7. The corresponding magnitude for Test Site 2 is 6. For Test Site 3, we have to extrapolate from the curve to get an estimate. We estimate that the site is likely to liquefy for any event with magnitude 4.5 or greater.

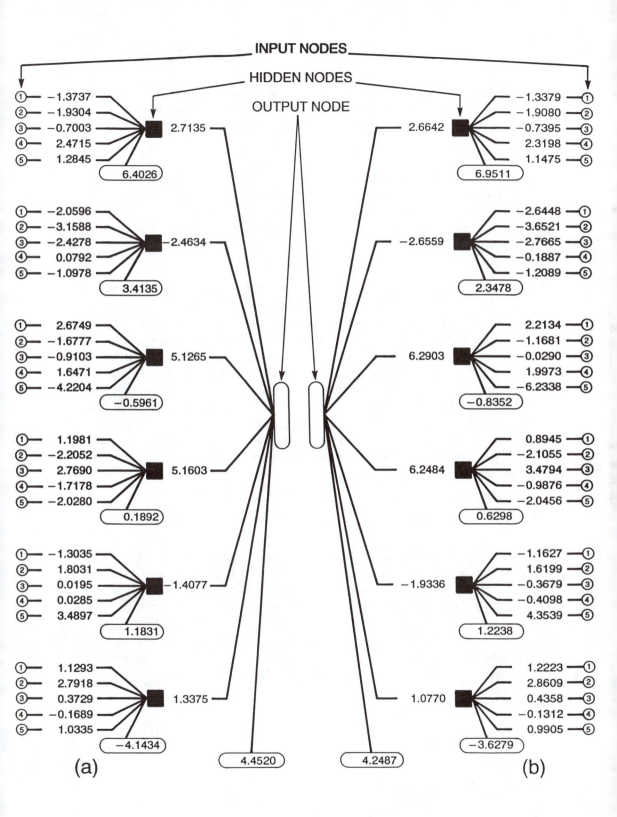

Figure 4. Weights at End of Final Training: (a) Case 5; (b) Case 6

205

A plot such as those in Figure 6 can be generated for a site where we need to evaluate the seismic risk. Combined with other information, this would help evaluate the overall risk as discussed in the next section of this chapter.

Variation with distance from source of energy release: Figure 7 is the result of the final experiment we conducted with the trained networks. The results are equivalent to those in the previous trial (Figure 7 is almost a mirror image of Figure 6). This information could be used to assess the impact of various seismic sources on a site.

From our knowledge of the physical processes involved, we know that the trends shown by the curves in Figures 5 to 7 reflect reality: an increase in the *N*-value means an increased resistance to failure under cyclic loading and hence a smaller possibility of liquefaction; and a seismic event of larger magnitude or a seismic event occurring much closer to the site would result in greater destructive energy reaching the site and this would result in an increased possibility of liquefaction. The results of the parametric trials provides qualitative evidence that the trends from the neural network are in the right direction. This gives us some confidence that even though the input-output mapping embodied by *the operation of the network ensemble is not a physical model, it has learned to successfully reproduce the effects of some of the physical processes that comprise the phenomenon of liquefaction.*

9.6 Concluding Remarks

If all of the data were from cases with unambiguous evidence for or against liquefaction, then data sets for which the output of the network is between 0 and 0.5 could be said to represent sites with no liquefaction and those with an output of between 0.5 and 1.0 would represent sites with liquefaction. This is indeed the traditional view. But looking at the results of classification from the point of view of the entropy of classification, we say that as the fuzzy entropy approaches 1 (possibility of liquefaction approaches 0.5), the evidence becomes ambiguous and no definite statement can be made about the "correct" classification.

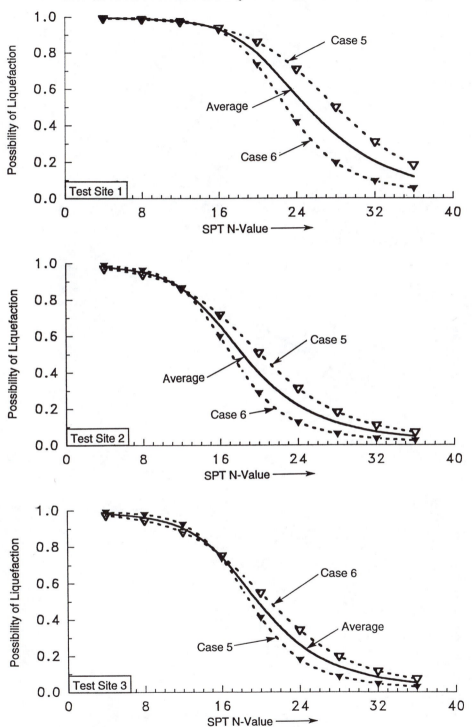

Figure 5. Variation in the Possibility of Liquefaction with change in N, the uncorrected SPT blow count

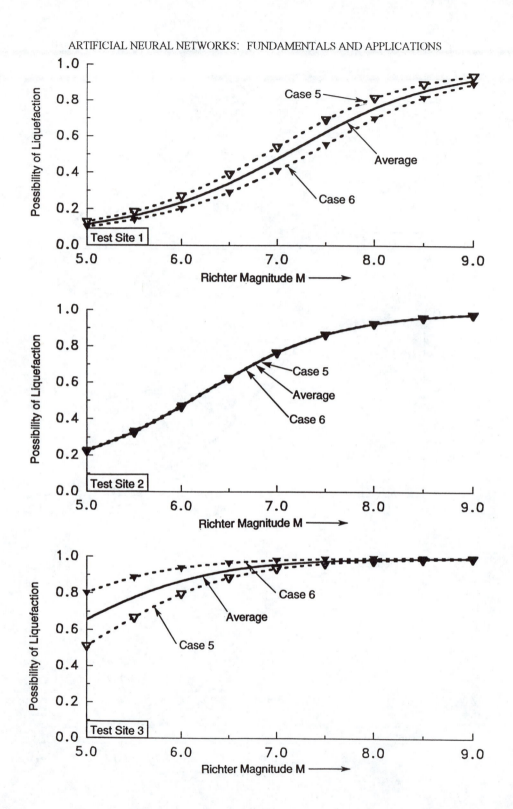

Figure 6. Variation in the Possibility of Liquefaction with change in M, the Richter Magnitude of the Earthquake

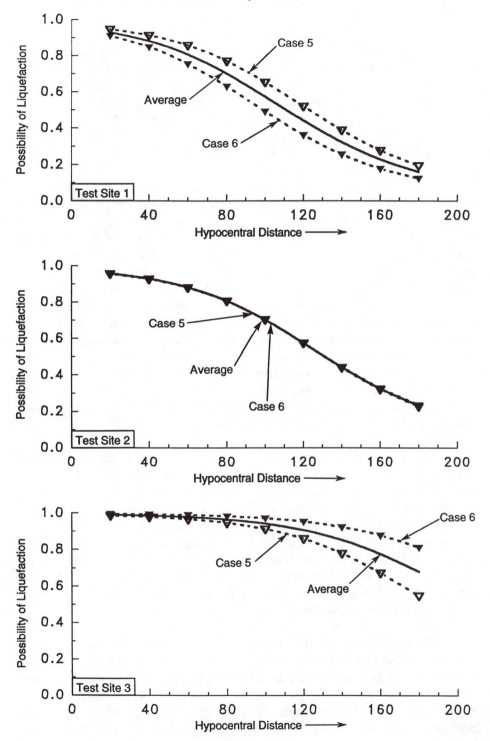

Figure 7. Variation in the Possibility of Liquefaction with change in R, the Hypocentral Distance (in km)

A very low entropy of classification is not desirable for the training set as it would imply over-fitting and this tends to reduce the ability of the network to generalize. The intent is to obtain a good approximation and not a perfect fit. From the point of view of approximating and predicting the behavior of an ambiguous or ill-understood process, our goal should not only be to obtain a good fit to a particular set of data, but also to gain the ability to predict. That is, the trained network should be able to generalize.

Neural-network training procedures are inherently statistical techniques. As White (1989) points out, the backpropagation algorithm is a special case of the stochastic approximation procedure of Robbins and Monro (1951). An implicit assumption in using backpropagation to train the network is that of statistical independence of the input parameters, *i.e.*, it is assumed that the value of one input parameter does not have any effect on that of another. It is further assumed that all the available input/output data vectors are random instances of the underlying pattern (which in the present case characterizes or is labelled as— the behavior *liquefaction*). Statistical discriminant analysis makes not only this assumption of independence but it also involves some stronger assumptions. For instance, it is assumed that the variates of parameters are normally distributed and that the variances and covariances of each of the two sets of cases one for liquefaction and one for non-liquefaction are the same as those for all cases taken together. With the neural network procedure, no such assumptions need be made concerning the underlying distribution of parameters.

Using the concepts of fuzzy sets in conjunction with a technique based on neural networks also allows the engineer to combine information from many sources, including non-numerical and subjective information. For instance the overall seismic induced risk may be assessed by combining information about seismic hazards and land use impact with the information about the possibility of liquefaction (available in terms of the degree of liquefaction). This is important as the range of consequences arising from the possible behavior of a site is large, depending on the importance and behavior of the structures affected. The more serious the consequences of liquefaction, the greater the risk and the lower the level of uncertainty that can be tolerated.

Finally a comment about "modelling" using all available data for training a network. This would be valid if our only goal was to use a trained network as a storage device, *i.e.*, using the trained network as an encoder for an input-output transformation that uses a significantly lower number of bits than were contained in the database used in its training. We must never lose sight of the fact that *all back-propagation does is stochastic approximation* (White, 1989), and that *neural networks are adaptive model-free estimators*. This implies that a neural network encodes a mathematical transformation from some input space to an output space and this transformation may or may not have anything to do with physical reality. The best we can do is to use validation techniques (such as crossvalidation) along with an "enhanced" database wherein we use our existing knowledge of the physical process of which the existing database is a sample. Then if the system behaves as expected (for instance, a reduction in the possibility of liquefaction with an increase in the N value) we may reasonably call it "a model."

9.7 References

Abramson, N. (1963). *Information theory and coding*. McGraw-Hill, Inc., New York, 201 p.

Agrawal, G. (1992). *Geotechnical Data Analysis: prediction and modelling using a neural-fuzzy methodology*. Ph.D. dissertation, Purdue University, August 1992, 104p.

Agrawal, G., Frost, J.D., and Chameau, J.-L. A. (1994). Data analysis and modeling using an artificial neural network. Proc. XIII ICSMFE, 5-10 January, New Delhi, India, Vol. 4:1441-1444.

Agrawal, G., Weeraratne, S., and Khilnani, K. (1994). Estimating clay liner and cover permeability using computational neural networks. *Proc. First Congress on Computing in Civil Engineering*, June 20-22, 1994, Washington, D.C.

Annaki, M., and Lee, K.L. (1977). Equivalent uniform cycle concept for soil dynamics. *Journal of the Geotechnical Engineering Division*, ASCE, 103(GT6):549-564.

Bennet, M.J., McLaughlin, P.V., Sarmiento, J.S., and Youd, T.L. (1984). *Geotechnical investigation of liquefaction sites, Imperial valley, California*. USGS Open-File Report 84-252.

Castro, G. (1987). On the behavior of soils during earthquakes—liquefaction. In A.S. Cakmak (ed.), *Soil Dynamics and Liquefaction*, proceedings of the Intnl. Conf. on Soil Dynamics and Earthquake Engineering, Elsevier.

Chameau, J.-L., Clough, G.W., Reyna, F.A.M., and Frost, J.D. (1990). *Liquefaction response of San Francisco Bayshore fills*. Geotech. Report 90/10, Purdue University, West Lafayette, Indiana.

Chameau, J.-L., Reyna, F.A.M., Clough, G.W., and Frost, J.D. (1991). *Ground motion analyses at several sites in San Francisco after the Loma Prieta earthquake.* Geotech. Report 91/9, Purdue University, West Lafayette, Indiana.

Christian, J.T., and Swiger, W.F. (1975). Statistics of liquefaction and SPT results. *Journal of the Geotechnical Engineering Division*, ASCE, 101(GT11):1135-1150.

Fu, Li-Min (1990). Analysis of the dimensionality of neural networks for pattern recognition. *Pattern Recognition*, 23(10):1131-1140.

Garson, G.D. (1991). Interpreting neural-network connection weights. *AI Expert*, 6(7):47-51.

Haldar, A., and Tang, W.H. (1981). Statistical study of uniform cycles in earthquakes. *Journal of the Geotechnical Engineering Division*, ASCE, 107(GT5):577-589.

Hansen, L.K., and Salamon, P. (1990). Neural network ensembles. *IEEE Transactions on Pattern Analysis and Machine Intelligence*, PAMI-12(10):993-1001.

Ishihara, K., and Yasuda, S. (1975). Sand liquefaction in hollow cylinder torsion under irregular excitation. *Soils and Foundations*, JSSMFE, 15(1):45-59.

Kosko, B. (1992). *Neural Networks and Fuzzy Systems.* Prentice Hall, Inc., Englewood Cliffs, N.J., 452 p.

Law, K.T., Cao, Y.L., and He, G.N. (1990). An energy approach for assessing seismic liquefaction potential. *Canadian Geotech. Journal*, 27:320-329.

Levin, E., Tishby, N., and Solla, S. (1990). A statistical approach to learning and generalization in layered neural networks. *Proc. IEEE (Special Issue on Neural Networks)*,C. Lau, Guest Ed.

National Research Council (1985). *Liquefaction of soils during earthquakes*, Report No.CETS-EE-001, Committee on Earthquake Engineering, Commission on Engineering and Technical Systems, NRC, National Academy Press, Washington, D.C., 240 p.

Rantzen, H.B. (1968). *Uncertainty in nature and communication.* Hutchinson & Co. Ltd., London, U.K., 151 p.

Reyna, F.A.M. (1991). *In-situ tests for liquefaction potential evaluation— application to California data including data from the 1989 Loma Prieta earthquake*. Ph.D. dissertation, Purdue University, December 1991, 502 p.

Robbins, H., and Monro, S. (1951). A stochastic approximation method. *Annals of Mathematical Statistics*, 22:400-407.

Rumelhart, D.E., Hinton, G.E., and Williams, R.J. (1986). Learning internal representations by error propagation. In: *Parallel Distributed Processing: explorations in the microstructure of cognition, Vol. 1: Foundations*. D.E. Rumelhart and J.L. McClelland, Eds., MIT Press, Cambridge, MA.

Seed, H.B. (1979a). Soil liquefaction and cyclic mobility evaluation for level ground during earthquakes. *Journal of the Geotechnical Engineering Division*, ASCE, 105 (GT2):201-255.

Seed, H.B. (1979b). Considerations in the earthquake-resistant design of earth and rockfill dams. *Geotechnique*, 29(3):213-263.

Seed, H.B., and Idriss, I.M. (1971) Simplified procedure for evaluating soil liquefaction potential. *Journal of the Soil Mechanics and Foundation Engineering Division, ASCE* 97(SM9):1249-1273.

Seed, H.B., and Idriss, I.M. (1982). *Ground motions and soil liquefaction during earth- quakes*. Monograph series, Earthquake Engineering Research Institute, Berkeley, California.

Seed, H.B., Tokimatsu, K., Harder, L.F., and Chung, R.M. (1984). *The influence of SPT procedures in soil liquefaction resistance evaluations*. Report No. UBC/EERC- 84/15, Earthquake Engineering Research center, University of California, Berkeley, California.

Shibata, T., and Teparaska, W. (1988). Evaluation of liquefaction potentials of soils using cone penetration tests. *Soils and Foundations*, JSSMFE, 28(2):49-60.

Sietsma, J., and Dow, R.J.F. (1991). Creating artificial neural networks that generalize. *Neural Networks*, 4(1):67-79.

Toussant, G.T. (1974). Bibliography on estimation of misclassification. *IEEE Trans. Information Theory*, IT-20:472-479.

White, H. (1989). Neural-network learning and statistics. *AI Expert*, Dec. 1989:48-52.

Youd, T.L., and Wieczorek, G.F. (1982). Liquefaction and secondary ground failure. *The 1979 Imperial Valley Earthquakes*, U.S. Geological Survey Professional Paper 1254, pp. 223-246.

Appendix I - Fuzzy Entropy

A *fuzzy entropy* measure, E, can be used to assess the confidence that may be placed on the classification system. Entropy is a measure of the uncertainty in our knowledge and a fuzzy set describes the uncertainty in our knowledge of some process. Fuzzy entropy provides a measure of this uncertainty (vagueness or ambiguity as distinct from randomness). Let a denote the smaller of the difference between the possibility value (the network output L) and 0 or 1, and let b denote the larger distance. Then the fuzzy entropy equals the ratio of a to b:

$E(L) = a/b$

An event with a L value of 0.2 or 0.8 would thus have a fuzzy entropy of 0.25. For the examples discussed in this chapter, an L value of approximately 0.5 would mean that there is almost as much possibility the site would liquefy as there is that it would not. In other words, there is insufficient information for the net to successfully categorize the site. Such an ambiguous event has entropy equal to 1. When the available information is such that L equals approximately 0 or 1, then the entropy is 0 and we say that we have sufficient information to successfully categorize the site. This agrees with the information theoretic interpretation of the probabilistic entropy measure: Let E be some event which occurs with probability $p(E)$. If we are told that event E has occurred, then we say we have received

$$I(E) = \log \frac{1}{p(E)}$$

units of information (Abramson, 1963; Rantzen, 1968). The occurrence of a sure event ($p = 1$) is minimally informative (zero entropy) and the occurrence of an impossible event ($p = 0$) is maximally informative (infinite entropy).

SUBJECT INDEX

Page number refers to the first page of paper

AUTHOR INDEX

Page number refers to the first page of paper